BEYOND
COMMON
SENSE

BEYOND COMMON SENSE

Child Welfare, Child Well-Being, and the Evidence for Policy Reform

Fred Wulczyn | Richard P. Barth | Ying-Ying T. Yuan
Brenda Jones Harden | John Landsverk

ALDINETRANSACTION
A Division of Transaction Publishers
New Brunswick (U.S.A.) and London (U.K.)

Second paperback printing 2006
Copyright © 2005 by Chapin Hall Center for Children.

This book is printed on acid-free paper that meets the American National Standard for Permanence of Paper for Printed Library Materials.

Library of Congress Catalog Number: 2004063678
ISBN: 0-202-30734-4 (cloth); 0-202-30735-2 (paper)
Printed in the United States of America

Library of Congress Cataloging-in-Publication Data

Beyond common sense : child welfare, child well-being, and the evidence for
  policy reform / Fred Wulczyn ... [et al].
        p. cm.
Includes bibliographical references and index.
ISBN 0-202-30734-4 (cloth : alk. paper) — ISBN 0-202-30735-2 (pbk. :
  alk. paper)
    1. Child welfare—United States. 2. Social work with children—United
States. 3. Child welfare—Government policy—United States. I. Wulczyn,
Fred.

HV741.B487 2005
362.7'0973—dc22   2004063678

Contents

Tables and Figures

Figures

problem of well-being as a system outcome, the absence of a coherent approach to child development will become increasingly problematic. A third meeting in October of 2003 focused on this latter point.

The Annie E. Casey and the David and Lucile Packard Foundations provided general funding for the meetings and editorial support. John Mattingly from the Casey Foundation and Lucy Salcido Carter, who was at the time with the Packard Foundation, provided critical support, although they, too, bear no responsibility for the final product. Moreover, the views expressed are ours, and do not necessarily reflect the views of either Foundation. Walter R. McDonald Associates, Inc. provided a grant to Chapin Hall for the third meeting, in October of 2003. It was during that meeting that many of the ideas pertaining to well-being were discussed, if not entirely resolved. Again, as a group, the authors benefited tremendously from the exchange with our colleagues.

It often happens that acknowledgments directed to individuals who provide editorial support are reserved until the end. However, the task of coordinating the work of five individuals with different perspectives, different backgrounds, and different vocabularies was bigger than usual. The extent to which the volume has stylistic coherence is because of Anne Clary, Rosemary Gill, Pattie Bengston, and Matthew Brenner and the dedication they brought to pulling the final draft together.

It is important to acknowledge state child welfare directors and the Children's Bureau at the Department of Health and Human Services. Both the National Child Abuse and Neglect Data System (NCANDS) and the Multistate Foster Care Data Archive would not exist if state child welfare directors were not willing to support the underlying data collection. In 1990, comparative maltreatment and foster care data for individual states and counties simply did not exist. Because there is so much work yet to do, it is hard to remember how far the field has come. To a very large extent, progress is directly attributable to the Children's Bureau. The Bureau has guided the development of NCANDS, provided early seed money for the Multistate Foster Care Data Archive and funded the State Automated Child Welfare Tracking System (SACWTS). These systems are to a large extent the source of administrative data that make tracking children possible. Through the Adoption and Foster Care Analysis and Reporting System (AFCARS), the Bureau has demonstrated why a commitment to data and information is important. Similarly, the

Acknowledgements

This project grew out of a series of meetings held at Chapin Hall Center for Children at the University of Chicago and the University of North Carolina in late 2000 and early 2001. In 2001, Congress was due to reauthorize the Safe and Stable Families program, but it was not clear how much enthusiasm existed for putting more money into child welfare services. Evaluations of family preservation programs carried out in the late 1990s were disappointing, and there was some anxiety in policy circles about the direction the debate would take. The goal of those meetings was to review the scientific evidence pertaining to effective interventions, with the hope that by looking beyond the family preservation evaluations, we would be able to identify successful programs.

In those meetings, the discussion focused on two central questions: Are some children more likely to be involved in the child welfare system than others, and are there effective therapies to address the human problems facing the clients served by the child welfare system? The findings were compiled and presented at a meeting involving senior policymakers in Washington. In the end, the meetings did not push the debate in one direction or another, in part because tensions over whether the Safe and Stable Families Program would be reauthorized had passed. After taking office, President George W. Bush promised to increase funds for child welfare services, the anxiety abated, and the policy debate more or less fizzled.

Policy impact notwithstanding, two conclusions were supported by the research that was synthesized. The first concerned the fundamental importance of child development in relationship to child welfare services. Time and again, the data pointed to distinct patterns of risk, service utilization, and outcomes linked to groups of children differentiated by age. The second conclusion pointed to the fact that child welfare policy and practice lack a coherent approach to issues of child development. Both of those themes are reflected in this volume. As the child welfare system tackles the very difficult

Administration on Children, Youth and Families has been behind the development of National Survey of Child and Adolescent Well-Being (NSCAW), the single most ambitious effort to understand children engaged in the child welfare system. Finally, the Annie E. Casey Foundation has provided generous support to the Archive, prompting its expansion. The integration, in this volume, of information from these three data sources offers only a glimpse of the possibilities of the interplay between these data.

We, as a group, owe the organizations and the individuals listed above a deep debt of gratitude. As individual co-authors, more thanks are in order.

Fred Wulczyn:

I want to express my gratitude to the co-authors who willingly and generously gave their time to the project. Each exchange of ideas was a reminder of how important it is to talk with colleagues about issues of mutual interest *because* we see the problems differently. If any of us hopes to make even a small difference for children, we cannot afford to be narrow-minded. It is for the same reason that I so value the vibrant intellectual community that is Chapin Hall Center for Children. Harold Richman wanted it that way, and Mark Courtney has kept it that way. It is a pleasure to be a part of that tradition.

I work every day with a group of dedicated and talented people who manage the state data we have the privilege of using. Kristen Hislop has done an extraordinary job turning the Foster Care Data Archive into a real research tool. Britany Orlebeke, Jennifer Haight, Jianyu Wang, and Lijun Chen use that data everyday, exploring the limits of what we can learn with administrative data and how we can best use what we learn. By the way they have seized on the opportunity to study child welfare, they have contributed more to this one piece of work than they know.

Finally, a passion for doing one's level best to make the world a better place for children does not come by accident. My parents taught me compassion, my teachers taught me what I needed to know, and my wife and children taught me just about everything else and then some. For all of that I am eternally grateful.

Richard P. Barth:

I am grateful to many colleagues and students at UC Berkeley, UNC, and across the land who have planted ideas in my mind—

some of which I have shamelessly cloned and some of which I have nurtured into my own creation. Although the most important material in this volume arises from the delightful collaboration and interplay between the authors, we have included considerable reliance on evidence from other large research projects. In my case, I drew heavily on findings from the NSCAW, which is a collaborative effort between the Research Triangle Institute (RTI), the University of North Carolina at Chapel Hill (UNC), the Administration on Children, Youth and Families (ACYF, DHHS), and many other colleagues who have contributed to the understanding of the data. I am deeply indebted to Mary Bruce Webb of ACF, Katy Dowd and Susan Kinsey of RTI, and my colleagues (Mimi Chapman, Becky Green, Shenyang Guo, and Judy Wildfire) and students (Carl Craig, Claire Gibbons, Julie McCrae, and Ariana Wall) at UNC for providing the ingenuity and effort that undergirds NSCAW's findings. Although all of the material based on NSCAW is in the public domain, and available on the ACF website, I hope to have augmented the utility of that work through the culling and refocusing of the findings presented herein. The interpretations are those of the authors of this book, and should not be taken to reflect in any way on the federal government. I also hope that those sections excerpted here offer reason for interested readers to look at the full reports that NSCAW continues to generate because these have far more detail and include more complex and telling analyses. I am also grateful to Ashley Butner and Priya Kapoor for assistance in preparing this manuscript and to the Frank A. Daniels Distinguished Professorship that provided me with resources to devote to this work. I am thankful to the members of my family, who continue to abide and support my mad passion about improving child welfare services.

Ying-Ying T. Yuan:
    I would like to thank Dr. Gila Shusterman, who analyzed the NCANDS data with creativity and enthusiasm. I would also like to thank Dr. John Gaudiosi for permission to use the NCANDS data. These interpretations are only the opinions of the authors and do not present the opinions of the federal government. Finally and most importantly, I thank the child welfare staff and administrators of the many states who have over the years participated in providing data to the three main research and analysis programs discussed in this volume. We have not yet fully plumbed all aspects of the data, but

we fully recognize and appreciate their contributions. Without their commitment to serving children and maintaining data, this book would not have been possible.

John Landsverk:

I wish to acknowledge Barbara J. Burns for her valuable advice and seminal work on evidence-based interventions, which were important to the development of Chapter 6.

Brenda Jones Harden:

I would like to gratefully acknowledge the mentorship of Dr. Edward Zigler, who taught me the value of applying a developmental perspective to child policy issues.

Part 1

Origins and Purpose

Introduction to Part 1

In this volume, we examine the use of child well-being as an outcome for children involved with the child welfare system. Until the Adoption and Safe Families Act of 1997 (ASFA) was passed, child safety and permanency were the two primary outcomes used to judge whether the child welfare system was fulfilling its responsibilities. Since the Adoption and Safe Families Act, well-being has moved closer and closer to the center of the debate guiding child welfare reform.

It should come as no surprise that attention would one day turn to the well-being of children involved with the child welfare system. Helping vulnerable children develop their full potential is an attractive idea because it has broad, common-sense appeal, especially if the government is providing alternative living arrangements for the children.

However, as is often the case when policy choices have to be made, finding a place for well-being on the list of outcomes used to manage the child welfare system is not as easy as it first seems. Holding a system accountable for outcomes assumes that the resources needed to influence those outcomes are available. Historically, the child welfare system has focused on the question of parental fitness—can the parents provide a safe and stable family for the child? Well-being is a much broader concept, influenced by factors that are often beyond the direct control of parents. Because family autonomy is closely guarded in the United States, the legislative mandate for addressing well-being in the context of the child welfare system is not particularly clear.

Despite the challenges, it is unlikely that the avowed interest in child well-being will wane. As we show in later chapters of this volume, the well-being of children involved in the child welfare system has to be a concern, given what we now know from the National Survey of Child and Adolescent Well-Being. Policymaking will move forward. The question is, what will the policies look like and how will the choices be defended?

With this volume, we offer one approach to this question. The book is divided into three parts. Part 1 explores the theoretical foundations for the argument. The main thrust of the argument, laid out in chapter 1, is that policy should be evidence-based. We note that two types of evidence are needed. First, because policymakers have to make decisions that allocate resources, a basic understanding of incidence in the public health tradition is important. Second, evidence that speaks to the question of what works clinically is also needed. In addition to evidence, policymakers, program planners, and child welfare workers need a working definition of child well-being. Contemporary theory focuses on bio-ecological and life course perspectives as a way to understand how children develop over time. The second chapter integrates the bio-ecological and public health perspectives so as to give the evidence base coherence.

The second and third parts of the book are devoted to evidence. In Part 2, chapters 3 and 4, evidence from the National Child Abuse and Neglect Data System, the Multistate Foster Care Data Archive and the National Survey of Child and Adolescent Well-Being is combined to offer an unprecedented profile of children as they come into the child welfare system. These data point to the fact that rates of involvement reveal strong developmental themes and that children who come in contact with the child welfare system have pervasive developmental challenges.

In Part 3, chapters 5 and 6 address the broad question of what works. Following the developmental theme established in the previous chapters, we focus the discussion on very young children and older children with behavioral problems. Infants are the children most likely to come in contact with the child welfare system, and any systematic attempt to improve the safety, permanency, and well-being of children in the child welfare system has to address the particular needs of children under the age of 1 and their families. Although fewer in number relative to infants, the needs of older children with mental health issues are striking. Meeting their needs for safety, permanency, and well-being means combining child welfare services with specialized mental health services that are not now widely available for children in the child welfare system.

The concluding chapter focuses on policy. The basic conclusion is that the child welfare system will have to partner with other service delivery systems in order to meet the challenge of improving well-being. Service integration is not a new idea. What the evidence suggests, however, is that simplistic models of service integration will not work. In order to connect child welfare services with those provided by other systems, the strategy has to focus on partnerships that are explicitly developmental in their structure. As a starting point, the data suggest that children starting out, children starting school, and children starting adolescence are high-risk populations for which explicit strategies have to be formed. The analysis also suggests the child welfare system ought to act as an advocate for children in high-risk situations, helping families get the services their children need. However, expectations that the child welfare system can be held accountable for those outcomes stretch the child welfare system well past its limited resources.

1

Beyond Common Sense to Evidence-Based Policymaking

Introduction

Safety and permanency are the two outcomes that have long guided policy and practice. With the passage of the Adoption and Safe Families Act of 1997, the list of outcomes expanded to include well-being. After Congress passed ASFA with overwhelming bipartisan support, the U. S. Department of Health and Human Services (HHS) declared unequivocally that "our national goals for children in the child welfare system are safety, permanency, *and* well-being" (Administration for Children and Families, 1998, emphasis added).

Common sense suggests that interest in child well-being is a positive, albeit belated development. Yet as of 2005, the Department of Health and Human Services had not incorporated any direct measures of well-being into the Child and Family Services Reviews (CFSR), the main tool used to monitor state child welfare programs.

Unfortunately for policymakers and practitioners, common sense does not always transform easily into practical reality. The reasons for this are easy to understand. Well-being is not a particularly well-defined outcome despite its common-sense appeal. The concept of well-being draws on a very different knowledge base, one that will have to be imported into child welfare before practice can be modified to reflect the latest thinking. Moreover, child welfare workers have had their hands full learning how to assure safety and permanency, often with very mixed results. Although a child's well-being has to be considered as part of the safety assessment that follows a report of maltreatment, developing explicit assumptions and guidelines that account for how well-being unfolds under a variety of circumstances (including closing cases, providing in-home services, and placing children into foster care) is a significant and critical challenge. Designing interventions that expressly promote well-being is harder still. From a treatment perspective, research has so far struggled to find effective services for maltreatment, placement prevention, and family reunification (Littell & Schuerman, 1995; Macdonald, 2001). Designing services that influence well-being will not be easy (DiPietro, 2000).

Definitional issues are not the only challenges that go along with an interest in child well-being. Context and timing are always very important, and the child welfare system in the United States already faces numerous difficulties. Rates of reported maltreatment, following a period of decline between 1993 and 1999, have stabilized. Although the foster care population in some states started to fall in the 1990s, the downturn has not been observed everywhere. In addition, legal action taken against states over the past decade has tended to focus on the fact that casework practice, the linchpin of the system, is often substandard. On the policy front, the field is polarized by ideological debates that divide those who favor limited state intervention in the lives of families and those who would act more readily to protect the best interests of children (Bernstein, 2001; Roberts, 2002; Shapiro, 1999). Each side of the debate, aided mostly by hindsight, relies on a handful of anecdotes to illustrate what happens when the state acts too quickly to remove a child and what happens when the state does not act quickly enough. On top of it all, the system of federal financing favors placement in foster care even though the weight of legislative language resonates with a commitment to placement prevention.

In existing child welfare policy, well-being and its developmental correlates are not taken into account to any large extent. There are special federal programs that focus on developmental goals for abandoned infants and children aging out of foster care, but these are small programs within the context of the larger child welfare system. In other important ways, there is virtually no sensitivity to well-being or child development. For example, the Child and Family Services Reviews rely on a single undifferentiated standard for reunification and adoption, despite the fact that research has shown repeatedly that placement outcomes and age are linked. The rule that states must pursue the termination of parental rights once the child has been in care for 15 out of 22 months does not consider well-being as a factor, except for a reference to the child's

best interest, itself a vague concept in practice. The rule has no developmental referent—it applies whether the child is 15 days or 15
years old at the time of entrance into foster care—a pretty sure sign
that its impact on well-being is not being carefully considered. In
short, the child welfare system has a long history of one-size-fits-all
solutions that ignore what is known about well-being and human
development.

The field also lacks the information needed to promote the idea of
well-being in a systematic, planful way. Until the mid-1990s, the
federal government was unable to produce a reliable count of children in foster care based on individual-level data. Today, although
the reporting of national statistics is dramatically improved, the published counts do not yet reflect any substantive appreciation for the
idea of well-being. The lack of evidence is hampered by theoretical
traditions that have given short shrift to the sort of developmental
perspective required to understand well-being in the context of child
welfare services. Without data and theory, it will be hard to organize
information in ways that reveal the influence of human development on fundamental issues of service utilization within the child
welfare system.

Finally, despite what common sense tells us about the importance
of well-being in the context of child welfare services, it is not at all
clear that the way we fund and regulate services can nurture a focus
on a child's well-being as the reason for intervention. Although federal funding for child welfare comes from a variety of sources (Bess,
Leos-Urbel, & Geen, 2001), the policy framework that guides state
intervention emanates from Title IV of the federal Social Security
Act (Committee on Ways and Means, 2000). In historical context,
the federal Title IV programs have been used to define how the state
should respond when parents are unable to carry out their various
responsibilities. Title IV-E, the program that provides federal funds
for eligible foster children, rationalizes state action by focusing on a
particularly narrow, sequential set of questions: Have the parents
failed to protect the child? Have the parents been given an opportunity to demonstrate their ability to provide a minimum and sufficient
level of care? Has the state done what it can to help the parents?
And, should the state seek new caregivers for the child?

On the one hand, the federal safety and permanency outcomes fit
this policy structure nicely. Good parents, even in tough circumstances, can protect a child's safety; when parents themselves pose

the safety threat, the state can step in and take whatever action it needs to take to protect the child. Permanency fits, too, because in the end the objective behind the permanency outcome has to do with establishing who will parent the child. Restoring the parents as the persons responsible for the child or finding new parents affirms the basic framework for allocating responsibility between the parent, the child, and the state (Mnookin, 1978).

On the other hand, pursuit of well-being outcomes strains the simplistic model at the heart of federal policy. Contemporary theories of child development link well-being to a system of bio-ecological influences that includes but is clearly not limited to parents and other family members (Bronfenbrenner, 1979; Elder, 1998; Rutter, Champion, Quinton, Maughan, & Pickles, 1995; Shonkoff & Phillips, 2000). The basic question behind state action–what should the state do when parents fail?—is inherently limited in the case of well-being because there is no easy way to acknowledge causal influences outside the parent-child dyad. If improved well-being is an objective, then a wider range of influences will have to motivate state action, and the solutions proposed will have to meet a wider variety of needs. There will be times when the traditional model of parent-child interaction will frame the intervention, but that will not be true in every case. Moreover, as time passes, we may find it is not true in a majority of cases that come to the attention of service providers.[1] A substantial proportion of reports are related to issues that bear on well-being, such as exposure to domestic violence, school nonattendance, and conduct disorders. For these children, the traditional rationale guiding child welfare programs will become increasingly anachronistic; the fit between federal policy and the everyday job facing caseworkers will become more disjointed; and long-term accountability within the child welfare system will suffer—precisely the opposite of the result intended.

How then does the child welfare field move beyond common sense and undertake a meaningful effort to weave well-being into the policy framework that guides the nation's system of child welfare services? Our argument is based on the idea that child welfare policy ought to be evidence based, and that the evidence no longer supports the current design of child welfare services. In part, this can be attributed to the fact that the evidence available at times when policy was being made was not particularly strong. Major federal programs and rules have been developed based on single studies in single locations—often with weak methodology. It can also be attributed to the role ideology has played in the development of child welfare policy, as some have argued was the case with family preservation (MacDonald, 1994). In either case, the available evidence is growing in both quantity and quality, so it is time to make deliberate use of that evidence for policymaking.

As it applies to the practice of medicine, *evidence-based* refers to the "conscientious, explicit, and judicious use of current best evidence in making decisions about the care of individual patients" (Sackett, Rosenberg, Gray, Haynes, & Richardson, 1996).[2] The widening interest in evidence-based medicine is tied to several concurrent developments within health care, but the central motivation is the idea that patients should receive treatments that afford them the best opportunity for a positive clinical outcome (Whynes, 1996). A similar movement is underway with respect to psychological services in schools, behavioral health services, and child welfare services (Curtis & McCullough, 1993; Hoagwood, Burns, Kiser, Ringeisen, & Schoenwald, 2001; Strein, Hoagwood, & Cohn, 2003).

By evidence-based policymaking, we mean the conscientious, explicit, and judicious use of evidence when making choices that shape child welfare policy. For this purpose, a definition of evidence that stresses efficacy at the clinical level is a necessary, but one-dimensional, perspective (Rychetnik, Frommer, Hawe, & Shiell, 2002). Clinical evidence of the efficacy of child welfare services must be augmented by evidence pertaining to the scope of the problem—information about who uses services and about basic indicators of risk. Without this kind of evidence, resources cannot be allocated in proportion to demand. Evidence-based policymaking does not replace ideology, social values, or political expediency in the policymaking process (Black, 2001). Rather, answers to questions about *who needs services*, *who uses services* and *what services work* form an evidence base that adds structure to policy discussions that other approaches to policymaking cannot (Petticrew & Roberts, 2003).

By child welfare policy, we are referring to the laws and regulations that rationalize the mission and purpose of the child welfare system.[3] Resource allocation (i.e., fiscal policy) is an important aspect of policy inasmuch as policy legitimates certain types of investment. Although there is a wide variety of government policy at the federal, state, and local levels directed at children and their families, our focus is on abused and neglected children and on federal policy.

Although state and local policy initiatives often pre-date changes in national policy (Wulczyn, 2003), the federal government's approach to child welfare issues sets an important tone. The approach adopted by the federal government to considering the fundamental issue of child well-being will be especially important in the years ahead as state and local governments interpret the federal mandate.

Frameworks for Interpreting Evidence

Two research traditions—the bio-ecological/life course perspective on human development and the public health approach to using observational data to understand the scope of a problem—provide frameworks for organizing evidence. The focus on developmental constructs in the bio-ecological/life course perspective highlights the fact that well-being is a dynamic, age-, and role-sensitive construct. In a developmental context, well-being is about transitions over the life course of childhood. For this reason, we use well-being and development interchangeably. (Chapter 2 will explore bio-ecological, life course, and public health perspectives and how they relate to defining child well-being and organizing empirical work.)

The public health perspective is associated with epidemiology, a basic science that reveals how social problems are distributed from place to place and over time. Because a principal aim of policymaking is deciding where, when, how, and toward what end resources should be distributed, the epidemiological study of child maltreatment and service use provides invaluable insights. Moreover, with its emphasis on multi-factor analysis, the eco-epidemiological paradigm fits comfortably with the bio-ecological model of child development. Finally, the public health perspective stresses prevention services over reactive approaches to the organization of services. A common thread in the criticism of child welfare services is their residual or reactive nature. When well-being is viewed through the joint lenses of developmental theory and public health, the limitations of residual child welfare services are accentuated.

Two types of evidence have been developed for this book: original evidence and reviews of existing research. The original evidence (which is presented in chapters 3 and 4) comes from three large studies of child maltreatment, foster care, and child well-being: the National Child Abuse and Neglect Data System (NCANDS), the Multistate Foster Care Data Archive (FCDA), and the National Study of Child and Adolescent Well-Being (NSCAW). Although other studies may give a better view of children in need or children at risk, the immediate policy challenge facing the nation's child welfare system has to do with the needs of children coming through the front door, and these data sources provide the least ambiguous, most current profile of those children.

As for our approach to the data, we use age as proxy for development. Our hypothesis is that absent developmental effects, the risk of maltreatment and placement will be even across developmental stages. That is, children belonging to one age group will be no more or less likely to be maltreated or placed in foster care than children belonging to a different age group. We also examine whether age-differentiated patterns differ depending on place and time. The importance of age and its developmental correlates is magnified if age effects turn out to be durable across changing contexts. In a number of respects, our argument regarding the use of age (as a proxy for child development) in relation to policy design is similar to ideas put forward in Heckman (2000) and Carneiro, Cunha, and Heckman (2003). In those papers, Heckman takes a multiperiod view of child development and uses it to understand human capital formation in children over time. The main assumption in their multiperiod model links the factors that influence human capital formation (e.g., parent's social capital, innate ability, and education) to change over time with respect to how much each factor influences the process during different stages of development. Heckman and his colleagues go on to evaluate the cost/benefit tradeoffs associated with policies that target human capital formation (e.g., schooling and job raining), an analysis we do not attempt. Nevertheless we are trying to inject into the child welfare policy debate a more conscious effort to learn how policy, programmatic, and practitioner efficacy is affected by the life cycle of children.

The test of both these hypotheses relies on the administrative data (found in NCANDS and FCDA). The survey data (NSCAW) provides detailed descriptions of the physical and behavioral status of children connected to the child welfare system. The specific goal of linking NSCAW to the administrative data is to better understand how children are doing at the time their experience with the child welfare system starts. Together, the data suggest that human development is implicated in the constellation of factors that determine whether a child will come into the child welfare system, and that when children do arrive for services, their well-being is often already seriously impaired.

The second source of evidence draws more directly on the clinical literature to identify examples of effective programs to pair with our primary data sources. In this context, the use of the term *evidence* is a bit more within the clinical tradition in that we use studies to build a case for interventions that fall into the category of best or promising practices. We have taken this approach because public policies should support programs that work and should deemphasize those that do not. At the same time, we realize that the list of programs that have been demonstrated to work is short and contentious. Consequently, we focus on broad themes rather than specific prescriptions for services. The epidemiological data, together with the data about successful programs (the subject of chapters 5 and 6), illustrate how developmentally sensitive programs evolve. Public policy will have to be generous with the opportunities it creates if the inevitable gaps in knowledge are to be worked out.

Safety, Permanency, and Well-Being: Underlying Tensions

ASFA thrusts the topic of well-being into the center of the discussion regarding outcomes for the child welfare system. Common sense suggests that well-being should be on the list, but more careful thought leads to the conclusion that it is not so simple. Are safety, permanency, and well-being the best way to articulate what the outcome framework should look like? Can we conceptualize a policy structure that is more amenable to providing services that promote child well-being?

These are important questions because they speak to bedrock assumptions that shape the overarching policy context. Well-being is a broad concept that touches on all phases of development throughout childhood. A commitment to child well-being could transform the child welfare system in the United States, leading it away from the largely residual system it is today to one that engages children and their families in a more proactive way that does not require a child maltreatment report for entry. The sweeping changes to current law that such refocusing implies are neither impossible nor inevitable. The history of child welfare policy in the United States has been conservative in the sense that government has been loath to open up family life to public scrutiny.[4] An emphasis on well-being could invite an expanded role for government in the way services are delivered in the community that goes against these more conservative tendencies. A children's agency that is designed to help families with a wide range of child-raising problems (e.g., children who run away from home, obese children, or children with conduct disorders) could also become an agency that mandates certain child-raising approaches. Worries that formalized preferences for certain parenting styles or approaches might emerge may seem esoteric, but the issue was addressed in the Adoption and Safe Families Act. Section 401 of ASFA specifically notes that the Act is not intended to "disrupt the family unnecessarily or to intrude inappropriately into family life, to prohibit the use of reasonable methods of parental discipline, or to prescribe a particular method of parenting." At the same time, child welfare administrators and service providers alike are worried about having expanded responsibilities without additional resources. They find some solace in being primarily responsible for safety and permanency—outcomes that are more manageable and countable.

Although modest alternatives that would strengthen the emphasis on well-being without triggering a counter-reaction that tilts away from an interest in well-being might prove valuable, arguments for or against a particular strategy will be more fruitful if core assumptions are scrutinized openly. In the end, if the best the child welfare system can do is take good care of the children and youth who wind up in foster care for more than a few months, our ability to help them will be aided immeasurably by the time we take to think about core assumptions in the broadest possible terms.

As child welfare policy has evolved in recent years, the working assumption has been that "safety, permanency, and well-being" is an accurate expression of priorities for the child welfare system. Research certainly suggests that there are substantive reasons to be concerned about well-being when children are maltreated and placed in foster care (Rutter, 2000). Safety and permanency outcomes were the first to be codified as part of the Adoption Assistance and Child Welfare Act of 1980. The phrase "well-being" was introduced later as part of the family preservation and family support provisions of the 1993 Omnibus Budget and Reconciliation Act of 1993.

Although the term well-being has gained wide usage among professionals, it is not entirely clear whether lawmakers intended to move well-being so close to the center of the policy and outcome framework now in place at the federal level. Well-being does appear in the legislative language of ASFA, but only because Congress modified an earlier statutory reference to well-being found in the definition of family support programs. Specifically, the 1993 OBRA amendments to Title IV defined family support services as services designed "to promote the well-being of children and families." ASFA amended the law, inserting the word "safety" ahead of well-being so as to shift the focus away from well-being. Similarly, the Safe and Stable Families legislation, which extended the authorization of federal Title IV-B, sub-part 2, contains no specific reference to well-being except in relation to court improvements originally authorized as part of 1993 OBRA legislation (section 107, paragraph a.2.A).

A more careful review of federal documents reveals that the pairing of safety and permanency with well-being is more a result of regulation and program instruction than legislative language. In her testimony before the House Committee on Ways and Means, then Acting Assistant Secretary for Children and Families Olivia Golden opened by noting that the Adoption Promotion Act of 1997 (as the Adoption and Safe Families Act was originally named) would further efforts "to ensure the safety, permanency and well-being of children in the child welfare system."

In fact, there is much less clarity about the goals than the pairing of well-being with safety and permanency implies. In the Adoption 2002 report, well-being is referenced only twice, once in the introduction and a second time in reference to non-adversarial case resolution (Children's Bureau, 1997). On both occasions, the reference to well-being includes safety and permanency. Moreover, there is no effort to explain exactly what well-being means. By comparison, the report goes to some length to define what the term *permanency* means.

Regulations that govern the Child and Family Services Reviews contain the most explicit references to well-being, but the references concern whether children are receiving the health and educational services they need.[5] The data for these measures come from on-site reviews, and judgments as to whether states are meeting the standards are largely subjective. However, there are no references to well-being that are expressed in the developmental terms normally associated with the idea.

Aside from a lack of clarity as to the meaning of well-being, there appears to be some ambivalence as to whether well-being ought to share such a central place in the outcome framework.[6] In its instructions to states clarifying the ASFA requirements, HHS left little practical room for well-being as a criterion for guiding child welfare services.

The safety of children is the paramount concern that must guide all child welfare services. The new law *requires* that child safety be the *paramount* concern when making service provision, placement and permanency planning decisions. The law reaffirms the importance of making reasonable efforts to preserve and reunify families, but also now exemplifies when States are not required to make efforts to keep children with their parents, when doing so places a child's safety in jeopardy. (Administration for Children and Families, 1998, emphasis added).

Even before the instructions were produced, there was notable ambivalence in the minds of progressive reformers who otherwise supported the aims of ASFA. MaryLee Allen of the Children's Defense Fund, testifying on the same day as Olivia Golden, noted that the proposed legislation would take "important steps to keep children safe and in permanent families" (Allen, 1997). Although she too mentioned well-being, Allen shied away from supplying a definition of well-being other than to say that it was contingent on having a safe and permanent home.

The reluctance to define well-being, if it can be called that, may be something more than an oversight. As an outcome, well-being represents a slippery slope. When well-being is defined broadly, the thresholds that guide state intervention become even more blurred than is already the case. Health and social/emotional well-being are measurable, but problems arise when one has to understand cause (parental action or inaction) and effect in the bio-ecological/life course perspective that best characterizes well-being. Cause and effect are often not linked closely in time, and ecological factors beyond the control of the parent may be as influential as how well the parents carry out their job (Coulton, Korbin, & Su, 1999). Moreover, children are not all affected to the same degree by adverse events like maltreatment. Experiences are absorbed over the life course of childhood, and events that are generally considered noxious influences may become sources of strength in other developmental contexts.

Without a looking glass, who is going to carry the responsibility for deciding whether the state should act when children are not doing as well as they could be? If we endeavor to protect children's capacity for well-being, rather than just their physical health, what will our yardstick be?

Responsibility for well-being thrusts the state into a large gray area where the decision-making rules and appropriate actions have yet to be defined. If children have been placed in foster care, the boundary of state responsibility vis-à-vis well-being is a little better defined because the state has physical custody of the child. However, should the state justify an ongoing placement because doing so enhances a child's chance of graduating from high school? Should a child be placed with a more prosperous, well-educated aunt rather than a poorer, uneducated grandmother . . . even if the child would be safe with either?

In short, well-being fits awkwardly into a framework built on safety and permanency. First, such a framework creates the expectation that well-being, safety, and permanency are on a par, but separable. Second, in the context of the Child and Family Services Reviews, the approach taken by HHS implies that national standards for well-being can be established and monitored routinely. Moreover, it suggests that HHS and state child welfare agencies will have enough information to know where a child involved with the child welfare system should fall on his or her age-specific developmental trajectory and the extent of change that can be expected. Finally, well-being measures and standards imply that the federal and state monitors will be able to isolate the impact of child welfare services from all the other influences that affect well-being so that they can render a judgment as to whether the services offered to children are of sufficient quality. Small wonder then that the full scope of well-being has yet to be defined.

Some potential solutions to the dilemma created when well-being is paired with safety and permanency are discussed in our concluding chapter, after we summarize the evidence from the research. Here, we will only point out that well-being is, arguably, the central outcome that subsumes both safety and permanency. Placing safety and permanency outcomes within the broader category of well-being underscores the notion that the child welfare system is foremost about well-being, while dispelling the idea that well-being is separate and apart. With this configuration, child welfare programs that successfully address safety and permanency gain credibility even as the difficult work on more conventional well-being outcomes is expanded. The scheme also allows for a recategorization of physician visits and school attendance as process measures that assess whether the child welfare system is doing all that it can to ensure that children are not denied access to health care and educational services simply because they have been placed in foster care.

Well-Being in the Context of Title IV of the Social Security Act

As the data presented in chapters 3 and 4 will show, the well-being of children is an issue the child welfare system will have to confront because the breadth and depth of the developmental problems of children receiving child welfare services are simply too profound to ignore. This will require the development of age-specific estimates of well-being and, in all likelihood, age-focused interventions. Program and service designs will have to respond to these needs earlier and more broadly, even if it means the traditional service boundaries have to be pushed outward.

With this in mind, a broader question has to do with whether programs focused on child well-being can be rationalized within the logical boundaries of Title IV of the Social Security Act. The difficulty well-being poses has to do with how Title IV rationalizes state action and decision making vis-à-vis parents and children. The conundrum is visible when the various parts of Title IV are considered as a whole. Much of the analysis of welfare in the United States has tried to account for the rise of American social policy in the broader historical context of developing industrial societies (Amenta, Bonastia, & Caren, 2001; Skocpol, 1992; Skocpol & Amenta, 1986). In the United States (and elsewhere), the tension has revolved around how benefits would be extended to the deserving poor. Social insurance for survivors and the aged established a preference for contributory schemes. For other classes of poor adults, the link to benefits was transmitted through their role as parents (Blank & Blum, 1997).

In response to concerns leveled by parties interested in limiting public support for the poor, the bundle of policies found in Title IV changed over time. However, the statute retained its view of parents as the adults who fail children in one way or another. The particulars can be seen in how each of the subtitles in Title IV disassembles parental duties and defines the boundaries of state action in the event parents do not or are not able to fulfill their role as "providers." It is particularly noteworthy to follow how the view of parents as economic providers limits state involvement in a manner that is consistent with family privacy. Specifically, Title IV-A deals with the issue of what happens when parents cannot provide adequate financial support—that is, when they fail in their role as breadwinners.[7] Title IV-B sets the boundaries of how the federal government supports families when the parents are unable to provide the non-financial resources needed to protect their children. In effect, the state recognizes that parents who sometimes fall into this position need crisis intervention and short-term social supports. Title IV-D deals with what happens when non-custodial parents do not meet their legal obligations to support a child financially.[8]

Finally, Title IV-E defines the federal role when parents do not meet their basic role requirements—protecting the safety of their children. The law creates a framework for deciding when this happens, what the state is required to do to make sure judgments about the fitness of the parents are sound, what the parent's obligations are to regain custody, and what to do when that is no longer a possibility. Compliance with and variability in the application of the laws are problematic, but the internal structure of the law is highly rationalized when it addresses the basic question of fitness.

The virtue of couching state intervention in terms of whether the parent has failed to carry out basic role functions is the way it balances the public interest in protecting children and in limiting state involvement in family life and regularizes decision making. The imperative to regularize decision making is best reflected in the structured decision making that some states use to guide their front-line caseworkers.

> The Response Priority process is designed to be used as a structured guide for *each* referral. Policies and procedures surrounding the process are directed toward assuring that each referral is evaluated against the *same* criteria by every CPS screener. It is expected that *increased consistency* in assessing each referral will result in the most effective and efficient application of available emergency response resources to the child maltreatment situations that come to the agency's attention. (emphasis added) (Children's Research Center, 2003)

In terms of evolving federal law and policy, regularized decision making connects everyday decision making to the formal rationality of the policies that balance family privacy and child protection. That is, decisions flow deductively from fixed legal concepts that are independent of other criteria. The general rules are used to decide individual cases.

The importance of regularized decision making and formal rationality is the internal coherence and legitimacy they generate within social institutions. Regularized decision making also creates certain tensions; as social conditions change, formalized systems of rationality lose relevence. If that relevance is lost, then the underlying paradigms lose their ability to guide decision makers. In the process, decision making becomes much more idiosyncratic as decisions are governed instead by personal interests and passions (Stinchcombe, 1986).

Maintaining the relevance of a rationized system of decision making is an evolutionary process, a matter of what has been called adaptive rationality. "Adaptive rationalization refers to the attempt to make legal systems congruent with other forms of structural rationalization" (Sterling & Moore, 1987, p. 86). According to Sterling and Moore, the state's legal system must be responsive to the social environment and the "intrusion of economic, sociological and ethical criteria, upon formal-rational reason and decision making" (Savelsberg, 1992, p. 1,346).

The argument presented here is that knowledge about child well-being will ultimately intrude upon the internal logic of federal policy, focused as it is on parental fitness. Well-being, because it relies on a multifactor model of causality, cannot be accommodated logically within a system of rules based on whether parents have fulfilled their role as caretaker. Keeping federal policy locked into Title IV limits the adaptability of the law to the growing realization that well-being is often about whether the parents have failed—and often about much more than that. To give policy predictability and coherence, the framework for action has to be broader. Otherwise, the caseworkers, given their day-to-day experience with families and children, will develop the sense that they know better than the institutions they represent.

The alternative to the relatively narrow construction of Title IV is to connect child welfare policy to more flexible policy doctrines that more easily recognize the multi-factor model that determines well-being in a developmental context. This is where the public health and bio-ecological perspectives enter the argument. The bio-ecological perspective provides a way to rationalize services in keeping with knowledge about human development. The public health perspective shifts the analysis away from the individual onto the population. With its focus on prevention and treatment, the public health perspective offers a way to rationalize community-based, interagency services. Combining the perspectives with the original intent of Titles IV-B and E creates a framework for rationalizing (and financing) the entire continuum of child welfare services.

Notes

1. One indication of this possibility is the large number of maltreatment reports relative to the number of founded, indicated, or otherwise substantiated reports. If we assume these reports are based on credible worries about the well-being of the children involved, then the size of the population that warrants attention is considerably larger than the number of substantiated reports would lead one to believe.

Further, the 1993 National Incidence Study placed the number of children harmed or endangered at approximately 2.8 million (Sedlak & Broadhurst, 1996). This number compares with approximately 1 million children found to be abused or maltreated by state CPS agencies that year, according to the National Child Abuse and Neglect Data System (U.S. Department of Health and Human Services, 2003a).

2. Some of the confusion has to do with the fact that the phrase "current best evidence" is rarely as straightforward as it sounds. Randomized clinical trials are regarded as the gold standard when it comes to the question "What works?" Even so, Petticrew and Roberts (2003) point out that randomized clinical trials are not always superior. More importantly, Petticrew and Roberts note that the match between the study question and the method used to gather the evidence is the real issue. Hence our preference for a definition of *evidence-based* that is more about the process of using evidence than it is about the hierarchy of evidence.

3. Policymaking is the process by which society makes decisions about problems, chooses goals and the proper means to reach them, handles conflicting views about what should be done, and allocates resources (Institute of Medicine, 1988).

4. The use of the term *conservative* is not meant as a reference to political ideology.

5. See, for example, Code of Federal Regulations, Section 1355.34, paragraph (b)(1)(iii).

6. During the House debate prior to passage of ASFA, Congresswoman Kennelly of Connecticut read from three letters in support of H.R. 867, the Adoption Promotion Act of 1997. The first, from Donna Shalala, noted that the bill would "further the President's effort to ensure the safety, permanency and well-being of children in the child welfare system and we strongly support the enactment." The second letter, from the Children's Defense Fund, was more guarded: "The bill takes some important steps to keep children safe and to provide them with permanent homes." The Heritage Foundation, the source of the third letter, declared: "This bipartisan legislation is a responsible attempt to speed up the adoption process for children who have been abused and have been neglected." In summary, Congresswoman Kennelly pointed to the bipartisan support engendered by the legislation. However, a closer reading suggests that the supporters saw different things in the legislation. Only Secretary Shalala invoked well-being. The others interpreted the law much more cautiously (*H. Res. 134, 105th Cong., 143 Cong. Rec. H2022 (1997) (enacted)*).

7. Of course, TANF is less about this than AFDC was. TANF has more to do with what happens when adults fail in their role as workers. This transformation of Title IV-A speaks to the fact that the original ideas embedded in AFDC slowly lost salience given the newer realities of the urban poor. That mismatch forced a shift in the underlying rationale.

8. For example, when a child is in foster care, both the mother and the father are noncustodial parents. Although states rarely pursue child support for children in foster care, regulations do allow for that.

2

Well-Being: Bio-Ecological, Life Course, and Public Health Perspectives

The common-sense appeal of considering well-being as a key outcome for the child welfare system may be confounded by the practical challenges of incorporating it into an accountability framework. There have been only a few systematic attempts to define well-being that have potential relevance to child welfare policy, child welfare practice, *and* accountability.[1] With that in mind, we start this chapter with three interrelated goals: to identify a useful way to think about well-being; to describe a corresponding approach to the analysis of observational data; and to interpret the results in a way that informs child welfare policy and practice.

With regard to well-being, the bio-ecological and life course theories of development offer a useful perspective, which we will explore in connection with the developmental, maltreatment, and service trajectories that unfold for children who come into contact with the child welfare system. We will also borrow from the public health perspective to explore the incidence, or epidemiology, of events that bring children to the attention of the child welfare system. Taken together, these perspectives—applied to the observational data now available on children in the child welfare system—will enable us to develop information useful in policy formation and practice.

We first turn to bio-ecological/life course theories of child development and child well-being. Contemporary research suggests that well-being is most easily understood as a developmental process influenced by both biological and contextual factors (Bronfenbrenner, 1979; Elder, 1975; Shonkoff & Phillips, 2000). Viewed from these bio-ecological/life course perspectives, well-being can be seen as a relative estimate of how a child is doing given certain assumptions and prior knowledge about his or her developmental path or trajectory. Maltreatment occurs in a developmental context accompanied by a stream of related risks and protective factors that also influence developmental outcomes. Increasingly, the impact of maltreatment is evaluated in developmental terms (Cicchetti & Manly, 2001; Manly, Kim, Rogosch, & Cicchetti, 2001; Thornberry, Ireland, & Smith, 2001), and child welfare services are part of the ecological context that influences progression along a developmental trajectory. There is broad consensus that successful services should be expected to create more favorable transitions through childhood, regardless of a child's developmental status when services begin, although how large and lasting these developmental advantages should be, or can be, is less clear because of our limited understanding of successful interventions.

Bio-ecological/life course perspectives encourage age-differentiated analyses of maltreatment and foster care placement. Elder (1975) notes that "age differentiation is expressed in the sequence of roles and events, social transitions and turning points that depict the life course" (p. 167). Successive cohorts of children may experience the same events, but they do so at different times relative to their ontogenetic path of development. Age-differentiated analysis of successive cohorts organizes the population so that it is possible to sort out age, cohort, and period effects, all of which impinge on our understanding of how maltreatment affects children's outcomes and how welfare services can counteract adverse influences on child well-being.[2] We are just beginning to understand the impact that maltreatment of different types has on children of different genders and ages (Stouthamer-Loeber, Loeber, Homish, & Wei, 2001; Thornberry, Ireland, & Smith, 2001; Wall & Barth, in press).

We are not arguing specifically for a stage or life phase theory of development that requires that each child accomplish the same developmental milestones with the same order and timing. However, there is some value to recognizing the substantial developmental homogeneity within age groups of children. Understanding the relationship between child welfare services and well-being, if that is the direction the field is headed, will depend on being able to isolate service effects from all of the other influences that have an impact on developmental trajectories. The empirical requirements of this work are substantial and go well beyond the data that are routinely available. As a starting point, though, we do have substantial amounts of data about children involved with the child welfare system that are organized by age. Age-differentiated analyses provide a modest control for other developmental influences by initializing service events within a more narrowly defined developmental context. If age-specific patterns in the data emerge, regardless of community or service contexts, this may suggest how interventions might be organized in relation to developmental trajectories.

We also introduce a public health perspective to the discussion about child well-being that is useful because it identifies risks in the general population and frames how those risks are linked to outcomes for a subset of the population. From this understanding, a range of policy, program, and practice changes can be designed. This is the link between policy and practice. Fundamentally, child welfare services represent a response to circumstances in which there are threats to a given child's well-being. Although these threats may be immediate or cumulative, the construct of maltreatment implies that underlying conditions will affect adversely the physical and emotional development of the child. At the same time, the response to maltreatment is a social construct, governed by the interaction of formal social institutions (public policy and bureaucracies) and community-level sensibilities that shape whether and how citizens respond to parents who violate community childrearing norms (Maas & Engler, 1959). The differences reported in the National Incidence Study (which estimates the underlying occurrence of child maltreatment) and NCANDS (which tallies the total number of reports of maltreatment) are testimony to this duality. Context is clearly important when thinking about whether any given child and family will be engaged by the child welfare system (and whether maltreatment is a dispositive factor in the decision).

Among the contextual factors, family and community are especially important. Maltreatment, referrals to home-based services, and placements into foster care are not randomly occurring events, changing over time without rhyme or reason. Over the decade of the 1990s, reported rates of victimization first increased and then dropped slightly, a pattern that suggests a link between maltreatment and broader socioeconomic trends. Spatially, both maltreatment and placement into foster care are on average more likely in poor urban communities. However, maltreatment rates and the likelihood of placement away from home differ in communities that are demographically similar in terms of, for example, poverty rates, family structure, etc. There is also substantial evidence to suggest that children are placed into foster care for somewhat different reasons depending on whether they live in rural or urban areas and on their age. For example, several sources of information converge on the finding that younger children are more likely to become involved with the child welfare system in urban areas and that adolescents are considerably more likely to receive child welfare services in nonurban areas (Barth, 2003; Wulczyn & Hislop, 2002). More broadly, from a national perspective, the child welfare system clearly does not have horizontal equity, in that similar families are not treated the same in all locales (Currie, 1997). Similar families living in different communities may be more likely to become involved with child welfare services because of where they live. In some communities, alternative services are available so the child welfare system would not be involved, and in other communities, no child welfare services or other services would be available. Coulton and her colleagues (1999) have started to expose additional factors that might be involved, but it is still not known specifically how the individual, familial, and community-level processes work in conjunction with one another.

Finally, there are system-level effects that influence the response to maltreatment. States differ in the types of maltreatment that they respond to, and whether they have any formal child welfare services response to assist families in which there is high parent-child conflict, without maltreatment. These differences in response vex the comparison between states. As an instance, states that exclude educational neglect from the formal reporting system have observed (i.e., reported) rates of maltreatment that are understandably lower than the rates reported for states with a different operating context (U.S. Department of Health and Human Services Administration for Children, Youth and Families, 2003). More subtle effects on child welfare service dynamics, measured at the system level, include the number of workers, the number of beds, the caliber of the workforce, and whether the child welfare system is administered by the state or by the county with state supervision (Mitchell et al., 2005). Each of these constructs is likely to influence the probability, appropriateness, and quality of any action taken in response to maltreatment.

These attributes of time and place are part of the ecological context that defines maltreatment and the social response to children in need. To view how maltreatment and placement are influenced by these factors, the population perspective is essential.

The Bio-Ecological Perspective

The bio-ecological perspective on human development (Bronfenbrenner, 1979; Bronfenbrenner & Ceci, 1994) has framed much of the knowledge and research on children in the last few decades. Originally conceptualized as the ecological theory of human development, this perspective responded to the singular focus in psychology on the effects of genetics and other biological phenomena on development. The basic premise of this theory is that human development is a result of the complex interaction between a child and his/her environment. It is a useful framework for child welfare because it allows for consideration of child well-being in a broader context that includes the child's genetic and prenatal experiences as well as the familial, social, cultural, and political environments.

Along with its focus on the environmental contributions to development, the bio-ecological perspective acknowledges that characteristics of the individual child determine the developmental trajectory. Thus, demographic attributes (e.g., age and gender) influence children's developmental trajectories. For example, male children are more vulnerable to a variety of adverse developmental outcomes, including infant mortality, learning disability, and autism (Prior, Lynch, & Glaser 1999). Additionally, such constitutional characteristics as the child's health, intelligence, and temperament affect developmental outcomes. With regard to health, a large proportion of children in the child welfare system have been prenatally exposed to toxic substances (e.g., nicotine, alcohol, cocaine), poor nutrition, or stress, which may have a significant impact on their development across domains.

Bronfenbrenner and Ceci (1994) have incorporated the mounting evidence from biological research in recent formulations of the ecological theory. For example, research on the impact of early experience (e.g., child maltreatment) on the developing brain has major implications for our understanding of children in the child welfare system. This line of evidence suggests that the underlying brain structures and processes may be permanently affected by such adverse experiences as neglect and trauma (DeBellis et al., 1999; Gunnar, 1998; Perry & Pollard, 1998), thereby rendering maltreated children persistently vulnerable to mental health problems and other developmental difficulties.

One virtue of the bio-ecological perspective is its multilevel orientation to the life experience of people. Bronfenbrenner proposed four interconnected, or nested, systems that have multiple but differing levels of influence on the human organism. The *microsystem*, the most important from a developmental perspective, includes the people and settings that are proximal to the child. For the child in the child welfare system, this level may include maltreating and/or foster parents, unstable home environments, child welfare workers, and social service agencies. The relationships between people and settings in the *microsystem* are defined as the *mesosystem*. In child welfare, there are multiple interrelationships that affect the developing child, for example the relationship between biological and foster parents, and between the social workers and attorneys responsible for a child's "case."

Developing persons are also influenced by settings with which they do not interact, which comprise the *exosystem*. Many larger settings may affect the child in the child welfare system, including the service sectors that intervene with maltreating parents (e.g., drug treatment programs, anger management services, parent education groups, and mental health agencies). Finally, the *macrosystem* consists of cultural ideologies, behavioral patterns, and artifacts that shape the content of what occurs in the various sub-systems in which developing persons participate. Policies created to address the needs of maltreated and foster children and cultural ideologies about the child protection system and families in poverty are among the many *macrosystem* influences on the development of children in the child welfare system.

Three premises of the bio-ecological theory are particularly germane to an understanding of the experiences of children in child welfare: the primacy of proximal relationships, the interconnectedness of individual and environmental influences, and the effect of ecological experiences—such as the quality of communities and social policies—on children's development.

In this vein, children's optimal development is supported by their interactive experiences with persons with whom the child has a "strong and enduring emotional attachment" (Bronfenbrenner, 1979, p. 60). As Bronfenbrenner and Ceci (1994, p. 572) assert, "...such patterns of behavior as neglect, abuse, or domination necessarily imply low levels of proximal process because they reduce possibilities for progressively more complex reciprocal interaction." In other words, maltreatment presupposes that affected children will experience compromised interactions with their family members that will ultimately jeopardize their development. The instability that often characterizes the familial and service environments experienced by maltreated and foster children has a particularly detrimental effect on their developmental outcomes (Jones Harden, 2004). Evidence from an 18-year study of maltreated and non-maltreated children suggests that transitions in living environments have an independent relationship to major indicators of adolescent deviance (e.g., delinquency and school dropout); further, the risk of poor outcomes experienced by maltreated children is exacerbated by changes in living environments (Herrenkohl, Herrenkohl, & Egolf, 2003).

Another premise of the bio-ecological approach is the reciprocity of individual and environmental influences. In other words, individual characteristics influence the environmental experiences the child has, and environmental factors have a major impact on the individual outcomes of the child. Multiple strands of evidence support this postulation for children in the child welfare system. For example, studies have identified age as a salient factor that catalyzes the reciprocal relationship between children and caregivers. Thus, because of developmental delays or early socialization to sexually aggressive behavior, caregivers may not engage in the reciprocal relationships that a child needs, resulting in a less-than-optimal response to the child. The reciprocal relationship between caregivers and children reaches further—and involves a reciprocal relationship between children and child welfare services. Age may be a child characteristic that influences how the child welfare system responds to maltreatment (for example, younger children are more likely to be maltreated, to be placed in foster care, and to be adopted) and each system response to infants has a developmental effect. Horwitz and colleagues (Horwitz, Balestracci, & Simms, 2001) have suggested that the child's developmental status is also related to placement stability and outcome. With regard to environmental effects on individual functioning, there is good evidence pointing to the negative impact of maltreatment (Azar & Wolfe, 1998; Cicchetti, Toth, & Maughan, 2000; Hildyard & Wolfe, 2002) and unstable foster care placement (Herrenkohl, Herrenkohl, & Egolf, 2003; Newton, Litrownik, & Landsverk, 2000) on children's developmental trajectories. The evidence is less clear about the impact of adoption on foster children, but European studies suggest that adopted children have better developmental outcomes than children raised in foster care (Triseliotis, 2002).

Finally, an underlying assumption of the developmental approach is that children's development may be facilitated or hindered by specific ecological experiences, such as hazardous communities and unresponsive social policies. One of the most devastating larger environmental influences on children's development is poverty (Duncan, Brooks-Gunn, & Klebanov, 1994; McLoyd, 1998). Poverty has a pernicious impact on children's development across domains, and it is particularly detrimental when experienced in the early years of life. Although maltreatment is not experienced only by children from low socioeconomic backgrounds, poverty does render children more vulnerable to maltreatment experiences, particularly the most common form—child neglect (Sedlak & Broadhurst, 1996).

In addition, social policies such as welfare reform that influence how parents meet certain role demands may affect their children. For example, there has been some suggestion that even with high-quality welfare reform interventions, children may be adversely affected (Duncan, Brooks-Gunn, & Klebanov, 1994; Yoshikawa, 1999). Several studies have documented that mandated parental employment may lead to negative child outcomes through associated changes in parenting quality (Menaghan & Parcel, 1995; Raver & Spagnola, 2002), in parental mental health (Galambos, Sears, Almeida, & Kolaric, 1995; McLoyd, 1998), in family routines (Lowe & Weisner, 2001), and in use of child care (Singer, Fuller, Keiley, & Wolfe, 1998; Yoshikawa, 1999). Infants and young children seem to be particularly affected by their mothers' mandated work experiences (Brooks-Gunn, Han, & Waldfogel, 2002; Duncan, Brooks-Gunn, & Klebanov, 1994).

Child welfare policies that are ostensibly designed to address the needs of children have the potential to hinder children's development as well. Newton and his colleagues (Newton, Litrownik, & Landsverk, 2000) looked at children who had normal behavior at entrance into foster care. They compared those who experienced many placements (evidently because of administrative moves rather than because the children were unmanageable) and those with few placements. After just one year, the children with many placements had significantly worse behavior than those who had started with normal behavior but had few placements.

Developmental Trajectories

Although stage theory has met with controversy in the developmental field in recent years, conventional developmental thought still maintains that children progress through different developmental periods, pushed toward maturity by multiple biological, cognitive, and social factors (Dawson, 2003; Lerner, Easterbrooks, & Mistry, 2003). From this vantage point, child development is conceptualized as a series of systematic, successive age-related changes that occur within and across developmental domains. Developmentalists have identified four global developmental periods: (1) infancy; (2) early childhood; (3) middle childhood; and (4) adolescence. Although research on developmental periods is becoming more refined and beginning to examine such developmental periods as early vs. late middle childhood, early vs. late adolescence, and the neonatal period vs. infancy vs. toddlerhood, these categorizations are too new to provide ample guidance for interpretation. Nonetheless, it will be important to track theoretical refinements as part of an overall effort to understand how development and child welfare services are linked. For example, adoptions involving children under age 1 are more likely than adoptions involving older children. However, the likelihood of a child's being adopted vs. reunified varies dramatically between children placed into foster care at ages younger than 1 month and more than 6 months (Wulczyn, Hislop, & Harden, 2002).

Thus, age or developmental period is a useful heuristic for a consideration of child well-being and the impact of child welfare experiences. Although most of child welfare research is not grounded in a developmental perspective, there is some evidence from interdisciplinary work that points to the value of such a perspective. Using the four global developmental periods identified above, it is possible to examine the age-specific outcomes of maltreatment and foster care placement, as well as to delineate the age-specific needs of children to inform policy and program development. Although it is difficult to disentangle the developmental outcomes of the foster care experience from those emanating from pre-placement experiences such as maltreatment, several studies provide evidence that children often show developmental improvements across domains when placed into foster care (Kerman, Wildfire, & Barth, 2002; Wald, Carlsmith, Leiderman, Smith, & French, 1988). Many other studies have documented negative outcomes of maltreatment across all the developmental periods of childhood. The next sections explore the attributes and milestones of the four global developmental periods and how maltreatment and involvement with the child welfare system is likely to impact development and well-being.

Infancy

Infancy, which roughly spans the period from birth to 3 years of life, is arguably the most complex period of development. Developmental changes occur at the most rapid rate of any point in childhood, and are intertwined across developmental domains. For example, advancement in visual perception leads to enhanced social development (e.g., recognition of maternal facial features, attachment). Important developmental milestones during this period, such as the emergence of language and the solidification of an attachment relationship, have important implications for infants in the child welfare system. Much empirical work has documented that maltreated and foster infants are more likely to exhibit language delays (Culp, Little, Letts, & Lawrence, 1991; Leslie, Gordon, Ganger, & Gist, 2002) and attachment disorders (Zeanah, Boris, & Leiberman, 2000).

In the physical domain, growth and ambulation are important developmental foci. Maltreated infants are more susceptible to growth delays such as failure to thrive (Black et al., 1994; Drotar & Robinson, 2000) and motor deficits (e.g., Leslie, Gordon, Ganger, & Gist, 2002). Very young children in the child welfare system are also prone to a variety of physical insults and illnesses, such as prenatal drug exposure and HIV (Dubowitz, 1999; Halfon, Mendonca, & Berkowitz, 1995). Additionally, findings in neuroscience have underscored the rapid and complex development as well as the plasticity of the brain during this period, suggesting that environmental processes may have an enormous impact on the developing brain and associated functioning.[3] As indicated previously, there is evidence that some types of insults to the brain, such as neglect and trauma, are more difficult to overcome and may result in lasting cognitive and social-emotional impairments (DeBellis et al., 1999; Gunnar, 1998; Perry, Pollard, Blakley, Baker, & Vigilante, 1995).

Thus, infancy can be understood as a period of extreme vulnerability in which specific child welfare experiences have the potential to have devastating, long-term consequences. There is also evidence that parenting is most challenging during this developmental period because of the virtual full dependence of infants on parents for survival. This evidence can be viewed in the light of evidence from the child welfare literature showing that infants are the group most likely to be reported as maltreated and the most likely to have severe consequences from the maltreatment. Infants are also more likely to be placed in foster care and adoption due to the social workers' focus on their inherent vulnerability.

Early Childhood

During early childhood, children typically make substantial strides in their language, cognitive, social, and emotional development. During this time in their lives, unexceptional children growing up under usual environmental conditions come to speak in complex sentences, solve concrete problems, engage in symbolic play, understand the perspective of another, make moral inferences, interact collaboratively with their peers, and become more emotionally regulated. The unusual circumstances defining the lives of maltreated and foster preschool children lead to compromised developmental outcomes across domains. For example, maltreated preschoolers have been documented to have expressive and receptive language delays, with more severe deficits found among neglected children (Culp et al., 1991; Leslie, Gordon, Ganger, & Gist, 2002). In the social-emotional domain, there is evidence that maltreated preschoolers exhibit less moral internalization (i.e., reliance on internal controls), display more aggressive social interactions, and have less emotional understanding and regulation than non-maltreated children (Koenig, Cicchetti, & Rogosch, 2000; Pollack, Cicchetti, Hornung, & Reeda, 2000).

Despite their increased competence, preschoolers still require adults to guide their actions and meet their dependency needs. In the area of behavioral compliance, researchers have found that preschool children can internalize parental standards, but still require parental regulation and support to behave in socially acceptable ways (Kochanska, Coy, & Murray, 2001). An interesting finding in this arena is that abused preschoolers may display *compulsive compliance*—i.e., immediate compliance with maternal demands and suppression of negative affect (Crittenden & DiLalla, 1988; Koenig, Cicchetti, & Rogosch, 2000). On the other hand, neglected children express more negative affect when interacting with their parents

(Koenig, Cicchetti, & Rogosch, 2000). Also during the preschool period, individual differences (e.g., in body size, intelligence, mental health, etc.) become more pronounced as children begin to display the unique ways in which their constitutional characteristics and environmental experiences interact to produce specific developmental outcomes. For example, many researchers have found that children with high levels of persistent aggression are identifiable as early as the preschool period (Campbell, Pungello, Miller-Johnson, Burchinal, & Ramey, 2001). For preschool children in the child welfare system, the expression of such characteristics as persistent aggression may lead to such punitive responses on the part of parents as maltreatment by biological parents or request for removal by foster parents.

Early childhood can be conceptualized then as a time of increasing competence, but continued vulnerability. Preschool children in the child welfare system can use language and play to reveal their maltreatment experiences, but are sufficiently young that their ability to self-protect is limited. In fact, the evidence points to fairly high rates of maltreatment in this group (see chapter 3). Although they are still quite vulnerable developmentally and in terms of their maltreatment experience, they are far less likely to be placed in foster care than their infant counterparts. Additionally, despite the substantial proportion of maltreated children of this age who experience mental health difficulties (Burns et al., 2004), there are not many examples of child welfare services targeted for this group that focus on their age-specific difficulties and capitalize on their enhanced capacities for language and play.

Middle Childhood

Across cultures, middle childhood is perceived as a time when children can take on more adult-like roles and responsibilities. In Western cultures, this is manifested in children's participating in formal education and assuming more independent roles in their families. For maltreated and foster children, these two areas present particular challenges. Multiple strands of research point to the inferior academic achievement of maltreated and foster children when compared with their same-age counterparts. In addition, there is evidence that maltreated children tend to have negative representations of their relationships with family members, and may have to take on adult roles in certain situations (McCrone, Egeland, Kalkoske, & Carlson, 1994; Rogosch, Cicchetti, Shields, & Toth, 1995).

School-aged children have broader social networks in which they are actively engaged, including the peer group and adults outside of their families (e.g., teachers and coaches). They are more able to regulate their behavior without the assistance of parents and caregivers, display much less aggression than during the preschool period, and apply their enhanced cognitive capacities to reason about social situations. They also become much more aware of their psychological identities and how they are perceived by others. Maltreated and foster children do not show the same strides in their social-emotional development as do non-maltreated children. For example, maltreated children exhibit negative mental representations of their peer relationships (McCrone, Egeland, Kalkoske, & Carlson, 1994) and higher rates of behavior problems, particularly aggression (Manly, Kim, Rogosch, & Cicchetti, 2001).

From the perspective of child welfare, the increased competence of children in this developmental period may reduce their vulnerability to maltreatment. First, they are much less demanding for parents as they are able to care for themselves in myriad ways. Second, they can potentially protect themselves against maltreatment by providing for themselves (e.g., finding food and clothing) and seeking assistance and support from other adults in their environment. The evidence that children are less likely to be placed in foster care during this developmental period (see chapters 3 and 4) lends credence to the hypothesis that the child welfare service sector does not perceive middle childhood as a particularly vulnerable developmental period. Such a view is somewhat problematic, however, when one considers the mental health vulnerabilities during this developmental period. Middle childhood has been identified as a period when children begin to exhibit many mental health difficulties (e.g., school phobia, dysthymia, and oppositional-defiant disorder). Indeed, conduct problems—including delinquent behavior—among maltreated children aged 6-12 are markedly elevated beyond the norms for boys and girls in the general population (Wall & Barth, in press).

Adolescence

Adolescence is a developmental period characterized by complex changes across developmental domains. The peer group becomes a major influence and sometimes is a greater determinant of behavior than parental mandates. Adolescents are also struggling with creating an identity, which will guide their life decision making as they enter young adulthood. Although fewer studies have examined the developmental effects of maltreatment on adolescents as compared with younger children, extant research documents that peer-related aggression and delinquency are at higher levels in maltreated adolescents (Widom, 2000).

Because of the myriad changes during this developmental period, adolescence is often a time when children experience difficulties in their academic and mental health functioning. Lower grades and truancy are reported with adolescents who did not have prior academic difficulties (Dryfoos, 1997). Lower academic achievement scores and higher rates of school dropout have been documented among maltreated adolescents (Egeland, 1997; Perez & Widom, 1994). Academic failure is a major cause of parent-child conflict and may result in maltreatment reports. In one urban area, longitudinal data gathered over 6 years indicate that children who experience educational neglect at an earlier age are likely to experience parent-child conflict at a later point (Institute of Applied Research, 2002).

In general, serious mental health difficulties emerge during this period, including substance abuse, delinquency, and suicidal ideation and behavior. Mental health problems are more common in adolescents who have been maltreated. Higher rates of internalizing disorders and co-morbid psychiatric diagnoses (e.g., dual diagnoses) have been reported for adolescents (Egeland, 1997; Johnson, Smailes, Cohen, Brown, & Bernstein, 2000). Although adolescence may well start prior to the onset of puberty, the biological maturation that ultimately occurs during adolescence leads to many complex personal and relational changes, including the emergence of sexual relationships. The intimate relationships of maltreated and foster adolescents bear the mark of past negative interpersonal experiences; consistent evidence points to the elevated levels of inappropriate sexual behavior, such as prostitution, of sexually abused adolescents (Friedrich et al., 2001; Widom & Kuhns, 1996). Additionally, early experience of child abuse and neglect has been found to predict adolescent parenthood (Herrenkohl, Herrenkohl, Egolf, & Russo, 1998).

The vulnerability of this developmental period underscores the major challenge that the child welfare system confronts in meeting the needs of this population. The evidence does suggest that adolescents show increased rates of reported maltreatment and placement compared with children in middle childhood (see chapters 3 and 4). These rates do not approach those of newborns, but the reasons for placement appear to be vastly different and anchored in the relationship dynamics between adolescents and caregivers. Placement requires adolescents to connect in an intimate way with other adults at a time, developmentally, when they are attempting to separate from their families to move toward independence. Despite the adult-child interactional difficulties that often precipitate child welfare involvement for adolescents, services for this group have not tended to be based on parent-child interventions (see chapter 6). Evincing this contra-developmental perspective, parent-training programs for parents with children in foster care rarely combine parents and adolescents, and they are typically delivered in the same way as they are for parents with very small children (Barth et al., in press).

The Life Course Perspective

The life course perspective is an emerging body of inquiry that spans social science disciplines (Elder, 1994). The life course "refers to the interweave of age-graded trajectories such as work careers and family pathways, that are subject to changing conditions and future options, and to short-term transitions ranging from leaving school to retirement" (p. 5). The focus of life course research stresses the timing, sequence, and duration of events over the life course.

Several concepts are especially important to the life course perspective. Chief among these is the notion of a trajectory—a pattern in the timing, duration, spacing, and order of events (Elder, 1998). Development over the course of childhood is composed of multiple, interdependent trajectories. Developmental trajectories relate to normative, ontogenetic development and are modified by the child's family and community contexts. They also have a substructure of intertwining strands of cognitive development, biological development, and emotional development. As with other trajectories, there is a high degree of interdependence and reciprocity between these components of child well-being.

Because trajectories and the events out of which they are assembled can be defined in social, cognitive, biological, and other terms, the concept is flexible enough to be used in a multilevel, developmental model of child welfare services. For our work, we are specifically interested in three general trajectories. They are developmental trajectories, maltreatment trajectories, and service trajectories.

Developmental Trajectories

Developmental trajectories refer generally to the entire life course from childhood through adulthood, including social, emotional, and intellectual functioning in a social context. As discussed above, the developmental path forms around the biological endowments of people at different phases of life given their social context. We do not have a complete record of this type of data for a large population, so we use developmental theory as a substitute. With age as a crude developmental proxy, we organize trajectories for age-differentiated populations to learn whether maltreatment and service patterns organize in developmentally meaningful ways. If they do, then this suggests the need to organize interventions and, perhaps, policies, accordingly.

Maltreatment Trajectories

Maltreatment trajectories refer to the course of maltreatment in the family context. Maltreatment may involve several members of the family, as both victims and perpetrators. Types of maltreatment may change over time—with earlier manifestations of one type of problem often predicting later difficulties of another type. Our assumption is that there is often an objective clinical manifestation of maltreatment (Helfer & Kempe, 1968), but that the process of case identification involves clinical judgments that are shaped by the way policy and practice contexts interact with the social context. We also understand that there are subjective reasons why an allegation of child maltreatment can be viewed as desirable (if it provides access to scarce services) or undesirable from the perspective of the family, child welfare professionals, and the court.

Having said that, the NCANDS data we use offers the chance to study the observed maltreatment trajectories as recorded in an administrative system. The trajectory for a child involves the sequence of report, investigation, and disposition, a sequence that can be repeated multiple times. The maltreatment rate describes the number of times the initial sequence concluded with an affirmative disposition. Although data such as these are not a substitute for true incidence data, report data are a net indicator of how the opposing tendencies within social and bureaucratic processes are resolved. Trends in reporting represent a record of the dynamic equilibrium.[4] Thus, reporting and other measures of related behavior can serve as dependent variables in a model that ties a base rate of maltreatment to social processes that together affect whether a given incident of maltreatment is recorded.

Service Trajectories

With respect to service trajectories generally, our interest is in the timing, sequence, duration, and outcome of service events and how they ameliorate or otherwise influence the unfolding maltreatment trajectory and its developmental consequences. In child welfare, given its link to court procedures and policy-driven timeframes, administrative milestones or events demarcate points along a service trajectory and may interact with treatment regimens. For example, delivery of therapeutic services in the context of out-of-home placement may lead to a protracted stay in foster care. This is the argument against the 15/22-month rule contained in the Adoption and Safe Families Act (ASFA) of 1997, which states that children who have been in care for 15 out of 22 months should be moved to an adoption track. The rule is applied administratively, subject to exceptions based on child-specific circumstances. Critics argue that the course of treatment takes time to work and that children have such long ties to their caregivers that termination of parental rights should be the option of last resort. The therapeutic requirements can exceed the administrative milestones established as part of ASFA.

Developmental and clinical trajectories are embedded in the service trajectories, as evidenced by the fact that a child faces higher risks of placement or reporting, etc. at different ages or stages of development (these different risks will be presented in chapters 3 and 4, and their implications discussed in the concluding chapters). Service trajectories (patterns in the timing of services) are also likely to be a function of the administrative rules about case processing. Such system-level effects on service trajectories include the availability and deployment of resources that define how a service trajectory starts (e.g., demand for group care may be supply-induced as opposed to need based). These system effects may support the natural interplay of developmental trajectories and service trajectories (by providing an age-sensitive platform of resources and interventions) or may distort the clinical or developmental trajectories so that little progress can be made.

Researchers have long endeavored to identify service trajectories, but the data have been sparse and the tools crude (Fanshel &

Shinn, 1978). A general classification of child welfare services differentiates between those that are provided while the child is at home (in-home services) and out-of-home placements that involve a child moving into a home other than the one provided by the parents. There is no regular source of national in-home services data; what is available comes from specialized surveys (Erickson, Egeland, & Pianta, 1989; U.S. DHEW Children's Bureau, 1978; U.S. DHHS Children's Bureau, 1994). The placement data available through the Multistate Foster Care Data Archive provides a direct way to trace and measure placement trajectories (Wulczyn, Kogan, & Jones Harden, 2003). For this reason, we stress foster care trajectories, but in doing so we understand that the trajectories have not been fully explicated at the child level. This deficiency in the data, resolved in part with the National Survey of Child and Adolescent Well-Being, is an important area for future research.

Service trajectories may disrupt or buttress the development of the child. For example, the separation of the child from his or her parents disrupts family relationships, diminishing the benefits of continuous relationships with biological family members. For this reason, child welfare service agencies increasingly recognize the importance of maintaining sibling ties between children involved with the child welfare system. Separation may also disrupt relationships with schoolmates and other meaningful adults (unless careful casework draws on these relationships in the creation of a service plan).

By the same token, placement can act as a protective factor because it can interrupt destructive parent-child interactions. As the duration of service/administrative trajectories grows longer, the degree of interdependence between development and services increases. This is one of the reasons why reform often focuses on reducing length of care–shorter time spent in care reduces exposure to any adverse impact that service trajectories may have on child development. Yet, service trajectories can also be thought of cumulatively—that is, if a child has many short admissions into emergency foster care and is subsequently reunified, this can become an elongated and adverse service trajectory. If children cannot go home quickly, an accelerated adoption timeline increases the likelihood of a rapid move to an alternative permanent family. Some family foster care environments (especially kinship foster care) do not fit this framework, however, and cause havoc for policymakers and practitioners who are ambivalent about forcing short stays in care.

The idea of a trajectory shapes empirical research. Formally, trajectories are sequences of events that commence with an initial event. In the case of maltreatment, the event typically is maltreatment. One of the central concerns in maltreatment is the question of onset and whether the initial event is detected, or perhaps more specifically, when in the evolving maltreatment trajectory detection does take place. Part of the issue is the fact that the initial event is not necessarily a discrete action, but rather a condition that emerges incrementally, may be repeated many times before detection, and has a cumulative effect. Again, the interdependent nature of trajectories is such that whether the cumulative effect reaches a threshold may depend on the onset of an administrative/service trajectory—that is, whether a child abuse report is filed, accepted by the agency, and acted on with the provision of effective intervention services.

The initial event has as its complement the end event. Developmental trajectories, when considered over the full life span, have a specific end or terminal event: death. Other trajectories differ in that the end events are less discrete. For maltreatment, the end comes when the maltreatment ceases, but the specific event may be as hard to discern as the initial event. In-home services have an end too, but when efforts to assist a family really end is hard to measure with any given dataset. Court and child welfare system involvement may end, but families may continue to receive services that started during the formal in-home service period. Placement is a bit different because the days when a child enters and leaves each placement are quite discrete. Yet, the end of child welfare services is much less discrete. Many children experience repeated returns to foster care. Further, even in that small proportion of cases when the right to parent a child has been terminated and the child is in a non-maltreating adoptive home, the child welfare trajectory may continue with child welfare system-funded or delivered post-adoptive services. Ongoing contact with biological siblings is quite likely (Frasch, Brooks, & Barth, 2000) and contact with biological parents may be included as part of the post-adoption plan.

That trajectories have beginnings and endings establishes the central role of onset, duration, and recurrence as constructs for evaluating and understanding child welfare trajectories. Further, the initial event establishes a fundamental interest in the "frequency of occurrence" and its timing relative to the life course. Epidemiologists use the frequency of occurrence to illuminate basic etiology: explaining what factors are associated with the frequency of occurrence and how those factors are related to theories of causality and intervention.

In turn, these factors represent the targets of service investments in that interventions are designed to alter the frequency and intensity of occurrence. Child welfare scholars have been at their most productive in their efforts to understand the recurrence of maltreatment reports and return to foster care (U.S. Department of Health and Human Services Administration for Children, Youth, and Families, 2003; Wulczyn, 1991), despite the fact that program development has not yet built program investments on the analyses of these trajectories. Program investments are also designed to affect the duration of a service trajectory, and to the extent that trajectories are interdependent, interventions can attenuate or amplify those interdependencies, the specific effect being context sensitive. For example, several foster care reform initiatives have endeavored to find placements for children within their school district in order to minimize the impact on their education from the onset of their placement service trajectory. The secondary benefits may be a shorter service trajectory inasmuch as the potential (i.e., probability) for reunification is enhanced because the parent-child relationship has been preserved to a greater degree than might have otherwise been the case.

Although no systematic national data are kept on the intensity or severity of maltreatment, this is a significant factor in determining service trajectories. When the abuse is very severe, this has a significant influence on the decision about whether a child should remain at home or go into care. Extremely severe abuse may result in the rapid termination of parental rights and responsibilities. At the same time, some children who go home from foster care will reenter foster care even though no re-abuse has occurred—their reentry may be triggered by signs that re-abuse may occur (e.g., that a parent tested positive for using drugs).

The Public Health Perspective

The bio-ecological/life course perspective provides the lens needed to understand what well-being means in the context of childhood and child welfare services. Our interest in the public health perspective is two-fold. The primary interest is empirical inasmuch as existing national child welfare data (the NCANDS, FCDA, and NSCAW) are observational and the public health perspective provides a rationale for imbuing observational data with relevance for policy analysis and decision making. In particular, the emphasis on epidemiology as a unifying approach to the study of population-level phenomena offers a way to link the bio-ecological/life course perspective with risk and the demand for services.

Second, because it favors prevention over the "reactive focus of therapeutic medicine," the public health perspective pushes thinking about well-being into a broader service context (Institute of Medicine, 1988). The continuum of services between universal (primary) prevention and indicated (tertiary) services that distinguishes the public health perspective mirrors the desire to refocus child welfare services away from residual service traditions and toward greater emphasis on preventive strategies. This calls for new efforts to develop evidence-supported interventions that are more effective than the relatively inert approaches tried in the last two decades (Littell & Schuerman, 2002).[5] Our review of the bio-ecological perspective suggests that well-being is a function of continuous developmental processes. Reactive models of child welfare services may prove to be inherently less effective than strategies that match the many causes with multidisciplinary interventions. If child welfare evolves along a similar path, the expressed interest in well-being outcomes may accelerate the push for a broader conceptualization of preventive child welfare services because similar multi-factor explanations dominate our understanding of well-being.

Although no single mode of research or body of theory characterizes public health research, the field is unified by a commitment to the science of epidemiology (Institute of Medicine, 1988). Schoenbach and Rosamond (2000) characterize epidemiology as a field of applied research that works to advance public health. Epidemiological research focuses on the factors that affect health in order to provide a scientific basis for prevention of disease and the promotion of health. Milton Terris (1992) argued that epidemiology, properly applied, could establish the relative importance of causal factors in order to set priorities for research and action. He also promoted the idea that epidemiological research would help to identify the populations at greatest risk so that interventions might be targeted appropriately. Our interest in epidemiology builds on these two points.

Epidemiological research in the public health tradition is not new to maltreatment or child welfare research, although it is much less common in foster care research. Frequency of occurrence is a basic measure in epidemiological research, and the U.S. Department of Health and Human Services has funded three national incidence studies of maltreatment in an effort to better understand the full scope or incidence of the problem.[6] In Canada, the Ontario Incidence Studies from 1993 and 1998 represent that province's effort to describe the scope and characteristics of reported child abuse and neglect (Trocme et al., 2002). Djeddah and her colleagues (2000) have reviewed international studies of child abuse. Finally, there are a number of specialized studies of maltreatment that focus on maltreatment subtypes, such as child sexual abuse (Finkelhor, 1994).

In recent years, epidemiological research has adapted research methods to account for an emerging interest in multilevel theoretical models (Berkman & Kawachi, 2000). Examples of eco-epidemiological research, to use a phrase that characterizes the newer approaches (Earls & Carlson, 2001; Schwartz, Susser, & Susser, 1999), can also be found in the maltreatment literature. For example, in their study of child maltreatment in Cleveland, Ohio, Coulton and colleagues (1999; 1995) found that census blocks with concentrated poverty have higher incidence of child maltreatment even after controlling for attributes of the community (child care burden and instability) and individual demographic risk factors. Using multilevel statistical models, they also found that within-neighborhood variation in risk was greater than between-neighborhood risks, a finding that is somewhat at odds with research conducted using aggregate data. Among other insights, their results are indicative of how difficult it is to discern causal relationships when dealing with multi-factor models.

Although epidemiological research is growing increasingly sophisticated, our starting point is much simpler. The key methodological insight arising out of epidemiological research is the emphasis on a population perspective for deriving basic incidence rates for both substantiated maltreatment reports and foster care placement. Incidence rates provide a direct estimate of the probability, or risk, of developing a condition (maltreatment or placement) within a given period of time (Lilienfeld & Lilienfeld, 1980). Age-, race-, period-, or geographic-specific incidence rates isolate whether risk is associated with attributes of people, time, or place.

The analysis of population-level risks is important for two reasons. First, the population perspective is essential for understanding basic etiology. Studies of individuals who have already been diagnosed are necessarily limited because the at-risk population is excluded. Second, population-level analyses offer an opportunity to observe and interpret the interaction between underlying conditions and the organization of services. Small area analysis (the study of geographic variation) has been used productively in health care research to understand how system structures influence patterns of health care delivery (Wennberg, 1999).

The approach we take uses the risk of maltreatment and foster care placement, measured as the number of child-level events (substantiated maltreatment reports and initial foster care placements) per 1,000 children in the year 2000. We analyze age-specific incidence rates within populations differentiated by urbanicity, race/ethnicity, and poverty. The objective is to discern whether the association between risk and age holds up with various sectors of the large population. Durable age effects speak to underlying risk patterns that are connected to child development.[7]

The second step involves the use of the NSCAW data to describe, in developmental terms, how children involved with the child welfare system are doing. The approach provides the insight needed to understand the developmental status of children at the start of their service careers and allows for exploration of age-specific measures of well-being.

Linking the Bio-Ecological/Life Course and Public Health Perspectives

The hypothesis that guides the empirical work posits that age, the risk of substantiated maltreatment, and the risk of foster care placement are linked and that services that build on this linkage are most likely to result in the shortest and most beneficial service trajectories.[8] The bio-ecological/life course perspective suggests that risk and age ought to be related in such a way that risk is elevated during certain developmental stages. This may be due to child attributes that are developmentally specific (babies are more vulnerable than older children) or because of the social institutions that mold the experience of children (e.g., most children start school between the ages of 4 and 6). Previous research points in this direction. We postulate that the relationship between age and risk is persistent in that, controlling for place, poverty, and race, age-specific risks are unaffected. For example, age-specific rates may be greater in areas characterized by higher levels of poverty, but age-specific patterns remain distinctive across the United States.

The focus on age as a factor that differentiates risk echoes a theme articulated earlier: principles of child development apply regardless of context (Shonkoff & Phillips, 2000). The developmental principle that guides the analysis assumes that there are stage-specific equilibria between risk and protective factors in a family context. Maltreatment results when the equilibrium shifts, often as a result of developmental changes in the child or parent, and risks outweigh protective factors (Djeddah et al., 2000). The equilibrium is age-sensitive in that developmental stages introduce unique forms of stress to the balance between risk and protective factors because the needs of children differ according to their idiographic position along the developmental continuum (Belsky, 1993). For example, children left unsupervised or without adequate provisions will provoke different responses depending on age. Unsupervised children may be of concern to child welfare systems, for somewhat different reasons, up through early adolescent years, but very few early adolescents come to the attention of the child welfare system because of failure of parents to provide basic necessities (Barth, Wildfire, & Green, in press). Age affects the social construction of risk because certain threats to well-being, such as the failure to provide nutrition or medicine, are more virulent in younger populations. Context matters, too. So do the characteristics of the parent. However, all else being equal, the probability of maltreatment, given identical behavior by caretakers in similar situations, will be higher for some groups of children for reasons that are connected to development. Age, as a proxy for child development, may help reveal these within-group continuities.

Ordinarily, researchers are interested in age as a predictor of maltreatment in order to outline the etiologic course of maltreatment. Although we share that interest, we are more concerned with whether the pattern of incidence is stable with respect to place and time. In a policy context, stable patterns of demand imply that services ought to be organized to respond to those patterns. At least three reasons underlie the rationale. First, the developmental status of target children implies that the content of interventions (diagnosis and treatment regimen) has to be contoured to fit the clinical manifestation of maltreatment *and* the capacity of the parent(s) and child to absorb the intent of treatment. Just as interventions have to be culturally appropriate to be effective, interventions also have to be developmentally relevant. Second, to the extent that developmental patterns persist across place and time, the differentiation of service types will share that persistence, making investments in system capacity (worker skills and treatment technology) reusable. Agencies are making greater efforts to move services away from the central offices into social contexts (neighborhoods) where the demand is high. To borrow the metaphor, the developmental perspective suggests that *locating* services along a developmental continuum fulfills an analogous purpose.

Finally, accountability has to be adjusted to reflect the realities of service utilization. If the underlying etiology of maltreatment is sensitive to age, then the instruments used to monitor success have to adhere to the underlying truths. In sum, the timing of onset of maltreatment and placement provides a point estimate of the child's developmental status when the service trajectory starts, sets a context for designing the intervention, and establishes the baseline needed to evaluate how services influence trajectories (service and well-being) going forward.

Our goal in this volume is to integrate these perspectives and draw inferences for policy.

Notes

1. For example, Child Trends convened a group to identify relevant well-being indicators (Chalk, Moore, & Gibbons, 2003). It is interesting to note that although the group identified indicators that were worth tracking, the members of the panel did not attach any of the well-being indicators to an outcome/accountability framework. Instead, the indicators were recommended for descriptive purposes.

2. The whole subject of age, period, and cohort effects demands more attention than is possible here. For more background on the problem in psychological and sociological research, see Elder (1975); Rutter (1989); and Wohlwill (1970).

3. The evidence suggests that although brain development does occur across the lifespan, the brain is most plastic during the first few years of life.

4. The idea of competing social forces playing out in a dynamic equilibrium is a way of thinking advanced by Lewin (1976), among others. Empirical models for studying such phenomena were described by Tuma and Hannan (1984).

5. Promising approaches to primary prevention and early intervention will be discussed in chapters 5 and 6.

6. The National Incidence Studies are an important source of incidence data (Sedlak & Broadhurst, 1996). Their principal value lies in the effort to track the true incidence of maltreatment. The findings from NCANDS do differ from the results produced with the NIS because the NCANDS data are based on official reports. Nevertheless, we use the NCANDS for the following reasons. First, there are no NIS data that correspond to NSCAW in terms of timeframe. Second, as we noted before, policymaking entities have to respond to the cases before them. If levels of unreported abuse and neglect are very high, then the underreporting is a public policy

problem that needs to be addressed. However, until that happens, administrators have to address the children and families identified by the community.

7.   In one sense, the approach adopted is akin to the work developed by the World Health Organization to assess the life course impact of mortality and morbidity. Measures of mortality, the conventional way of evaluating the impact of medical conditions, understate the impact of disabling conditions that affect individuals over their lifetime. The newer approach, which assesses the burden of disease, summarizes the relative impact of both morbidity and mortality using a single measure—the Disability Adjusted Life Year (DALY). The DALY is calculated using the years of life lost because of morbidity and the years of life expected to be lived with a disability. The later component is weighted to reflect the severity of the condition. Researchers have since created other measures, such as the Healthy Life Years (HeaLY) and the Quality-Adjusted Life Year (QALY) in an effort to improve upon the basic concept. (See for example, Hyder, Rotlant, & Morrow, 1998; Schwappach, 2002.) The similarity of our approach rests with the use of a simple epidemiological model based on the incidence and duration of underlying conditions. In applications that involve morbidity, incidence and duration are used to understand how many individuals get sick and for how long. These measures form the basis of the DALY. We do not attempt to evaluate the burden of maltreatment. However, our analysis does suggest that reported maltreatment is more common in some populations than others. Maltreatment onset during infancy differs from onset during adolescence. The impact (or burden) is potentially greater when onset is early. Thus, policy development and planning for services ought to take these realities into account, especially if underlying conditions have salience for designing services.

8.   Child welfare services must also weigh the rights of parents to care for their children and the rights of children to remain with family members. There are no close parallels in epidemiology, although the prevention of disease must also be accomplished within a legal framework that protects privacy.

Part 2

The Epidemiology of Maltreatment and Foster Care Placement

Introduction to Part 2

In Part 2, we present the main empirical findings from our analysis of three datasets. These findings form the core evidence we use to better understand the fit between child welfare policy and basic notions of well-being. Before we present those findings, however, we want to provide a broad outline of the analysis and to briefly describe the data we draw on.

There are two chapters in this section. Each is organized in the same way. In chapter 3, we present the maltreatment data from the National Child Abuse and Neglect System (NCANDS). The data presented shows the risk of maltreatment, organized by age of the child, in order to ascertain how age as a proxy for child development is related to the risk of reported maltreatment. We then relate these findings to the NSCAW data, which reveals how children who have been reported for maltreatment are faring according to various age-appropriate screens. Chapter 4 examines placement data using the Multistate Foster Care Data Archive (FCDA). The data presented follow the approach used with NCANDS data. We describe the risk of placement by the age of the child, and then supplement that information with data from NSCAW that describe the developmental status of children when they enter placement. Again, we use age at onset of placement as a proxy for underlying developmental influences in relation to how children leave foster care. The foster care analysis is different from the maltreatment analysis in that we follow the children placed in foster care further along their service trajectories, until they leave placement. The analysis of maltreatment in chapter 3 focuses only on the initial report, and does not follow children through subsequent events (e.g., recurrence), although that type of analysis can be done with the NCANDS data.

Our approach to the data combines the bio-ecological/life course and public health perspectives. With bio-ecological/life course models of human development, the timing of events is as critical as their actual occurrence (Elder, 1998). This basic notion gives rise to two

ideas that we use to bridge development, maltreatment, and placement: onset and timing. Onset refers to whether something happens,
whereas timing embeds events in the developmental trajectory underway at the point of onset. By concentrating on the time when
involvement with the child welfare system begins, maltreatment and
placement are placed in a developmental context. More specifically,
well-being outcomes imply both an initial status and movement along
a developmental trajectory. Designing child welfare services that have
an impact on well-being involves understanding where the child
started and the path of development given that starting point. Public
policy has to be responsive to these dynamics.

We emphasize rates of maltreatment and placement in order to
identify age-based patterns in the data. This is a standard public health/
epidemiological approach designed to reveal the magnitude of the
problem. To capture developmental influences, age-specific rates
are calculated. The null hypothesis would state simply that the likelihood of onset is equally probable across the age span of childhood. Departures from the hypothesis highlight the importance of
age and its developmental correlates within the spectrum of influences that define risk and service use. To further establish the relevance of age-differentiated patterns in the data, we also examine
rates by age and place. Stable age-based risks would suggest that
variation in local ecologies is not enough to trump the importance of
age as a defining determinant of maltreatment and placement.
Shonkoff and Phillips (2000, p. 341) argue that "the general principles of development apply to all children independent of…the range
of environments in which they live." The analysis of maltreatment
and placement rates is intended to explore the relevance of this perspective to the children who came into contact with the child welfare system in the year 2000.

Data Sources

The data used for the analysis come from three sources. The NCANDS
and FCDA are both administrative datasets extracted from the information systems states have developed to monitor their child welfare programs. The NSCAW data are based on a survey of children and families involved in the child welfare system. Although the data from these
sources are not linked physically, the data are synchronized in that the
analysis of NCANDS and the FCDA focuses on calendar year 2000,
the period when the initial NSCAW sample was identified.

The use of administrative data together with survey data strengthens both sources in important ways. Administrative data sources typically contain fewer data elements, but the data are gathered routinely over time. Moreover, the data usually refer to an entire population. The weakness of the administrative data is the limited range of detailed individual-level data that can describe who the children are. Survey data typically contain a great deal of detailed individual-level data, but the expense of collecting the data usually limits how frequently the data are gathered. With these three datasets, we are able to amplify what the administrative data say about the risk of placement by using the NSCAW data. With the administrative data, we are able to explore age effects during time periods that are not covered by NSCAW.

National Child Abuse and Neglect Data System (NCANDS)

The Child Abuse Prevention and Treatment Act of 1974 (Public Law 93-247), as amended, directed the Secretary of the U.S. Department of Health and Human Services to establish a national data collection and analysis program on child abuse and neglect. In response, HHS established the National Child Abuse and Neglect Data System (NCANDS) as a voluntary national reporting system for states. The Children's Bureau in the Administration on Children, Youth and Families maintains the national data collection and analysis program. NCANDS represents an effort to develop and improve state and local child welfare services information systems, to implement a national child abuse and neglect data system, and to develop a data source able to respond to a wide range of policy and program analysis needs. For the most recent year, 2002, NCANDS received data from forty-two states representing about 85 percent of the nation's population.

The NCANDS system has two parts. The Summary Data Component (SDC) consists of aggregate child abuse and neglect statistics from states that are not able to submit case-level data on children. The SDC contains data on reports, investigations, victims, and services. The Child File (formerly named the Detailed Case Data Component) contains detailed case-level information from state child protective services agencies able to provide electronic child abuse and neglect records. The NCANDS Child File encompasses all reports of suspected child abuse and neglect that result in an investigation (about one-third of reports are screened out before the investigation stage). Reports are included in the Child File if an investigation or alternative response has been conducted following an allegation of abuse or neglect. The results of the investigation or alternative response are in terms of dispositions or findings in the following categories: "substantiated," "indicated," "unsubstantiated," "alternative-response-victim," "alternative-response-non-victim," and "closed without a finding."

Regardless of how the investigation is resolved, the Child File contains report data (with state, report date, report identification number, report source, disposition, disposition date, and so on) and data describing the child who was the subject of the report (age, sex, race, Hispanic ethnicity, living arrangements, county of residence, military dependent status, and maltreatment history).

NCANDS also records additional information:

- Child risk factors—for children, data indicating the presence of substance abuse, mental or physical disability, emotional disturbance, behavior problem, or other medical problem
- Maltreatment—data on the type of maltreatment alleged (physical abuse, neglect, medical neglect, sexual abuse, psychological/emotional maltreatment), the disposition for each of up to four "maltreatments" (substantiated, etc.), and whether the child died
- Perpetrator—for up to three perpetrators (if the allegation is substantiated), data on relationship to victim, age, sex, race, ethnicity, military status, and whether the perpetrator had abused before
- Caretaker risk factors—for the primary/family caretakers, data on the presence of substance abuse, mental or physical disability, emotional disturbance, domestic violence, financial strain, and inadequate housing (for all children in the file)
- Services provided—family support/preservation services, petition to juvenile/family court, removal from home, and several other services (for all children in the file)

With the implementation of the Child File starting with the 2000 data year, complete data are requested on each child, regardless of the disposition.[2]

The Multistate Foster Care Data Archive[3]

The Multistate Foster Care Data Archive (FCDA) is maintained by Chapin Hall Center for Children at the University of Chicago. The Archive is similar to NCANDS in that the data are constructed from information drawn directly from the administrative databases that state agencies use to manage and operate their child welfare programs. States provide data to the Archive on a voluntary basis. At last count, the Archive included the placement records of 1.3 million children placed into foster care. From a point-in-time perspective, on September 30, 2000, the federal government estimated that there were 556,000 children in foster care (U.S. Department of Health and Human Services, 2003b). The states contributing data to the Archive accounted for approximately 50 percent of the nationwide total.

The core module of the Archive contains a limited set of child characteristics and placement events. The child characteristics are date of birth, gender, ethnicity, and a unique identifier. The placement events are date of placement, type of placement, and exit destination (e.g., reunification and adoption). The placement data from each state are linked to a general schema so that the data are as comparable as possible. Three features of the Archive design are relevant. First, the advent of computerized child tracking in the participating states differs. Illinois, one of the first states to adopt computerized tracking, contributes data from July 1, 1976 forward. This means the Archive has sequential event records for every child placed in foster care since that date. In other states, the available data begin somewhat later. Michigan, Missouri, New York, and New Jersey initiated computerized tracking in the early to mid-1980s. In the late 1980s, California and Alabama implemented child welfare tracking systems, while the remaining states contribute data from systems that permit child tracking from 1990 through the most recent update, which in the case of this study is December 31, 2001. In some states, such as California, newer computer systems led to changes in the legacy databases that altered the time period covered by the Archive. The specific time period associated with the analysis is noted in the discussion.

Second, the idea of a *spell* in foster care is a key methodological concept that influences how the data are analyzed. Most of the descriptive work done with the Archive has focused on spells because of their conceptual simplicity and their substantive importance—a child is either in foster care or not. A spell is defined as a continuous period of time spent in placement. A spell begins with a new foster care placement and continues until reunification, adoption, or any other discharge from the foster care system. Once the spells are derived from the event sequence, spells that lasted fewer than 5 days are excluded because shorter spells tend to be reported only in certain states. Also, when spells in foster care end for reasons other than reunification or adoption, and reentry then follows within 1 week, the gap is "bridged" and the two separate spells are treated as one single spell. This adjustment was needed to remove certain "paper changes" that reflect idiosyncratic reporting practices.

Third, to further ensure comparability, the Archive includes the records associated with children who meet the following criteria: children must have entered foster care before the age of 18; children must be in state care for reasons of dependency, abuse, or neglect; and the foster care placement must be state supervised and supported with a board and maintenance payment.

The National Survey of Child and Adolescent Well-Being[4]

In 1996, Congress directed the Secretary of the Department of Health and Human Services to conduct a national study of children who are at risk of abuse or neglect or who are in the child welfare system, as set forth in the Personal Responsibility and Work Opportunity Reconciliation Act of 1996, Sec. 429A, National Random Sample Study of Child Welfare (P.L. 104-193). In response, the Administration on Children, Youth, and Families undertook the National Survey of Child and Adolescent Well-Being. NSCAW is the first source of nationally representative longitudinal data developed from first-hand reports of children, families (or other caregivers), and service providers. Moreover, this is the first national study that examines child and family well-being in detail.

This volume primarily includes data from the first round, or baseline, data collection begun in late 1999 and concluded at the end of 2000.[5] Living in 36 states and 92 counties, the children in NSCAW represent all children whose families were investigated (or assessed) for child abuse and neglect during that timeframe.[6] The intent of NSCAW is to follow, and continue to assess, children and their caregivers regardless of the form of continued child welfare services receipt—even if their cases are closed after investigation and never reopened. Although the study design collects data relevant to the substantiation of child abuse cases, cases that were not substantiated following the investigation are also included in the sample.

The NSCAW cohort includes children from birth to age 14 (at the time of sampling). The NSCAW findings discussed in this volume are based on information from 5,501 children and their caregivers, child welfare workers, and teachers. (In addition, NSCAW includes another 727 children who had been in out-of-home placement for 8-18 months at the time of sampling.) The findings reported here are based on the children who were entering child welfare services at the time of sampling. These children may have previously been involved with child welfare services.

NSCAW is unique among national child welfare studies in providing information from children and caregivers as well as child welfare personnel. There are four possible types of respondents for each "case": the caregiver (either the biological parent, another responsible adult, or the out-of-home caregiver), child welfare worker, the child, and the child's teacher (when the child is old enough to go to school) (U.S. DHHS, 2005; Dowd et al., 2002). The information reported here is primarily from "baseline" interviews with these respondents, which were conducted following the close of the investigation. The findings referenced in this document are a small proportion of those reported in the full baseline report (U.S. DHHS, 2004).

Notes

1. For details on the data elements contained in the files available to researchers: National Data Archive on Child Abuse and Neglect (NCANDS), page at http://www.ndacan.cornell.edu/.) For details on the complete Child File (*The national child abuse and neglect data system (NCANDS): The detailed case data component (DCDC) child data file record layout*, June 2000), see http://www.acf.dhhs.gov/programs/cb/dis/ncands98/record/recorda1.pdf

2. Perpetrator data are present only if the allegation is substantiated.

3. More information about the *Multistate Foster Care Data Archive* can be found at: http://www.chapinhall.org/article_abstract_new.asp?ar=1322&L2=61&L3=130

4. For additional information on the NSCAW study, please see NSCAW Research Group, 2002. Methodological lessons from the National Survey of Child and Adolescent Well-Being: The first three years of the USA's first national probability study of children and families investigated for abuse and neglect. *Children & Youth Services Review*, 24, 513-543.

5. Data on these same children have also been collected at 18 and 36 months, but are not included in this volume.

6. In a handful of states in which state law required that the first contact of a caregiver whose child was selected for the study be made by child welfare services agency staff rather than by a NSCAW Field Representative, response rates were unacceptably low. Thus, the target population for the NSCAW child welfare services sample is, technically, "all children in the U.S. who are subjects of child abuse or neglect investigations (or assessments) conducted by child welfare services and who live in states not requiring agency-first contact."

3

The Epidemiology of Reported
Child Maltreatment

Among the most significant contributions of the data now available on child maltreatment and foster care is the finding that although rates of reported maltreatment vary across the age spectrum of childhood, they occur in a pattern that is largely unchanged when one controls for poverty status, urbanicity, and race/ethnicity. Specifically, regardless of the family's area of residence, income level, or race/ethnicity, infants are more likely than any other age group to be maltreated—a finding that should drive policy formation and service delivery.

In this chapter, we analyze child maltreatment trajectories from both epidemiological and developmental perspectives. First, we use the child's age at *first* victimization to probe age-differentiated patterns in the likelihood of being the subject of a substantiated maltreatment report.[1] We do this by isolating first-time victims from all other reported victims in the NCANDS data using the report date and the date of birth. In effect, we examine substantiated maltreatment as close to its onset as possible, given the limits of current reporting data. The report date is only a proxy for the onset of maltreatment because of how and when states receive reports; maltreatment and service trajectories are necessarily intertwined and the reported date of maltreatment may not always serve as an accurate proxy for the onset of maltreatment.

The second component of the analysis examines data from the National Study of Child and Adolescent Well-Being. Whereas we use the NCANDS data to provide a broad overview of reported maltreatment in relation to age, the NSCAW data are used to enrich our understanding of maltreated children in two important ways. First, NSCAW data supply the information needed to better understand the development and circumstances of children investigated for maltreatment. If, somehow, the outcomes for children identified by child welfare agencies are going to include well-being, then agencies will identify what services or supports will be needed, given a developmental starting point. The NSCAW data provide the only national estimates of these issues.

Second, service trajectories that start with an investigation divide along two distinct paths. One path starts with placement; the other path starts with in-home services (although some children who have been the subject of a substantiated maltreatment report may not get services at all).[2] To the extent that children who follow one trajectory or another share certain characteristics, the NSCAW data offer an opportunity to identify those characteristics at a point in time that coincides closely with a child's initial contact with the child welfare system.

The Incidence of Maltreatment

We begin by outlining briefly how reports alleging maltreatment are processed. State laws and regulations differ with respect to the ways in which allegations of maltreatment are handled.[3] This is one reason why epidemiological research in child welfare has not flourished to the extent it has in some other fields. Legal context and the level of worker discretion during the investigation are thought to create an environment that renders comparisons between jurisdictions meaningless because these influences on the data are hidden. That said, the National Study of Child Protective Services Systems and Reform Efforts points to the fact that certain core features of child protective services systems are in fact present in many if not most states (U.S. Department of Health and Human Services, 2003b). Moreover, the extent to which the epidemiological perspective has salience is largely an empirical question. As we show later in this chapter, different localities have strikingly similar victimization rates. Although administrative processes are undoubtedly important, the data suggest that the causes of maltreatment have as much if not more to do with who enters the system than how the system operates. The epidemiological perspective helps to reveal the underlying patterns.

A traditional state child welfare services agency has jurisdiction over child protective services, preventive services, foster care, and adoption. Some states have a consolidated agency that oversees child welfare services, children's mental health, and juvenile justice.[4] Still other states have child welfare agencies that control only two of these service areas. All told, the child protection system consists of more than 2,600 local agencies and about 42,000 workers who respond to allegations of maltreatment. In virtually all of the states, maltreatment is defined in statute and regulation (U.S. Department of Health and Human Services, 2003b). Statutes also outline the steps workers must follow once a report has been accepted. For example, most states provide a timeline that describes when various activities related to the investigation should be completed. The investigation involves interviews with family members, the child when warranted, and others, all in an effort to determine what happened, what is happening at the present, and what might happen in the future. Ultimately, the goal is to determine whether the child was maltreated, is currently safe, or is at further risk of harm. When the process results in an affirmative finding of maltreatment, the report is said to have been *substantiated*, *founded*, or *indicated* depending on the jurisdiction. [5]

In 2001, there were approximately 5 million child referrals to the child welfare agencies (U.S. Department of Health and Human Services, 2003a). Of these referrals, about 3 million were accepted as reports and followed with an investigation, and about one-third of the children were found to be victims of abuse and neglect. More than half of the investigated reports are from professionals.[6,7]

The investigation typically results in some sort of determination as to whether the child has been abused and a secondary determination as to whether services should be provided on a voluntary or court-ordered basis. When making a determination, slightly fewer than half the states use either the preponderance of evidence or clear and convincing evidence as the standard of evidence needed to substantiate maltreatment. The remaining states use a lower, credible evidence standard. Depending on the circumstances, all states allow for the removal of a child from his or her home. Although a parent may consent to removal, the court has to supervise both voluntary and involuntary placements.

NCANDS collects data from states on post-investigation services provided within 90 days of the disposition. According to the 2001 report, 58.4 percent of the child victims received services, including foster care, following the investigation. Among non-victims (children who were investigated for maltreatment, but not substantiated), 29 percent received services after the investigation, a figure that also includes foster care. Understandably, the likelihood of placement is much higher for victims of maltreatment (19 percent) than it is among non-victims (4.7 percent).

Prior to NSCAW, the most recent national study of in-home services was conducted in the mid-1990s (U.S. Department of Health and Human Services & Children's Bureau, 1997). For the most part, services focused on adults and their ability to parent, which is not surprising given that 50 percent of the caretakers lacked appropriate parenting skills in the opinion of the caseworker. One-third of the parents also had difficulty with employment, income, and money management. Services were offered to children, but direct service provision to children was less common. Health assessments were the most common service provided to children; 53 percent of the children had their health evaluated. Outpatient mental health services were provided to 27 percent of the children. Day care, the next-largest category of services for children, was provided to 16 percent of the children.

Maltreatment

In general, substantiated reports of maltreatment provided by states to NCANDS fall into three major domains—physical abuse, sexual abuse, and neglect—plus a fourth category that includes emotional abuse and "other" forms of maltreatment.[8] The most common form of substantiated maltreatment, neglect, accounted for 57.2 percent of all victims in 2001 (U.S. Department of Health and Human Services, 2001). Neglect refers to the failure to provide needed, age-appropriate care even though the parents are financially able or have been offered the financial or other means to do so. Neglect includes the failure to provide adequate food, shelter or supervision; it also includes medical neglect, which is the failure to provide adequate medical attention. According to the 2001 maltreatment report, the rate of neglect in the United States was 7.4 victims per 1,000 children, which was a slight increase over the previous two years.

Physical abuse is the second-largest category of maltreatment, accounting for 18.6 percent of all victims. Physical abuse refers to acts that cause physical injury to a child, ranging from inappropriate discipline, to excessive force, beatings, and scalding. Official reports of physical abuse from 1996 through 2001 showed a decline from 3.5 to 2.3 per 1,000 children.

Sexual abuse includes any sexual activity that provides gratification or benefit to the perpetrator. Molestation, statutory rape, prostitution, pornography, incest, exposure, and sexually exploitive activities with a minor child are included in the definition of sexual abuse. Of the primary maltreatment types, sexual abuse is the least common, accounting for less than 10 percent of the victims, according to NCANDS. The rate of substantiated sexual abuse declined between 1997 and 2001, from 1.7 to 1.2 per 1,000 children. Typically, rates of sexual abuse are higher for both older children and females.

States do track other types of maltreatment, but reporting is much more state-specific. For example, educational neglect and perinatal exposure to substances are two forms of maltreatment that states treat differently insofar as official reporting mechanisms are concerned. However, in total, other types of maltreatment account for about 26 percent of all victims.

Finally, it is important to note that children may become involved with child welfare services for reasons other than abuse and neglect. For example, if a parent has a child with very difficult behavior, severe mental retardation, or who repeatedly runs away, the parents may turn to the child welfare agency for help, using their inability to supervise their child (neglect) as the reason for seeking help. Recent studies by the U.S. General Accounting Office (2003), James Bell Associates (2004), preliminary findings of the Child and Family Services Reviews in FY 2001 and 2002, and NSCAW are beginning to describe the extent to which this happens. In their analysis of data collected as part of the federal Child and Family Service Reviews, James Bell Associates (2004) found that among 421 cases of children in foster care, 18 percent were in placement for reasons linked to the child's behavior. Thus, although child maltreatment reports are very useful for understanding the extent to which children and families are in need of services, they may not precisely label the need for such services.

NCANDS: The Risk of Reported Maltreatment

As noted, the most readily available source of data for epidemiological research pertaining to child maltreatment is the National Child Abuse and Neglect Data System (NCANDS). In 2003, the U.S. Department of Health and Human Services published the twelfth annual maltreatment report, *Child Maltreatment 2001*. The reports set a standard for collecting and analyzing administrative data. Each year since the first report was published, the number of states reporting and the level of detail covered have grown. The 2001 report covers reporting, investigations, victims, recurrence, fatalities, services provided, workforce, and perpetrators.

Since the federal government began publishing maltreatment statistics, surprisingly little has changed regarding the basic patterns that characterize reported maltreatment in the United States. Most reports of maltreatment are not substantiated; neglect is the most common form of maltreatment; and young children are the most likely victims of maltreatment. Overall, the one change that has taken place concerns the general incidence of maltreatment. Starting in the mid-1990s, rates of maltreatment declined from 15.3 per 1,000 children in 1993 to about 11.8 per 1,000 in 1999. The drop in victimization rates coincides with the decline in child poverty that occurred throughout the 1990s, so it is tempting to attribute a drop in maltreatment to lower poverty rates. However, since so little is known about the relationship between *changes in poverty rates* and *changes in maltreatment rates,* it is difficult to pinpoint why victimization declined in the 1990s.[9] As Jones and Finkelhor (2003) point out, official reports of maltreatment are influenced by a number of factors that include social and administrative norms that govern whether a report will be made, accepted, and substantiated.

Age-Specific Rates of Maltreatment

Although the rate of maltreatment overall is an important indicator of how well the nation's children are doing, we are more interested in who is maltreated. We are particularly interested in how old children are when they are first victimized. To understand how age and the likelihood of maltreatment are related, we carried out a special study using NCANDS data from four states representing 296 counties, 11,450,000 children under the age of 19, and 64,000 first-time victims.[10]

The analysis begins with a simple description of maltreatment rates by age at onset for single-year age groupings. The analysis then divides the counties into two groups based on the county's poverty level. Counties with low poverty levels are the counties that fall into the top 20 percent—that is, counties with child poverty rates (in 1999) between 2.3 percent and 12.2 percent. Counties with high poverty rates fall in the bottom quintile, a group that includes counties with poverty rates between 17.6 percent and 43.6 percent. The counties are then divided into three groups based on the level of urbanicity. *Primary urban counties* include the state's largest county; *secondary urban areas* include counties with other large cities; *non-urban counties* include all other counties not fitting the other categories.

The analysis is repeated using maltreatment type to further distinguish age-specific patterns in the data. The focus is on neglect and physical abuse because age-specific base rates for sexual abuse are quite low. Again, data are presented separately for counties grouped by their level of urbanicity and their poverty level. These analyses show that age distributions of maltreatment are strikingly similar in high-poverty and low-poverty counties, and in primary urban compared with secondary urban and the remaining non-urban counties. Finally, the analysis considers urbanicity and race-specific maltreatment rates to underscore the fact that fundamental patterns that relate age and maltreatment hold across place and race.

The basic relationship between age and the risk of reported maltreatment is displayed in Figure 3.1. In general, the rate of reported maltreatment is highest for children who were under the age of 1 at the time of the investigation. The rate reported for infants in 2000 was 16 per 1,000, more than twice the rate for 1-year-olds, the group with the next-highest rate of maltreatment. Rates of maltreatment decline with age, although there are small age-specific exceptions found in the data. Except for 5-year-olds, school-aged children have lower rates of maltreatment than children under the age of 5. However, among school-aged children, older adolescents (i.e., 15-year-olds) have a risk of maltreatment (4.76/1,000) that is about 13 percent greater than the maltreatment risk facing 11-year-olds.

Maltreatment and poverty. The risk of maltreatment, according to age and county poverty level, is displayed in Figure 3.2. The basic pattern showing an elevated risk of maltreatment for infants is found in both high- and low-poverty counties. The risk of maltreatment for infants is 2.8 times as great as it is for 1-year-olds, the group with the next-highest maltreatment rate in high-poverty counties, and 1.6 times as great in low-poverty counties. For children of all other ages, maltreatment rates are lower among school-aged children, regardless of poverty level. The data also indicate that age-specific differences in the risk of victimization are comparable within high- and low-poverty counties. For example, late adolescents (14- and 15-year-olds) have maltreatment rates that are about 15 percent as great as those

Figure 3.1
Rate of Victimization by Age: 2000
(initial victims)

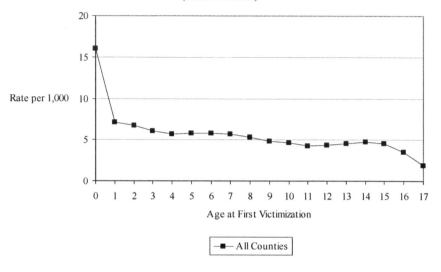

Figure 3.2
Rate of Victimization by Age and County Poverty Rate: 2000
(initial victims)

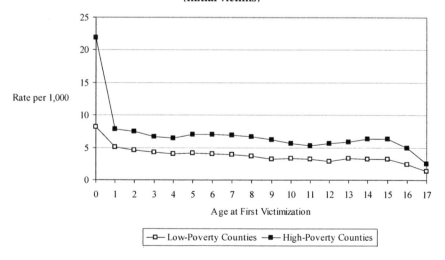

reported for 11- and 12-year-olds, regardless of poverty level. Finally, although maltreatment rates are generally higher in high-poverty counties, the differences among counties separated by poverty rates are most pronounced among infants. Among children between the ages of 1 and 10, maltreatment rates in high-poverty counties are about 1.5 times as great as the rates in low-poverty counties. Maltreatment rates among adolescents in high-poverty counties are about twice the rate reported in low-poverty counties. However, infant maltreatment rates are 2.7 times greater in counties with the highest poverty rates.

Maltreatment and urbanicity. Figure 3.3 shows maltreatment rates for counties characterized by their degree of urbanicity. These data tell a similar story with regard to the relationship between age and maltreatment rates, although the picture is a bit more complex. First, infants have the highest rate of maltreatment regardless of urbanicity. Second, except in the primary urban areas, maltreatment rates are typically higher among preschool children than among school-aged children. In primary urban areas, the rate of maltreatment for 14- and 15-year-olds exceeds the rate for 3- and 4-year-olds.

Differences in maltreatment rates between secondary urban areas and non-urban areas grow smaller with the increasing age of the child. A somewhat different pattern emerges when primary urban areas are compared with secondary and non-urban counties. For babies, maltreatment rates are highest in urban counties. For toddlers and preschool-aged children, maltreatment rates are highest in non-urban areas. The higher rates of reported maltreatment among

Figure 3.3
Rate of Victimization, All Maltreatment Types by Age and Urbanicity: 2000
(initial victims)

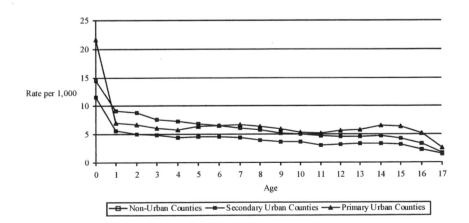

toddlers and preschool-aged children in non-urban areas may be attributable to case-finding effects among infants in urban areas. That is, at-risk children are identified earlier (reported as infants) in urban areas so that as that birth cohort reaches toddlerhood there are fewer at-risk children who have yet to be reported. The opposite pattern would account for the higher rates of maltreatment in non-urban areas. Lower reporting of at-risk babies means that more at-risk children reach toddlerhood without having come to the attention of a child welfare services agency.

Maltreatment type and urbanicity. Except for the significantly higher rates of maltreatment among infants, age effects in the maltreatment data are modest but persistent. The risk of maltreatment declines with age, although rates of maltreatment are higher among 13- to 15-year-olds than among children on the cusp of adolescence.

More distinct age patterns reveal themselves when maltreatment types are examined separately, and Figure 3.4 shows age-specific maltreatment rates for physical abuse. According to this data, the risk of maltreatment rises among infants, children entering school, and 13- to 15-year-olds. The most pronounced age effects are found in primary urban areas. However, in both primary and secondary urban areas, the rate of maltreatment among adolescents was higher than the rate for infants. Physical abuse rates in secondary urban

Figure 3.4
Rate of Victimization for Physical Abuse by Age and Urbanicity: 2000
(initial victims)

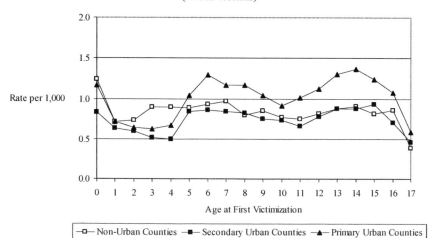

areas are the lowest. The data also indicate that among preschool-aged children physical abuse rates are highest in non-urban and primary urban areas.

These data suggest that entry into school brings children into contexts where surveillance is greater. The pattern is particularly pronounced in both secondary and primary urban areas. For example, the physical abuse rate for 6-year-olds in primary urban and primary urban areas was 1.29 per 1,000, more than double the rate for 4-year-olds.

Because neglect is so much more common than physical abuse, its incidence docs not differ too much from the general patterns already described. According to Figure 3.5, the rate of neglect for infants reached 16.7 per 1,000 in primary urban counties, by far the highest rate of neglect reported for any age group, regardless of urbanicity. Neglect rates are uniformly lower for children living in non-urban counties, although infants still face the greatest risk. In fact, the rate of neglect for infants living in primary urban areas exceeds the rate of neglect reported for all other age groups of children regardless of where they live. The data also point to the fact that in non-urban areas, rates of neglect among 1- to 5-year-olds exceed the rates found in other areas. This is a finding that has not been documented elsewhere.

In primary urban areas, there is an elevated risk of neglect among younger school-aged children (in kindergarten, first grade, and sec-

Figure 3.5
Rate of Victimization for Neglect by Age and Urbanicity: 2000
(initial victims)

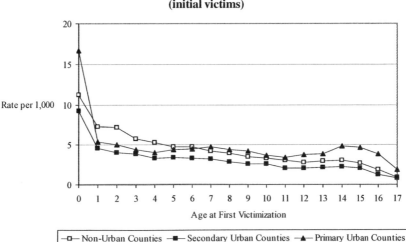

ond grade) and teenagers. Specifically, the rate of neglect rises to 4.8 per 1,000 among 7-year-olds from 4.1 per 1,000 among 4-year-olds. The neglect rate then falls steadily for children between the ages of 7 and 11. Thereafter, the rate rises again, reaching a peak of 4.8 per 1,000 among 14-year-olds. A similar pattern is found in the secondary urban and non-urban counties. That is, when compared with other children above the age of 7, 14-year-olds typically have higher rates of reported neglect.[11]

Maltreatment type and poverty. The next two figures will show that maltreatment rates are generally higher in poorer counties. According to Figure 3.6, the risk for physical abuse shows the same three peaks—infants, children entering school, and teenagers—as the risk for neglect. The risk is generally higher in the poorest counties, but the underlying pattern with respect to age is consistent. Figure 3.6 also demonstrates that relative risks are roughly proportional across the age spectrum of childhood. That is, age-specific differences between high-poverty and low-poverty counties are comparable across age groups. For example, in poor counties, the likelihood of reported physical abuse among toddlers and preschoolers is about 1.7 times as great as the rate reported in low-poverty counties. For children in elementary school (children between the ages of 6 and 11), the difference is on average about 1.8 times as great; among adolescents,

Figure 3.6
Rate of Victimization for Physical Abuse byAge and County Poverty Rate: 2000
(initial victims)

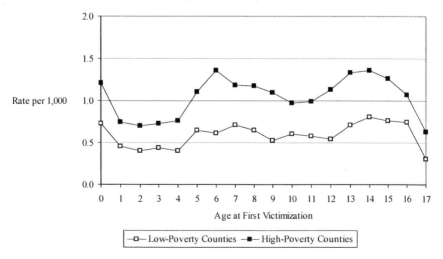

the rates of physical abuse in high-poverty counties are 1.7 times as great, on average.

Figure 3.7 shows age-specific rates of neglect according to county poverty level and age. The same fundamental pattern persists. Infants, regardless of poverty level, have the highest rates of reported neglect. Risk generally declines with age, with a slightly elevated risk reported for adolescents, especially those adolescents living in the poorest counties. Except for infants and teenagers, age differences in the rate of neglect are comparable when high- and low-poverty counties are compared. For example, rates of neglect are about 1.9 times as great in the poorest counties. Among babies, neglect is 2.7 times as likely in the poorest counties. For adolescents (13- to 17-year-olds), neglect rates are 2.2 times as high in high-poverty counties as in low-poverty counties.

Race, poverty, and maltreatment rates. Thus far, age effects have been explored in the context of place, with counties divided into groups based on either poverty or urbanicity. In this section, we add race and ethnicity as attributes of the children to further explore how age is related to maltreatment risk. Figure 3.8 shows the rate of victimization for children living in high-poverty counties, by both age and race/ethnicity. Once again, the underlying pattern is evident. Regardless of race/ethnicity, infants have the highest reported rates

Figure 3.7
Rate of Victimization for Neglect by Age and County Poverty Rate: 2000
(initial victims)

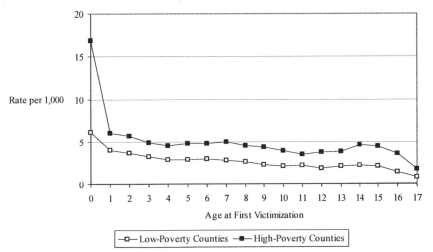

Figure 3.8
Rate of Victimization, All Maltreatment Types by Age, Race/Ethnicity, and
County Poverty Rate: 2000
(initial victims/high-poverty counties)

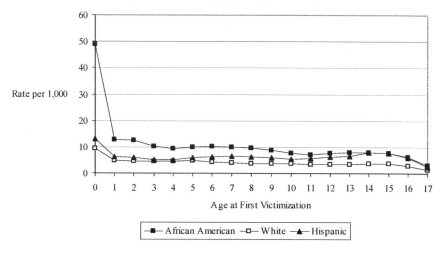

of maltreatment. Among African American infants, the risk of maltreatment is about 50 per 1,000 children, itself a striking figure when compared with infants of other races and ethnicities.[12] Nevertheless, white and Hispanic infants were about twice as likely as 1-year-olds to be reported for maltreatment. Hispanic children between the ages of 1 and 5 from high-poverty areas had maltreatment rates that were closest to those for white children. Among teenagers, however, the maltreatment rates among Hispanics most closely approximated the rate for African American children.

Figure 3.9 shows that in low-poverty areas, the patterns resemble what has already been described, with some notable differences. First, the generally higher rates of maltreatment among babies, regardless of race/ethnicity, are consistent with the findings reported earlier in this chapter. African American babies, in particular, have an exceptionally high rate of maltreatment, even in counties characterized by low poverty rates. For Hispanic and African American children, the risk of reported maltreatment begins to increase with 5-year-olds. The risk of maltreatment was elevated for teenagers as well, regardless of race or ethnicity.

In contrast to risk patterns observed in high-poverty areas, where age-specific differentials were more or less steady, in low-poverty areas, African American children under the age of 7 are much more

Figure 3.9
Rate of Victimization, All Maltreatment Types by Age, Race/Ethnicity, and
County Poverty Rate: 2000
(initial victims/low-poverty counties)

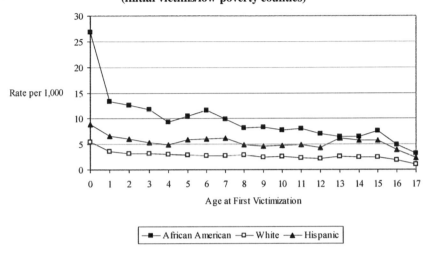

likely to be the subject of a substantiated allegation of maltreatment than white children of the same age. African American teenagers are also more likely to be victimized, but by this age the differences between whites and African Americans are much smaller. For example, the rate of maltreatment in low-poverty counties for African American 2-year-olds was 4 times as great as the comparable rate for white children. Among 15-year-olds, the rate for African American teens was three times as great. Across all age groups, the differential between African American children and white children was greatest in the low-poverty counties. These data suggest that to the extent that there is a disproportionate rate of reported maltreatment relative to the overall population, the problem may loom largest in counties where poverty is less severe.

NSCAW: The Status of Children Investigated for Maltreatment

As the NCANDS data clearly indicate, children of all age groups become involved with the child welfare system. However, the risk of reported maltreatment is significantly higher for children under the age of 1. Among African American infants residing in poor counties, the likelihood of a child under the age of 1 being the subject of a substantiated maltreatment report is 50 per 1,000. Even in counties with much lower poverty rates, the risk of substantiated maltreatment among African American babies exceeds 25 per 1,000. Moreover, although maltreatment rates differ depending on the type of maltreatment, there are important age-related patterns in the underlying data. Neglect is clearly concentrated among the very youngest children, whereas the relationship between age and physical abuse is more complex. As children enter school age and adolescence, the rates of reported physical maltreatment rise. In epidemiological terms, this may be due to a combination of factors that are age-related, but it may also be tied to social timetables and other normative patterns. For example, the upswing in the risk of reported physical maltreatment probably reflects entry into school and the fact that children are spending more time in the presence of mandated reporters (teachers).

The sample of NSCAW children looks similar to the children found in the NCANDS data (U.S. DHHS, 2005).[13] As the baseline NSCAW report details, nearly one in five children were younger than 3 at the time of investigation (U.S. DHHS, 2005). A much smaller sub-population of the sample was children between the ages of 3 and 5. From the perspective of race and ethnicity, almost half of the children were white/non-Hispanic, with African American/non-Hispanic children making up over one-quarter (28 percent), and Hispanic children being less than one-fifth of this population. Although the percentage of African American children who become involved with the child welfare system is larger than it is among children in the general population, this over-representation is far lower than typically found in national statistics for foster care.[14]

Types of Maltreatment

For the children in the NSCAW sample, child welfare workers who carried out the maltreatment investigations indicated the types of *alleged* maltreatment, whether the child experienced multiple types of maltreatment, the severity of maltreatment, and the onset of maltreatment. In the roughly 20 percent of cases in which there were multiple types of reported maltreatment, the child welfare worker indicated the most serious type of abuse. For nearly half of the children in the NSCAW sample, neglect was the most serious form of maltreatment alleged (U.S. DHHS, 2005). This is consistent to a large extent with the NCANDS data. Physical maltreatment is the most serious type of abuse for another quarter of the children (see Table 3.1). Children reported for sexual abuse accounted for 11 percent of the sample. All other maltreatment types accounted for 15.6 percent of the NSCAW cases, a figure that is somewhat lower than the comparable NCANDS figure (U.S. DHHS, 2005). Part of the reason for this disparity results from a peculiarity of the NSCAW sample. Even though these children had been classified as abused or neglected in the official records—and, therefore, eligible for inclusion in the study—interviews with child welfare workers indicated that reasons other than the ones listed were responsible for their involvement with child welfare.[15] (Indeed, when field interviewers were asked to encourage child welfare workers to consider coding more cases in the standard child maltreatment categories, they were met with objections because child welfare workers wanted them to know the real reasons for child welfare involvement.)

Although states and municipalities may classify child abuse reports in an enormous number of ways, NCANDS reports information on five types of maltreatment (physical abuse, neglect, medical neglect, sexual abuse, psychological maltreatment), *other*, and *unknown*. In the NSCAW analyses drawn on here (U.S. DHHS, 2005), maltreatment types have been consolidated into five major categories: physical abuse, sexual abuse, neglect—*failure to provide,* neglect—*failure to supervise* (including abandonment), and other types of maltreatment (e.g., educational neglect and emotional maltreatment).[16] The analysis excludes cases with abuse types described as

Table 3.1
Most Serious Type of Alleged Abuse

Type of Abuse in NSCAW*	%/(SE)
Physical Maltreatment	27.1/ (1.4)
Neglect: Failure to Supervise	26.9/ (1.6)
Neglect: Failure to Provide	19.5/ (1.5)
Abandonment	1.6/ (0.3)
Sexual Maltreatment	11.0/ (1.2)
Emotional Maltreatment	7.3/ (1.1)
Educational Maltreatment	1.6/ (0.5)
Moral/Legal Maltreatment	0.5/ (0.2)
Exploitation	0.1/ (0.1)
Other	4.5/ (0.8)

* The NSCAW sample includes 5,504 children, with a weighted count of 2,397,504 children. Abuse type refers to alleged abuse type. Most serious type of abuse is missing for 452 children.

Table 3.2
Most Serious Type of Alleged Abuse Among Children Involved with the Child Welfare System by Age*

Age	Physical Maltreatment % (SE)	Sexual Maltreatment % (SE)	Failure to Provide % (SE)	Failure to Supervise % (SE)	Other % (SE)	Total
0-2	22.6 (2.2)	6.1 (1.7)	29.9 (2.5)	36.6 (3.0)	4.8 (1.7)	100%
3-5	23.6 (2.9)	12.8 (2.8)	23.8 (3.8)	30.3 (2.6)	9.5 (2.3)	100%
6-10	31.2 (2.6)	11.1 (2.4)	18.9 (2.4)	26.1 (2.4)	12.7 (2.1)	100%
11+	32.7 (3.1)	14.9 (2.1)	12.7 (2.3)	29.7 (2.5)	10.0 (1.8)	100%
Total	28.4 (1.5)	11.5 (1.2)	20.4 (1.5)	29.8 (1.5)	9.9 (1.2)	100%

Actual percentages may not total to 100 due to rounding. Abuse type refers to alleged abuse type.
* Children 0-2 are more likely than children 6-10 to have a most serious abuse type of failure to provide ($c^2=7.4, p < .01$). Children 0-2 are more likely than children 11+ to have a most serious abuse type of failure to provide ($c^2=25.9, p < .001$). Children 0-2 are more likely than children 6-10 to have a most serious abuse type of failure to supervise ($c^2=8.7, p < .01$). Children 6-10 are more likely than children 0-2 to have a most serious abuse type of physical maltreatment ($c^2=6.9, p £ .01$). Children 6-10 are more likely than children 0-2 to have a most serious abuse type of Other ($c^2=7.4, p < .01$). Children 11+ are more likely than children 0-2 to have a most serious abuse type of sexual maltreatment ($c^2=11.9, p < .001$).

non-maltreated-*other* (signifying other reasons for placement, as discussed above), as well as cases with *don't know, refused,* or *missing* responses (*don't know, refused,* and *missing* responses account for a weighted 7 percent of the total population).

The distribution of the most serious abuse types according to age, following this recoding of the data, is found in Table 3.2. This simple table reinforces the significant truths about the intersection of development and child maltreatment in child welfare services. The most serious type of alleged abuse experienced by children who reach the point of investigation by child welfare services is linked to children's age (U.S. DHHS, 2005). In general, and consistent with much previous research (e.g., Berrick et al., 1998), the youngest children are the most likely to have a most serious abuse type of neglect (i.e., failure to provide or failure to supervise) and the least likely to have a most serious abuse type of physical or sexual maltreatment, or one of the other abuse types. As would be expected, the oldest children are the most likely to have a most serious abuse type of sexual maltreatment. Still, the data show a surprisingly even distribution of sexual abuse cases across the age groups. We had expected a much steeper age gradient.[17]

Onset of Maltreatment

Onset is significant in that it places maltreatment in a specific developmental context. Onset during early childhood means that a greater proportion of a child's life may unfold under adverse developmental conditions depending how long maltreatment lasts. Onset of maltreatment during adolescence clearly represents an altogether different developmental context that alters how one thinks about both the impact of maltreatment on a child's developmental trajectory and the types of services that have ameliorative potential (Cicchetti and Toth, 2000). Early onset of maltreatment can be viewed as the most serious form of maltreatment, but exposure to a prolonged period of adversity has been linked to developmental problems (Egeland, Yates, Appleyard, & van Dulmen, 2002).

Table 3.3 divides the children studied in NSCAW according to their current age and their age at the time maltreatment reportedly began.[18] Across all age groups, about 80 percent of the children experienced the onset of maltreatment in close developmental proximity to when the maltreatment was reported.[19] For example, 80 percent of the children who were between the ages of 6 and 10 at the time of investigation experienced the onset of maltreatment between the ages of 6 and 10. About 5 percent of those same children experienced onset much earlier in life, between the ages of 0 and 2. The

Table 3.3
Age at Onset of Maltreatment by Current Age*

Current Age	Age at Onset of Maltreatment % (SE)			
	0-2	3-5	6-10	11+
0-2	100	N/A	N/A	N/A
3-5	11.6 (2.1)	88.4 (2.1)	N/A	N/A
6-10	5.6 (1.7)	14.5 (2.9)	80.0(3.0)	N/A
11+	0.2 (0.1)	1.1 (0.4)	12.6(2.0)	86.1 (2.0)
Total	22.3 (1.6)	22.7 (1.7)	32.5(1.8)	22.5 (1.6)

*Rows may not total to 100% due to rounding.
N/A – not applicable.

data also suggest that reported maltreatment among adolescents was also contemporaneous with onset. Fewer than 2 percent of the adolescents in the NSCAW sample reported onset between the ages of 0 and 5. Thus, although long-term maltreatment is problematic, the data suggest that it may be relatively rare. The data in Table 3.3 do, however, underscore the fact that the onset of maltreatment among very young children (0 to 2) means that maltreatment is a potential developmental influence over a greater proportion of the child's life, depending on how well services address the family's needs.

Child Welfare Service Trajectories

Generally speaking, after an investigation, a child welfare worker has to decide whether services are needed to further protect the child. This decision ought to be reached by weighing the perceived threat to the child relative to the family, community, and protective services resources that can be mustered on the child's behalf. In essence, the worker is making a decision regarding how a child's service trajectory will begin—with no further action, in-home services, or out-of-home care.

As both the NCANDS and NSCAW data clearly indicate, age and abuse type are related. Abuse type is also related to what happens following the maltreatment investigation. To illustrate this point, the population of maltreated children from NSCAW was divided into two primary groups depending on whether the child was or was not placed in out-of-home care following the maltreatment. Children who remained at home were then divided into whether they received child welfare services or not. Table 3.4 classifies these groups of children based on age and maltreatment type.

The majority of children who are investigated for maltreatment will not receive any ongoing services, following any single investigation. Generally, one in ten children who were the subject of a maltreatment investigation was placed into foster care. Of children who remained at home, about one-quarter received child welfare services. In total, about one-third of the children were either placed or served in the home. We recognize that many children will be involved with child welfare services on more than one occasion, and their likelihood of getting additional services is higher than children in their first episode (U.S. DHHS, 2005).

The starting point of the service trajectory is, however, associated with both age and maltreatment type. Very young children (ages 0

Table 3.4
Most Serious Type of Alleged Abuse of Children Involved with Child Welfare Services by Age and Service Setting

Age and Maltreatment Type	All Children	All Children in the Study		Children in home*	
		Children in home % (SE)	Children Out of Home % (SE)	No Child Welfare Services % (SE)	Child Welfare Services % (SE)
All Ages					
Total	100%	89.2 (1.3)	10.8 (1.3)	73.7 (1.6)	26.3 (1.6)
Physical Maltreatment	100	91.5 (2.0)	8.5 (2.0)	76.0 (2.5)	24.0 (2.5)
Sexual Maltreatment	100	90.6 (2.3)	9.4 (2.3)	72.1 (4.2)	27.9 (4.2)
Neglect-Failure to Provide	100	87.9 (2.3)	12.1 (2.3)	72.0 (3.6)	28.0 (3.6)
Neglect-Failure to Supervise	100	86.7 (1.8)	13.3 (1.8)	72.3 (2.4)	27.7 (2.4)
Other	100	91.1 (1.7)	8.9 (1.7)	76.1 (3.5)	23.9 (3.5)
Ages 0 to 2					
Total	100%	83.9 (2.9)	16.1 (2.9)	72.6 (2.3)	27.4 (2.3)
Physical Maltreatment	100	89.8 (2.5)	10.2 (2.5)	75.6 (5.2)	24.4 (5.2)
Sexual Maltreatment	100	96.0 (2.6)	4.0 (2.6)	85.5 (7.3)	14.5 (7.3)
Neglect-Failure to Provide	100	79.9 (4.0)	20.2 (4.0)	67.5 (4.0)	32.5 (4.0)
Neglect-Failure to Supervise	100	80.7 (4.0)	19.3 (4.0)	73.8 (3.6)	26.2 (3.6)
Other	100	89.9 (5.6)	10.1 (5.6)	61.7 (14.5)	38.3 (14.5)
Ages 3 to 5					
Total	100%	94.2 (1.2)	5.9 (1.2)	72.2 (2.6)	27.8 (2.6)
Physical Maltreatment	100	95.9 (1.4)	4.2 (1.4)	75.6 (4.5)	24.5 (4.5)
Sexual Maltreatment	100	96.1 (1.9)	3.9 (1.9)	71.9 (9.1)	28.1 (9.1)
Neglect-Failure to Provide	100	95.0 (1.9)	5.0 (1.9)	72.0 (7.2)	28.1 (7.2)
Neglect-Failure to Supervise	100	90.3 (3.2)	9.7 (3.2)	70.4 (4.3)	29.6 (4.3)
Other	100	97.4 (1.4)	2.6 (1.4)	70.3 (7.3)	29.7 (7.3)
Ages 6 to 10					
Total	100%	90.5 (1.7)	9.5 (1.7)	77.1 (1.8)	22.9 (1.8)
Physical Maltreatment	100	91.5 (3.4)	8.5 (3.4)	78.6 (3.5)	21.4 (3.5)
Sexual Maltreatment	100	90.3 (3.9)	9.7 (3.9)	79.2 (5.3)	20.8 (5.3)
Neglect-Failure to Provide	100	89.2 (4.0)	10.8 (4.0)	79.5 (4.6)	20.5 (4.6)
Neglect-Failure to Supervise	100	89.2 (2.4)	10.8 (2.4)	70.0 (4.1)	30.1 (4.1)
Other	100	92.8 (2.5)	7.2 (2.5)	82.6 (4.6)	17.4 (4.6)
Ages 11+					
Total	100%	87.0 (1.7)	13.0 (1.7)	70.4 (4.0)	29.6 (4.0)
Physical Maltreatment	100	89.6 (2.4)	10.5 (2.4)	72.8 (4.3)	27.2 (4.3)
Sexual Maltreatment	100	85.3 (4.5)	14.7 (4.5)	59.3 (11.7)	40.7 (11.7)
Neglect-Failure to Provide	100	87.8 (3.8)	12.2 (3.8)	62.2 (8.9)	37.8 (8.9)
Neglect-Failure to Supervise	100	85.8 (3.3)	14.2 (3.3)	75.9 (5.5)	24.1 (5.5)
Other	100	83.3 (4.2)	16.7 (4.2)	73.4 (6.7)	26.6 (6.7)

Percentages may not total to 100 due to rounding. Abuse type refers to alleged abuse type.
* As a percent of all children in home.

to 2) and older children (ages 11+) are more likely to go into placement than are children between the ages of 3 and 10. If placement
setting were included here, the analysis would show that very young
children are placed in family settings, whereas the adolescents are
more likely to be placed in group settings. Within age groups, children between the ages of 0 and 2 investigated for neglect (the failure
to provide or supervise) are the most likely to go into placement.
Children between the ages of 3 and 5 are more likely to enter placement if the maltreatment investigation was related to the failure to
supervise. Among 6- to 10-year-olds, maltreatment type did not influence the likelihood of placement. Children in this age group are
somewhat more likely to enter placement than are 3- to 5-year-olds,
but less so than infants, toddlers, and adolescents. For adolescents,
physical abuse was associated with a reduced likelihood of placement.

If a child is not placed, then child welfare workers have to determine whether some form of child welfare services is warranted. As
noted in Table 3.4, about one-quarter of the children who did not
enter placement received some form of services after the investigation, although differences between age groups are less prominent
than among children who are placed. Adolescents are somewhat more
likely to receive services (29 percent), whereas 6- to 10-year-olds
are somewhat less likely (23 percent). Populations of children that
stand out as more likely to receive services include adolescents with
a maltreatment type of sexual abuse, 6- to 10-year-olds investigated
for failure to supervise, and 0- to 2-year-olds whose parents were
not providing for them.

When the data pertaining to the likelihood of receiving services
of any type (either placement or child welfare services while at home)
are combined, the results indicate that very young children and adolescents are the children most likely to receive some attention beyond the investigation. Figure 3.10 illustrates this point.

Developmental Status of Children

The NSCAW data allow us to explore the well-being of children
who were not placed in foster care at the time of their most recent
contact with the child welfare system. Children that fit this category
may or may not have received some type of child welfare services
after the investigation, and we describe the well-being of children in
both groups.

Figure 3.10
Children Investigated for Maltreatment Who Were Either Placed or Received
Child Welfare Services by Age

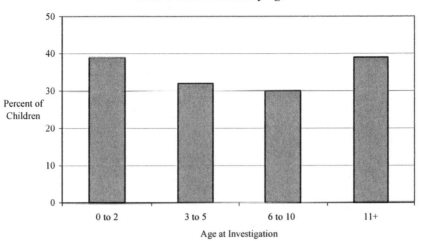

The findings are based on direct measures of the child's well-being as well as caregiver reports. The results are organized roughly according to children's developmental stages beginning with the youngest. Within each developmental stage, the findings are organized in a way that reflects age-specific concerns. For example, developmental issues facing infants are best reflected in terms of the physical growth, development, and responsiveness to their environment, whereas verbal skills and school-based achievement are more central to understanding the developmental standing of older children (U.S. DHHS, 2005).

Infancy and Early Childhood

Young children are the most difficult to assess because they are least able to contribute personally to our understanding of how well they are doing. That said, physical status offers a meaningful place to start an assessment of infants and toddlers (Mackner, Stair, & Blac, 1997). The NSCAW data assess the following: Body Mass Index, the risk of developmental delay, early language skills, and problem behavior as they affect the developmental trajectories of very young children who are maltreated.

Body mass index. Body Mass Index (BMI) can be used to identify individuals who are, or are at risk of becoming over- or underweight. BMI takes height and weight into account—percentile scores show whether children are in the normal range (Kucznarski et al., 2000). In general, the mean BMI for 2- to 3-year-olds who stayed home after the maltreatment investigation was close to average (U.S. DHHS, 2005).[20] BMI percentiles were lower, however, for African American children who stayed home and received services than for children of other races and ethnicities.

Risk of developmental delay. Predictions of later functioning based on measures of infant well-being lack precision, but there is a long history of measurement of children's risk for developmental delays. More than half (53 percent) of the NSCAW sample are classified by the Bayley Infant Neurodevelopmental Screener (BINS) as being at high risk for developmental delay or neurological impairment (U.S. DHHS, 2005). This rate is far greater than would be found in a normal population and is much more like a group of children found in a clinical setting (Aylward, 1995).[21] Further, assuming that the BINS is capturing risk equally across racial/ethnic groups, the findings indicate that African American infants under the age of 2 who are involved with the child welfare system may be at particularly high risk for developmental delay or neurological impairment.

In NSCAW, early cognitive development was assessed with the Battelle Developmental Inventory (BDI) for children ages 3 and younger. On this measure, about one in three children had an extremely low score (U.S. DHHS, 2005)

Problem behavior. Although children may outgrow early childhood problems, problems that begin early in a child's life often persist (Stormont, 2001). Overall, the 2- to 3-year-olds who enter child welfare services are reported as having borderline or clinical behavior problems at a rate approximately five times as high as the norm (U.S. DHHS, 2005). Many of these children are not receiving early intervention or mental health services (Burns et al., 2004).

Developmental trajectories for young children. The overriding message from the measures of young children's well-being is that they are facing multiple developmental challenges. (U.S. DHHS, 2005). These children risk poor adjustment in a variety of life domains, including school. The much-reported failure of children involved with child welfare services to make adequate educational progress begins, for many children, at a very early age.

These children are also commonly exposed to unpredictable parenting, which contributes to lasting behavior problems (Stormont, 2001). One of the most central needs that young children have is for stable and safe parenting; without stability, the likelihood of developing difficulties in relationships and in other cognitive and behavioral realms is substantial (Ackerman, Brown, D'Eramo, & Izard, 2002; Berlin & Cassidy, 2001). Yet, some of the young children in this study had had previous episodes in foster care, and more than a few of these young children are residing in group care despite their imcompatibility with children's need for close relationships (Berrick, Needell, Barth, & Jonson-Reid, 1998; Jones Harden, 2002).[22,23,24]

Middle Childhood

Although children who are early school age (ages 3 to 5) have many developmental differences from those who are between the ages of 6 and 10, both groups are rapidly developing social and academic capacity for school and extrafamilial success. In this section, children in these age groups will be discussed together, with a focus on cognitive and social developmental tasks.

Reading and math achievement. The reading and mathematics sections of the Mini-Battery of Achievement (MBA) were administered to children age 6 and older in the NSCAW study (U.S. DHHS, 2005). In general, the mean reading scores (98) and math scores (92) of children are below the normed mean of 100, although well within one standard deviation of 15 points. Yet a full 5 percent of the children in this population have a reading score lower than 70 and 12 percent have a math score that is this low. The NSCAW data has a striking finding regarding the relationship between age and reading scores. The oldest children in the study—ages 11 and older—have significantly lower reading scores than children ages 6 to 10. Because these children have, generally, just entered child welfare services, the greater lags for older children cannot be readily attributable to exposure to child welfare services.

Behavioral problems. Much has been written by the authors of this volume and others about the high rates of mental health problems among foster children in urban settings (Garland, Landsverk, Hough, & Ellis-MacLeod, 1996; Landsverk, 1997), but far less is known about children in the general population who receive child welfare services. NSCAW offers information that is especially pertinent to the design of child welfare services because it includes assessments of mental health problems at the time children start child welfare services.

The Child Behavioral Checklist (CBCL) was used by primary caregivers to assess child behavioral problems. As shown in Table

3.5, the findings of high rates of behavioral problems among children receiving child welfare services at home confirm that children become involved with child welfare services with substantial behavioral problems (Burns et al., 2004). Nearly half (44.6 percent) of children entering child welfare services between the ages of 4 and 15 have a borderline or clinical CBCL. This is true regardless of age, although the oldest children have the highest rates of borderline or clinical behavioral problems. This is also true whether children and their families receive in-home services or not.

Overall well-being of preschool and elementary school children. Overall, 2- to 3-year-olds were reported as having approximately five times as many problem behaviors as found in the general population (27 percent vs. 5 percent). As reported by caregivers in the NSCAW study, more than one-third of children ages 4 to 5 years who are involved with child welfare services exhibit borderline or clinical levels of problem behaviors. High rates of problem behavior are not insignificant for younger children—especially those who are also from violent families (Stormont, 2001; Qi & Kaiser, 2003)—as they portend a difficult future.

The evidence from NSCAW suggests that maltreated children of elementary school age are also compromised in several developmental areas (U.S. DHHS, 2005). Academic deficits are quite widely experienced by this group of children and very serious for a sizable segment of youth. Youth who enter child welfare services after age 11 have, in general, more academic deficits than those who become

Table 3.5

Caregiver Report of Clinical/Borderline Total Problem Behaviors (4 to 15 years) as Measured by the CBCL*

Age	Total In-Home (SE)	No Child Welfare Services (SE)	Child Welfare Services (SE)
4-5	37.4 (4.1)	37.2 (5.6)	37.9 (7.2)
6-10	38.4 (3.0)	35.0 (3.9)	49.4 (4.6)
11+	55.3 (3.5)	55.6 (4.7)	54.8 (4.6)
Total	43.5 (2.4)	41.6 (3.0)	48.9 (3.1)

*Proportion of borderline/clinical scores for children 11+ years is higher than for 4- to 5-year-olds (c^2=19.8, $p \leq .001$). Proportion of borderline/clinical scores for children 11+ years remaining at home is higher than for 4- to 5-year-olds remaining at home (c^2=15.0, $p \leq .001$). Proportion of borderline/clinical scores for 11+ years remaining at home is higher than for 6- to 10-year-olds remaining at home (c^2=13.4, $p \leq .001$).

involved earlier. From a more positive perspective, reading scores are at the norm and tend to be higher than math scores for children in the 6- to 10-year-old group; 6- to 10- year-olds reported fewer school problems than did children over age 10.

Adolescence

Children ages 11 to 14 are in less need of protection from serious physical abuse at the hands of their caregivers, but have substantially more behavior problems and are more likely to experience physical and sexual abuse than their younger counterparts (U.S. DHHS, 2005). By virtue of age and greater extent of exposure, the oldest children are the most likely to have had more previous reports, more previous substantiated reports, and more out-of-home placements. They also have the highest rates of prior psychiatric hospitalizations, which reflects the high rates of placements of children with mental illness into child welfare supervised placements (U.S. General Accounting Office, 2003). Adolescents are more likely than other children, with the exception of infants, to receive services in out-of-home care. Early adolescents are 25 percent of the sample but represent 29 percent of the children in out-of-home care (U.S. DHHS, 2005). They more often live in family-like out-of-home care, yet they represent approximately 75 percent of all the children living in group care—a setting that has not been shown to reduce behavior problems (Barth, 2002).

The weak educational performance of early adolescents (Crozier & Barth, in press) is coupled with high rates of school problems, including increased difficulty of work, incomplete homework, and behavior problems (U.S. DHHS, 2005).

It appears from other analyses of NSCAW data (Barth et al., in press), that a sizable proportion of children who become involved with child welfare services do so because they have behavior problems. In several states, these children are formally admitted to child welfare services under a designation such as "child-parent conflict cases." Although this practice has been more widely used in conjunction with involuntary placement of children, it is also very likely that some children who receive in-home services do so primarily because of their behavior problems. Certainly many child welfare services-administered family preservation programs have made note of this phenomena as well (Fraser, Pecora, & Haapala, 1991). If so, and we need to find out, this has major importance for the design of child welfare services and allied children's services.

Conclusions

This chapter provides substantial support for continuing to examine ways that a developmental perspective can help to shape the design of child welfare services and the allied service systems that are also involved in addressing the needs of these vulnerable children and families. Younger children tend to be most vulnerable and are most likely to receive in-home and out-of-home services in contrast to having their cases closed at intake (U.S. DHHS, 2005). Evidence of many family risk factors is not enough, on the other hand, to result in out-of-home placements, for many older children. When the older children do enter care, the problems are somewhat more likely to be based on their behavior problems than a broad set of indicators of family dysfunction.

Children who are entering child welfare services are clearly in need of a range of supportive activities. Yet, the vast majority of these children will not receive ongoing child welfare services and, if they do, they will receive in-home services (U.S. DHHS, 2005). These children are substantially less likely to receive specialized services than children who are in foster care or group care (Burns et al., in press), although we cannot determine whether or not the likelihood has increased over what would have occurred had there been no child welfare services involvement. Nor have we determined whether those children who become involved with child welfare services for the first time receive fewer services, all else equal, than those who have had child welfare services contact before.

The developmental context for children in NSCAW includes, at minimum, alleged harms and very often includes a history of repeated events indicating exposure to an unsafe and compromised environment. This would seem to predict futures beset with significant health and mental health problems.

Notes

1.   Language is particularly important in distinguishing between reports and victims. Because reports of maltreatment often involve more than one child, *substantiated reports* can be a confusing term. *Substantiation* is an umbrella term that refers to indicated, founded, or alternative response categories. *Substantiation* is the term we have opted to use when the alleged maltreatment was affirmed following the investigation. For the counts of maltreatment used in this chapter, *only* those children

whose specific report was substantiated or indicated are included. In this section, unless noted otherwise, victims refer to children who are the subject of a substantiated maltreatment report. We use the terms *victimization* and *substantiated maltreatment* interchangeably.

2.   This is something of a simplification. The tacit assumption built into the discussion thus far is that service trajectories start with an investigation. However, some families start child welfare services voluntarily. Also, the number of potential trajectories developed from a sequence of investigation, service, and placement events is quite large. Some sequences are more common than others. Here, we have chosen to simplify the presentation by dividing children who have been investigated into two groups: those who did not receive continuing child welfare services and those children who did. The latter group can then be divided into children who received services in their home and those who were removed.

3.   These differences include thresholds for accepting reports for investigation and the response time that defines the period between when a report is filed and when the investigation must begin. For example, about one-third of all referrals are screened out. However, in some states, 60 percent of the referrals to the state are screened out. In other states, almost all of the referrals are screened in. The average response time between report and investigation can be as little as 5 hours and as long as 340 hours.

4.   Tennessee is a state with an umbrella child welfare agency. In New York City, the Administration for Children's Services includes day care and child support together with more traditional child welfare services (i.e., protective, preventive, foster care, and adoption). Vermont, Colorado, and Iowa are among the states that provide services to children involved with juvenile justice.

5.   States have modified their approach to the disposition of maltreatment reports. In an effort to increase flexibility, some states are using an "alternative response" to sort high-risk cases from lower-risk cases. For more information, see National Study of Child Protective Services Systems and Reform Efforts (U.S. Department of Health and Human Services, Administration on Children Youth and Families/Children's Bureau, & Office of the Assistant Secretary for Planning and Evaluation, 2003).

6.   Child Abuse and Neglect: Case-Level Data 1993: Working Paper l.

7.   Based on analysis of data from ten states, 63 percent of referrals from legal and law enforcement professionals, 55 percent of referrals from medical professionals, 47 percent from social services professionals, and 44 percent from educators are substantiated or indicated. This contrasts with 34 percent of referrals from friends and community members.

8.   See the description of the NCANDS data in the introduction to this section for more information.

9.   As shown later in this chapter, areas with higher poverty rates have higher maltreatment rates. Data such as these are usually interpreted to mean that changes in poverty rates will produce changes in the rate of maltreatment that follow the basic trend. However, research that tests this hypothesis in several jurisdictions at different points in time is surprisingly limited given how important the basic question is. Paxson and Waldfogel (2001) have tried to unravel the relationship between maltreatment and economic well-being, with mixed results.

10.   In these analyses, only victims with no known prior substantiated or indicated victimization are included. Each victim is counted only once. Also, the four states (Missouri, New Jersey, Illinois, and New York) were selected because those states overlap with states that are found in the Foster Care Data Archive.

11.   Although this may seem counterintuitive, we expect that it is a function of the classification of these children as neglected, when their parents are judged as unable to supervise them or provide (treatment) for them because of parent-child conflict.

12.   Although the terminology used to designate race differs among the data sources, we use the terms African American and Hispanic. The coding of "other" races and ethnicities (beyond Hispanic, African American, and white) also varies considerably. Unfortunately, there is insufficient detail in the source data to be more precise.

13.   NSCAW cases were limited, at intake, to children 0-14, so the percentages of children in the younger age groups are likely to be higher than NCANDS because children ages 15 to18 are not part of the denominator.

14.   The proportion of African American children in foster care at the end of 2000 was 43 percent; whites were only 36 percent of the children in foster care; and Hispanics were 15 percent (U.S. Department of Health and Human Services, 2003b).

15.   A direct comparison between the NSCAW maltreatment type proportions presented here with the NCANDS data has some limitations because of the way that maltreatment types are recorded. The states that supply the NCANDS data allow for multiple maltreatment types for each victim and are based on state-reported data. Whereas NSCAW also collected data on all reported maltreatment types (see later discussions on number of main abuse types), researchers developing NSCAW have generally limited their analyses to the most serious abuse type identified for each victim.

16.   However, the maltreated-*other* category was not included in most analyses that employ an abuse type because the interpretation for this group is too difficult. The less common types of abuse (i.e., *emotional maltreatment, educational maltreatment, moral/legal maltreatment*, and *exploitation*) were combined into a maltreated-*other* (types of abuse) category.

17.   Although not shown in this table, gender plays a significant role in the most serious abuse type, with males significantly more likely to be victims of physical maltreatment and females significantly more likely to be victims of sexual maltreatment (both findings are robust, at $p < .001$). No bivariate association between race/ethnicity and most serious abuse type is evident in the data.

18.   The question does not explicitly indicate whether it refers to the age group that any maltreatment began for this child or to the most recent episode of maltreatment.

19.   This is an example of where the use of age groups may conceal as much as is revealed. In developmental terms, 6- and 10-year-old children are quite different, and we do not mean to imply that onset at age 5 for a 6-year-old is different than onset at age 6 for a 10-year-old, as categories used in Table 3.3 imply.

20.   A Body Mass Index for children 1 and under was not gathered.

21.   Because of the subjective elements involved in the BINS, the NSCAW Research Group checked to determine whether raters were consistent in their ratings of children, regardless of the race/ethnicity of the child and rater. White children were found to receive significantly lower scores from Hispanic interviewers than from white interviewers ($p< .001$). There was also a trend toward African American interviewers scoring white children higher than Hispanic interviewers ($p=.03$). Hispanic children were found to receive significantly lower scores from African American interviewers than from either Hispanic interviewers or white interviewers. Finally, children of "Other" races/ethnicities were found to receive significantly lower scores from African American interviewers than from Hispanic interviewers ($p<.001$). There were no significant differences with regard to how African American and white interviewers scored African American or white children, which are the interviewer/child, race/ethnicity combinations that account for the majority of the NSCAW interviews.

22.   It is possible that some of these very young children are in congregate health care facilities because of special medical needs, although these group care placements do not include "other" placements such as hospitals.

23. Intensive, early interventions may be key to minimizing the long-term effects of early trauma on children's brain development, and children who become involved with child welfare services should have access to early intervention programs. Most models of early intervention programs for young children involved with child welfare services involve a home-based component. Health-oriented, professionally provided home-based interventions for mothers with infants have shown program effectiveness (Kitzman et al., 2000). Although the clientele served in the aforementioned study are not as disadvantaged as the child welfare clientele, there is some evidence that other home-based interventions aimed at improving mother-infant interaction show positive results influencing the relationship between mothers' drug use and lack of maternal responsiveness (Schuler, Nair, Black, & Kettinger, 2000).

24. Although NSCAW children ages 0- 2 show physical and cognitive needs and experience relationships with their caregivers that lack sufficient physical affection, verbal attention, and safe play environments, very few are assessed and treated for developmental difficulties. Children in this age category are the least likely to receive special education services, despite having at least one clinical score. About one in eight caregivers with children in this age group reported their child had been tested for special education services since the investigation. A small proportion (4 percent) of 0-2-year-olds reportedly had an IEP/IFSP, and 3 percent of children in this age group were receiving special education services at the time of the baseline interview.

  Children in this age group are also unlikely to be receiving mental health services. Just 3 percent of children ages 0-2 were receiving early intervention services and an even smaller proportion were receiving mental health care (1%) at intake to child welfare services. These findings from NSCAW do not converge with other research concluding that younger children (under age 4) receive more child welfare services overall, and greater caseworker activity than older children (Freeman, Levine, & Doueck, 1996). In either case, the level of unmet need for direct services to children is significant. Opportunities to begin a long trajectory of compensatory services are squandered under the current delivery of child welfare services.

4

Placement in Foster Care

The epidemiological evidence that is featured in this chapter is drawn from the Multistate Foster Care Data Archive, which contains the foster care histories of children in eleven states, accounting for approximately 51 percent of the nation's children in foster care. We also draw on NSCAW for information on the developmental status and well-being of these children.

In keeping with the analytic approach developed in chapter 3, we evaluate placement patterns using the following events: onset (admission), duration (time in foster care), and exit (e.g., reunification or adoption). The unique combination or sequence of events represents the placement trajectory (Wulczyn, Kogan, & Jones Harden, 2003). We use attributes of place and time to better understand the risk of placement in relation to age. Exit patterns are also linked to age. Then, we draw on the NSCAW data to describe what is known about the well-being of children who are admitted to foster care.

The overarching goal of the placement trajectory analysis is to test whether placement trajectories—the likelihood of entry, placement duration, and so forth—are tied to age in a way that can provide evidence to guide the reform of child welfare policy and programs. Placement patterns are generally known to vary based on time and location. For example, during the 1990s, the likelihood of placement declined in a number of states, suggesting that placement risk may depend on general social and economic conditions. Similarly, the recent emphasis on community-based services is testimony to the fact that placement rates are typically higher in areas with above average poverty rates. What is not known—and what will be explored in this chapter—is how age adds to our understanding of the underlying patterns.

Our basic measure is the placement rate. Rates per unit population (i.e., placements per 1,000 children) are measures of risk that indicate the likelihood of placement within a given population. The assumption is that age-stratified populations have different placement rates for reasons linked to age, its developmental correlates, and the institutional context of childhood. A second assumption is that placement rates may be different depending on place and time, as we saw with child maltreatment rates, because general social conditions (including policy) contribute to the overall magnitude of the placement rate. Learning how rates change given unique combinations of age, place, and time provides the basis for judging the relative importance of each factor.

In addition to the placement rate, data pertaining to placement duration and exit patterns are presented. Each subsequent part of the placement sequence is studied in a slightly different way, but the central purpose remains the same. We want to establish that when age is used to stratify the population, specific patterns emerge in the data that support the idea that age is an important factor influencing how a child moves through the child welfare system.[1]

Onset and Timing

Onset, or admission to care, together with the timing of placement relative to the child's age, is the most important link between human development and child welfare policy. This is because the point at which placement occurs initializes the placement experience in a given developmental context. From that point forward, the developmental trajectory is forever tied to the child's experiences within the child welfare system and vice versa. Short placements may, on average, have less impact on development than much longer placements. Nevertheless, our ability to understand the developmental sequelae of placement and other child welfare experiences will depend on how well the initial developmental conditions are understood. Distinct, age-differentiated patterns of placement and any subsequent similarities in trajectories (e.g., exit and reentry) are evidence for the basic role of age as a factor that organizes how we think about children in the child welfare system. Well-being, as a monitored outcome, has to be understood within this context.

FCDA: Placement Rates

In this section, we examine placement rates in relation to age, race and ethnicity, urbanicity, and poverty. Although we know that the likelihood of placement is higher among African American and

Hispanic children, less is known about the within-racial and ethnic group differences across the age spectrum of childhood. We also know that placements are higher in urban areas and in counties with higher-than-average poverty rates. Data that describe age-related placement risks are evaluated next, with the idea that urban areas and poor counties are defined by unique social and economic circumstances as well as policy and practice regimens. The graphs in the first part of this chapter look very much like the graphs in the previous chapter. Such stable age patterns suggest that the link between risk and age is robust, even though the local ecological or policy contexts may differ. If age-specific risks are the same regardless of the socioeconomic conditions found in a given community, this would argue for the organization of services around developmental issues within the context of community.

Placement rates by age and race/ethnicity. Our analysis of age-specific placement risks begins with a baseline placement rate per 1,000 children at any age. In Figure 4.1, the data reveal three distinct patterns that define the relationship between age and the likelihood of placement. The most notable feature is the elevated placement risk for children under the age of 1. In 2000, there were almost 10 infant placements per 1,000 children falling in that age group. This figure is more than 2.5 times the rate reported for 1-year-olds, the group with the next-highest likelihood of placement. Second, placement rates for children between the ages of 1 and 11 were considerably lower than those reported for infants. Moreover, the likelihood of placement dropped steadily from 3.5 per thousand 1-year-olds to 1.8 per thousand 11-year-olds. Third, the likelihood of placement was higher for adolescents. In 2000, the rate of placement for 15-year-olds was 2.8 per thousand, a full 50 percent higher than the placement rate reported for 11-year-olds. Placement rates generally rise from age 12 through 15, reaching a peak at age 15.

Age-specific placement rates for different racial and ethnic groups are presented in Figure 4.2. These data reflect the same fundamental pattern. Placement rates are significantly higher for infants than for all other children. Among African American children, the infant placement rate is about 3.4 times as high as the rate for 1-year-olds. The comparable figure for Hispanic and white children is 2.4. Across racial and ethnic groups, placement rates decline with age between ages 1 and 11. The placement rate reported for African American 1-year-olds in 2000 was 2 times the rate reported for 11-year-olds and

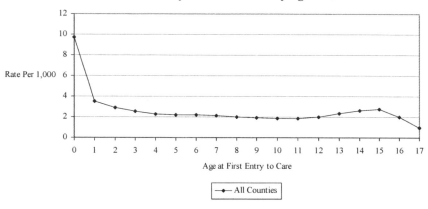

Figure 4.1
Rate of First Entry into Foster Care by Age: 2000

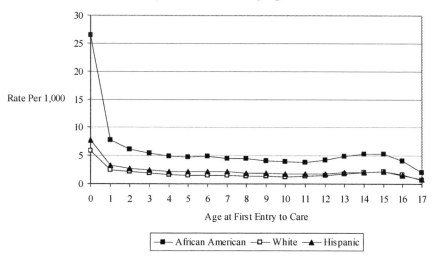

Figure 4.2
Rate of First Entry into Foster Care by Age and Race: 2000

for Hispanic and white children was 1.8 times the rate reported for 11-year-olds. Finally, for all three racial/ethnic groups, children who were age 15 at the time of initial placement had the highest placement rate among any age group of children over the age of 4. These rates were substantially higher than those for pre-adolescents or adolescents. Specifically, the placement rate for 15-year-old African Americans was 40 percent higher than the figure reported for African American 11-year-olds. Comparable figures for Hispanic and white children were 25 percent and 64 percent, respectively.

Age-based differences in the likelihood of placement in foster care are essentially the same, regardless of the child's race and/or ethnicity. Generally, children between birth and 2 years of age face the highest risk, and 14- and 15-year-olds are the group with the next-highest likelihood of placement. In between these age groups, age and the likelihood of placement are negatively correlated. The most striking finding involves African American infants, who are 3.4 times as likely to enter care as the group with the next-highest likelihood of placement (African American 1-year-olds).

Placement rates by age, urbanicity, and poverty. In this section, we explore attributes of place as factors that are known to influence placement rates. Urban areas such as New York City, Chicago, Detroit, and Los Angeles are widely recognized as being difficult environments in which to operate child welfare programs, although why this is true is not understood fully. Non-urban environments may have less drug use and crime, but appear to have a greater demand to serve children with mental health problems (Barth, Wildfire, & Green, in press). Poverty is another factor thought to exacerbate the demand for child welfare services, in general, and placement into out-of-home care in particular.

The specific question addressed in this analysis is whether these attributes of place alter basic age-differentiated patterns in the risk of placement. Figure 4.3 presents data for all 615 counties in the FCDA. Counties were identified as a *primary urban county* (generally the state's largest urban area), a *secondary urban county* (all other urban counties, except those containing the primary urban area), or a *non-urban county* (all other counties).[2] Then, age-specific placement rates for 2000 were calculated.

These data point to an age structure that is nearly identical to the pattern observed for the population as a whole. As expected, urban areas—because of their generally higher poverty rates—have higher placement rates across all age groups. However, because the pattern of age-specific risks is basically the same, differences between urban, secondary urban, and non-urban areas are unremarkable. Again, the heightened risk of placement found for urban infants is the one exception. Infants from urban areas are about 1.6 times as likely to be placed into foster care as are infants from non-urban areas. For other age groups, children from urban areas are between 1.1 and 1.3 times as likely to be placed in foster care. The likelihood of a teenager entering placement in non-urban areas is nearly the same as it is in urban areas.

Figure 4.4 shows age-specific risks of entry into foster care after controlling for the poverty level of the county where the child resided. Again, the age-specific likelihood of placement is remarkably persistent. Placement rates are generally higher in counties with higher poverty rates, and the rate of placement is highest among infants, regardless of the county poverty rates. For example, the infant placement rate in the counties with the lowest poverty rates was 1.7 times as great as the rate for 1-year-olds; the same ratio existed in counties with the highest poverty rates. Children above the age of 11 also

Figure 4.3
Rate of First Entry into Foster Care by Age and Urbanicity: 2000

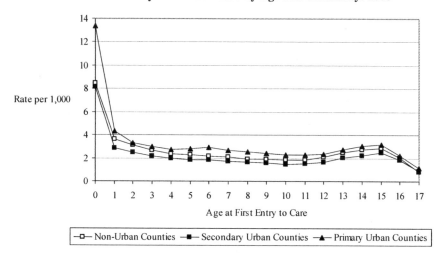

Figure 4.4
Rate of First Entry into Foster Care by Age and County Poverty Rate: 2000

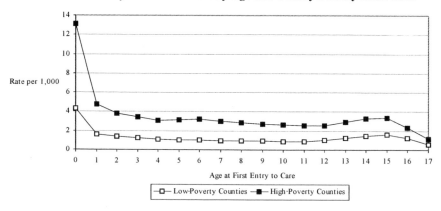

have higher placement rates, regardless of local poverty rates. Compared with 11-year-olds, 15-year-olds in low-poverty counties were about 80 percent more likely to be placed. In high-poverty counties, the rate of placement among adolescents was about 30 percent higher than it was among 11-year-olds.

Placement rates by age, race/ethnicity, and poverty. The risk of placement into foster care is associated with the race/ethnicity of the child and poverty measured at the county level. However, race/ethnicity and poverty are related to each other as well. To further establish age-based risk patterns, the data in Figure 4.5 and Figure 4.6 show age-specific placement risks according to race/ethnicity and county poverty level. Specifically, Figure 4.5 shows the placement rate for African American, white, and Hispanic children in the counties with the lowest poverty rates, whereas the county-level data in Figure 4.6 is limited to counties with the highest poverty rates.

Age-specific patterns are consistent across racial/ethnic groups, regardless of poverty. Babies have the highest placement rates; placement rates increase through adolescence, from age 12 through 15, before falling again. Placement rates are most pronounced for African American babies. Indeed, the likelihood of placement for African American babies in low-poverty areas is higher than the likelihood of placement for any other group of children in higher-poverty areas except African American babies. The data also indicate that within counties that have similar poverty rates, differences between African American children and children of other racial/ethnic groups are nearly constant across childhood. Thus, in low-poverty areas, African American children are about twice as likely to be placed as Hispanic children and three times as likely to be placed as white children of the same age. The same is true in high-poverty areas, except for the fact that the differences between white and Hispanic children are much smaller. On average, across all ages, African American children from high-poverty counties are slightly more than twice as likely to be placed as Hispanic and white children of the same age.

Having said all of that, for each group of children, we observe the same pattern described in previous analyses—placement rates are highest among babies; placement rates decline through age 11; and placement rates among children above the age of 11 reach a peak at age 15.

Age structure in the context of change. The stability of the age-specific likelihood of placement even when checked against factors

Figure 4.5
**Rate of First Entry into Foster Care by Age, Race, and County Poverty Rate:
2000
(low-poverty counties)**

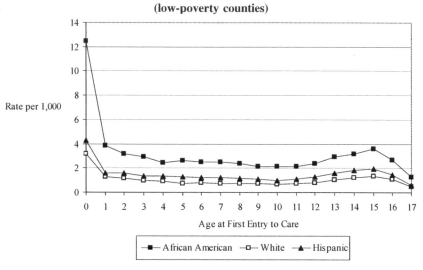

Figure 4.6
**Rate of First Entry into Foster Care by Age, Race, and County Poverty Rate:
2000
(high-poverty counties)**

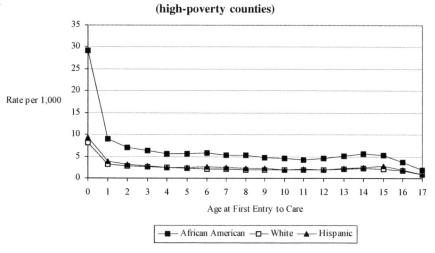

known to influence the general likelihood of placement suggests
that age is a durable predictor of placement risk. From the perspective of child welfare administrators, this means that incoming
caseloads of children will have distinct developmental needs that
will be quite stable across time, states, and regions of states. This

provides important evidence that should be brought to bear in shaping the structure of services in order to meet the needs of children and families, regardless of whether those services are designed to prevent placement or to expedite permanency.

Our final example of age effects on the incoming foster care population explores their durability over time. Figures 4.7 and 4.8 show the age distribution of children placed into foster care at the county level for 1990 and 2000.[3] The decade between 1990 and 2000 was marked by a substantial decline in the overall rate of placement; however, the likelihood of placement per 1,000 increased over the course of the decade in some counties and decreased in others.

Moreover, between 1990 and 2000, there were dramatic changes in the policy and practice context guiding the child welfare system. In 1990, the urban drug epidemic was still influencing placement patterns; the Family Support and Family Preservation legislation was passed in 1993; and the Adoption and Safe Families Act was passed in 1997. The question is, were these changes associated with changes in placement patterns?

Figure 4.7 shows the age distribution of children placed into foster care in counties where the overall placement rate per 1,000 children dropped most sharply between 1990 and 2000. The data show that the major component of the incoming population is babies. In 1990, in this selection of counties, babies accounted for about 28 percent of all the children placed for the first time. By 2000, babies

Figure 4.7
Age Distribution of Children Entering Care—Counties with Sharpest Drop in Placement Rates by Year of Admission: 1990 and 2000

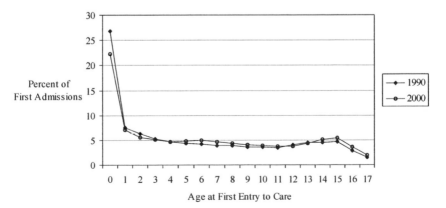

had dropped to about 23 percent of all first admissions to foster care, still the largest group of children entering care. The proportion of adolescents entering care increased, but only slightly. The proportion of children between the ages of 5 and 8 at the time of their initial placement increased modestly as well.

In Figure 4.8, we examine counties with the largest absolute increase in the rate of placement to determine whether the age mix of children entering care changes when the likelihood of placement increases. Again, the age structure of the incoming foster care population was largely unchanged between 1990 and 2000. The proportion of babies was smaller, even in areas where the risk of placement overall increased. In counties with higher placement rates, there was an overall increase in the proportion of children between the ages of 5 and 11. As we will show later in the chapter, this is a significant change in that the children most likely to still be in care after ten years belong to this age group.

NSCAW: Status of Children Entering Foster Care

The data presented in the first part of this chapter point to broad developmental themes that characterize the risk of placement and identify the type of child caseworkers refer to the foster care system. No age group approaches the rate of placement recorded for babies, particularly African American babies. Children ages 1 and 2 face a higher placement risk compared with other children under the age

Figure 4.8
Age Distribution of Children Entering Care—Counties with Largest Increase in Placement Rates by Year of Admission: 1990 and 2000

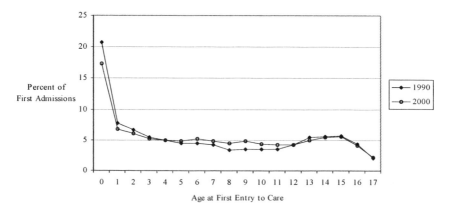

Age at First Entry to Care

of 10. Among children between the ages of 12 and 17, placement rates peak at age 15, regardless of race or poverty levels.

These findings agree very well with those of NSCAW (see Table 4.1). Among all children who are investigated for child maltreatment, only 11 percent enter out-of-home care. But among all the children who do enter out-of-home care, 28 percent are between the ages of 0 and 2. This is 1.6 times as great as the proportion of infants receiving in-home services. Among children receiving in-home services, more than half are between the ages of 3 and 10. There were more adolescents in the sample of NSCAW children that were placed than in the sample of children receiving in-home services.

Maltreatment History and Foster Care Placement in NSCAW

One particular advantage of the NSCAW data is the connection between the maltreatment data, foster care data (if placed), and developmental data for each child in the sample. States often have maltreatment data and placement data for individual children, but that information is generated during routine child welfare practice, and generally does not include direct measures of child well-being. Before looking specifically at the NSCAW data that describe how children placed in foster care are doing, we provide some basic information about the maltreatment histories of children placed in out-of-home care (which includes foster care, kinship care, and group care). For comparison purposes, we contrast the population placed

Table 4.1
Ages of Children Receiving In-Home vs. Out-of-Home Care

Age	All Children in the Sample % (SE)	Total In-Home % (SE)	Total Out-of-Home % (SE)
0-2	18.8 (1.0)	17.6 (1.2)	27.7* (2.8)
3-5	20.3 (1.1)	21.5 (1.2)	11.0 (1.5)
6-10	36.3 (1.4)	36.8 (1.7)	32.3* (2.7)
11+	24.6 (1.1)	24.0 (1.3)	29.1* (2.9)
Total	100	100 (1.2)	100 (1.2)

Percentages may not total to 100 due to rounding.
*Children 0-2, 6-10, and 11+ are more likely than children 3-5 to be in an out-of-home placement.

into out-of-home care with the population of children that received in-home services.

NSCAW data show that age is not the sole arbiter of who enters out-of-home placement (U.S. DHHS, 2005). As discussed in chapter 3, maltreatment type varies by age. In this chapter, we will show that maltreatment type is also associated with decisions about which children will enter out-of-home care. As a result, the population of children served at home looks quite different from the population of children placed into foster care. In Table 4.2, the in-home and foster care populations are differentiated by alleged maltreatment type. The most striking differences pertain to children who were investigated for physical maltreatment and failure to supervise. Almost 30 percent of the children served at home were reported to have been physically abused compared with 22.4 percent of children placed in out-of-home care. More than one-third of the children placed in out-of-home care were investigated because their caregivers failed to provide adequate supervision, while fewer than 30 percent of the children served at home fell into this category. With regard to the other maltreatment types, the differences between the in-home and the out-of-home populations were negligible.

According to Table 4.3, NSCAW data (U.S. DHHS, 2005) also indicate that, contrary to the belief that most children are reported for multiple reasons, more than two-thirds of children are assessed by child welfare agencies as having experienced just one of the main

Table 4.2

Most Serious Type of Alleged Abuse Among Children Involved with the Child Welfare Services by Child Setting

Maltreatment Type	All Children in the Sample % (SE)	Total In-Home % (SE)	Total Out-of-Home % (SE)*
Physical Maltreatment	28.4 (1.5)	29.1 (1.6)	22.4 (3.8)
Sexual Maltreatment	11.5 (1.2)	11.7 (1.4)	10.0 (2.2)
Failure to Provide	20.4 (1.5)	20.1 (1.7)	22.9 (2.7)
Failure to Supervise	29.8 (1.5)	29.0 (1.6)	36.6 (3.1)
Other	9.9 (1.2)	10.1 (1.3)	8.1 (1.7)

Percentages may not total to 100 due to rounding.
*Includes children in Other out-of-home placement settings (e.g., hospitals and runaway and homeless youth facilities). Abuse type refers to alleged abuse type.

Table 4.3
"Main" Abuse Types Among Children Involved with Child Welfare
Services by Child Setting**

Main Abuse Type Alleged	All Children in the Sample % (SE)	In-Home % (SE)	Out-of-Home % (SE)*
No main abuse types	6.7 (0.9)	7.2 (1.0)	3.2 (0.6)
One main abuse type (physical)	24.7 (1.5)	25.6 (1.6)	17.4 (2.1)
One main abuse type (sexual)	8.5 (1.0)	8.7 (1.1)	7.0 (1.9)
One main abuse type (failure to provide)	15.4 (1.2)	15.8 (1.4)	12.1 (1.2)
One main abuse type (failure to supervise)	24.4 (1.4)	24.1 (1.4)	26.9 (2.5)
Two main abuse types	18.1 (1.5)	16.8 (1.6)	28.8 (2.4)
Three main abuse types	2.1 (0.4)	1.8 (0.4)	4.0 (0.9)
Four main abuse types	0.1 (0.1)	0.1 (0.1)	0.7 (0.3)

Percentages may not total to 100 due to rounding.
* Includes children in Other out-of-home placement settings. Abuse type refers to alleged abuse type.
**Children remaining at home are significantly more likely than children in out-of-home care to have experienced none of the main abuse types in the current report ($c^2=10.7$, p <.01). Children remaining at home are significantly more likely than children in out-of-home care to have experienced the one main abuse type of physical maltreatment in the current report ($c^2=9.7$, p <.01). Children in out-of-home care are significantly more likely than children remaining at home to have experienced two of the main abuse types in the current report ($c^2=12.3$, p <.001).

types of maltreatment, described above. NSCAW findings are very clear that children who remain at home differ from children who go into out-of-home care in the extent to which they experience abuse that is other than the main abuse types (7 percent vs. 3 percent) or experience physical maltreatment (26 percent vs. 17 percent). Children in out-of-home care are also much more likely to have experienced two of the main abuse types in the current report (29 percent vs. 17 percent).

Severity of Maltreatment

Children remaining at home are more likely to have been reported for less severe maltreatment than children in out-of-home care. Although these findings may seem obvious, they do indicate that the decision to place a child into out-of-home care is often reserved for children who have experienced the greatest threats to their safety and well-being, an indication that the underlying decision-making process works on average.

Table 4.4 shows that the type of out-of-home placement does vary by maltreatment type, with children placed in kinship foster care less likely than other children in other placement settings to have been reported for physical abuse and more likely to have been investigated for neglect (failure to supervise). Children in group care are far and away the most likely to be linked to sexual abuse and the least likely to be tied to a failure to provide or failure to supervise. This is most likely an artifact of age, because children who have experienced sexual abuse are generally older and those who experience failure to supervise are younger.

Time since onset for children in out-of-home care. The extent to which the maltreatment continued between original onset and the most recent report was assessed in NSCAW (U.S. DHHS, 2005). The continuance of maltreatment may have been interrupted by formal actions (e.g., agency intervention, receipt of services, and/or placement into out-of-home care) or informal actions (e.g., the family intervened to end the maltreatment). A score was computed to reflect the proportion of the child's life by dividing the time in months, as reported by the child welfare worker, by the child's age in months (these ranged from less than 1 percent to 100 percent of the child's life).[4]

As shown in Table 4.5, children in out-of-home care have experienced a longer period of exposure to maltreatment than have chil-

Table 4.4
Most Serious Type of Alleged Abuse of Children Involved with the Child Welfare System by Child Setting

Abuse Type	All Children in the Sample % (SE)	Foster Family Care % (SE)	Kinship Foster Care % (SE)	Group Care % (SE)	Total Out-of-Home % (SE)*
Physical Abuse	28.4 (1.5)	22.8 (4.2)	16.3 (3.7)	24.1 (11.1)	22.4 (3.8)
Sexual Abuse	11.5 (1.2)	7.0 (1.8)	10.2 (2.5)	23.9 (10.3)	10.0 (2.2)
Failure to Provide	20.4 (1.5)	24.9 (2.9)	26.0 (5.7)	7.7 (3.7)	22.9 (2.7)
Failure to Supervise	29.8 (1.5)	36.6 (4.7)	40.5 (4.4)	31.0 (11.9)	36.6 (3.1)
Other	9.9 (1.2)	8.7 (2.6)	7.1 (2.1)	13.3 (5.8)	8.1 (1.7)

Percentages may not total to 100 due to rounding.
* Includes children in Other out-of-home placement settings. Abuse type refers to alleged abuse type.

Table 4.5
Mean Time (and SE) Since Onset of Abuse (as a proportion of child's life)

All Children in the Sample	Foster Family Care	Kinship Foster Care	Group Care	Total Out-of-Home *
0.11 (.01)	0.23 (0.02)	0.28 (0.06)	0.13 (0.04)	0.23 (0.03)**

* Includes children in Other out-of-home placement settings.
** Children in out-of-home care have significantly longer times since onset of abuse than children remaining at home (t=-4.9, p< .001). (See Table 2-7)

dren in the general child welfare services population—about twice as great a proportion of their entire lives (23 percent for children entering foster care vs. 9 percent for children living at home). Children in kinship foster care and family foster care are similar on this account. Children in group care have had the shortest periods of exposure to maltreatment.

The Well-Being of Foster Children

Information is just starting to emerge about the characteristics of children when they enter foster care. Most research has focused on children who have been in foster care for a considerable period of time. Some of the information gleaned from these studies shows that children and youth in foster care and group care are not doing well, but the inability of prior studies to compare how they were doing at intake makes it impossible to judge the contributions of child welfare services to children's outcomes.

Infancy and Early Childhood

This section on the well-being of children who entered foster care in 2000 draws on the same indicators of well-being used in chapter 3—albeit, just a sample of the many measures collected by NSCAW and presented in other NSCAW reports and papers.

Risk of developmental delay. The Bayley Infant Neurodevelopmental Screener (BINS) was used to assess the risk of developmental delay or neurological impairment in children ages 3 to 24 months. The serious risk of developmental delay or neurological impairment was pervasive. Service setting (i.e., open or closed in-home child welfare services or kinship or non-kinship foster care) is not significantly related to BINS scores (U.S. DHHS, 2005). African American infants under the age of 2 are at particularly high risk for developmental delay or neurological impairment.

On the cognitive domain of the Battelle Developmental Inventory and Screening Test (BDI), children in foster care are at very high risk of having below average cognitive development, with almost one-third scoring lower than two standard deviations below the mean on the overall measure (U.S. DHHS, 2005). These results apply to children who have become involved with the child welfare agency regardless of gender, race/ethnicity, or foster care or in-home setting.

Problem behavior: The child behavior checklist. Behavior problems that begin early in a child's life cause problems in parent-child relationships (Fisher, Gunnar, Chamberlain, & Reid, 2005) and also predict future problems in school and other settings (Qi & Kaiser, 2003). Total Problem Behaviors were measured in NSCAW using the caregiver-reported Child Behavioral Checklist (CBCL) as shown in Table 4.6. Overall about one in four of these young children are reported as having borderline or clinical behavior problems (U.S. DHHS, 2005).[5]

Middle Childhood

In this section, results of standardized assessments of reading and math achievement are presented for children placed in out-of-home care, with age, gender and race/ethnicity differences also considered. We compare children involved with child welfare services with children in the "general population," on whom measures were ostensibly normed, while recognizing that children involved with child welfare services are more often poor children than the children in the "general population" samples.

Reading and math achievement. In general, the mean reading (98) and math scores (92) of children whose families were investigated for maltreatment are below the normed mean of 100, but not significantly so (U.S. DHHS, 2005). Setting does not predict a child's mathematics or reading achievement, which indicates that at baseline, at

Table 4.6
Percentage of Children with Caregiver Report of Clinical/Borderline Total Problem Behaviors (age 2 to 3 years) as Measured by the CBCL

All Children in the Sample % (SE)	Foster Family Care % (SE)	Kinship Foster Care % (SE)	Total Out-of-Home* % (SE)
26.0 (2.5)	54.1(17.6)	23.0 (10.3)	37.3 (12.0)

*Includes group care and other out-of-home placements.

least, children who enter out-of-home care are just as far behind as children who remain at home. The broad concern about the academic achievement of children in foster care should extend to those children who become involved with child welfare services and remain at home.

Behavior problems. Children in out-of-home care have extraordinarily high rates of behavior problems, whether assessed by their caregivers, teachers, or by themselves. Although there is some inconsistency in the assessment of problems across reporters, the overall picture is the same; these children have substantial levels of behavior problems (U.S. DHHS, 2005). The proportion of children in the borderline/clinical range varies from 33 percent to 44 percent on Externalizing behaviors, from 24 percent to 36 percent on Internalizing behaviors, and from 36 percent to 44 percent on the Total Problems scale (see Table 4.7).

Among children ages 4 to 15 years, children in out-of-home care and older children are generally reported as having the most problem behaviors (U.S. DHHS, 2005). Caregivers of children in out-of-home care reported significantly more problem behaviors than caregivers of children remaining at home. Children in foster care have more problems than children in kinship care and those in group care have far and away the most (Table 4.8). The oldest children are identified as having significantly more problem behaviors than younger children. This difference is true for children remaining at home as well, with the older children reported as having significantly more problem behaviors.

Table 4.7
Children with Clinical/Borderline Problem Behaviors as Measured by the CBCL, TRF, and YSR

Rater and Age	Externalizing % (SE)	Internalizing % (SE)	Total Problems % (SE)
Parent report			
4 – 15 years	43.4 (2.3)	31.6 (1.6)	44.6 (2.3)
Norm*	5	5	5
Teacher report			
5 – 15 years	43.8 (2.4)	36.3 (2.1)	37.3 (3.2)
Norm*	5	5	5
Youth report			
11 + years	33.0 (3.0)	24.3 (2.5)	36.3 (2.6)
Norm*	5	5	5

* Norms are based on children up to 18 years of age.

Table 4.8
Caregiver Report of Clinical/Borderline Total Problem Behaviors (4-15 years) as
Measured by the CBCL**

Age	All Children in the Sample % (SE)	Foster Family Care % (SE)	Kinship Foster Care % (SE)	Group Care % (SE)	Total Out-of-Home % (SE)*
4-5	36.9 (3.7)	54.7 (12.0)	9.9 (4.8)	---	27.8 (8.7)
6-10	40.4 (2.9)	66.3 (8.0)	48.1 (9.6)	95.9 (3.7)	58.2 (6.4)
11+	55.4 (3.1)	47.4 (7.0)	42.2 (7.1)	79.6 (8.4)	56.1 (5.2)
Total	44.6 (2.3)	58.8 (4.3)	40.6 (5.3)	82.5 (6.7)	54.2 (3.5)

— Too few cases.
** Includes "other" out-of-home placement
Proportion of borderline/clinical scores for children in out-of-home placements is higher
than for children remaining at home (c^2=6.2, p < .01). Proportion of borderline/clinical
scores for children in group care is higher than for children in foster family care (c^2=6.7,
p < .01). Proportion of borderline/clinical scores for children in group care is higher than
for children in kinship foster care (c^2=8.7, p < .01). Proportion of borderline/clinical
scores for children 11+ years is higher than for 4- to 5-year-olds (c^2=19.8, p < .001).
Proportion of borderline/clinical scores for children 11+ years is higher than for 6- to 10-
year-olds (c^2=14.9, p < .001).

Adolescence

Youth who become involved with child welfare services are more
likely to score within the clinical range than the normative sample.
(See Table 4.9.) Teenagers in group care are judged to be within the
clinical or borderline sample at extraordinary rates. Although there
are many ways in which the young people in the NSCAW sample
express their problem behavior, they have especially high sub-scale
scores on conduct problems (Wall & Barth, 2005).

Whereas serious conduct problems are more common for the oldest children and for children living in out-of-home care, the levels of
problem behavior are substantial across all age groups and settings
(U.S. DHHS, 2005). The findings do indicate that there is a selection
of the most troubled children into the most intensive placements.
These findings also suggest the revisiting of David Fanshel's (1992)

Table 4.9
Youth Self-Report of Clinical/Borderline Total Problem Behaviors (11-15 years)

All Children in the Sample % (SE)	Foster Family Care % (SE)	Kinship Foster Care % (SE)	Group Care % (SE)	Total Out-of-Home % (SE)*
36.3 (2.6)	32.4 (8.2)	39.4 (7.4)	60.7 (11.3)	38.5 (4.9)

* Includes "other" out-of-home placements.

proposal that child welfare services should be explicitly designed and administered to achieve two basic purposes: (1) to achieve safety and permanency for maltreated children and (2) to "forestall the evolution of full-blown deviant careers" (p. 49). Child welfare services are, apparently, engaged in this work, albeit without a formal plan to accomplish this mission.

Differences in child setting very often show children in group care and non-kinship foster care as faring the worst, at the outset. Children in group care exhibit more behavioral problems than children in other settings. This was shown consistently through both caregiver and youth self-reported measures of problem behaviors, depression, delinquency, and substance abuse. In comparison to children remaining at home, children in non-kinship foster care appear to have poorer social and daily living skills, and more behavioral issues. Children in kinship care very often have scores more similar to those of the children remaining at home rather than the scores of children in other types of out-of-home placements. It may be that decisions about which children will enter which type of placement reflect consideration for their functioning—especially their level of problem behaviors.

In summary, children who have been placed into out-of-home care are entering the child welfare system with substantially lower cognitive and academic abilities, fewer skills, more problem behaviors, and even poorer physical health than their counterparts in the general population. According to Felitti et al. (1998), confluence of measured developmental risks, compounded by the high rates of exposure to poverty and violence described in earlier chapters, explains why the population of maltreated children is at such lifetime risk of health, mental health, and legal problems. In these data, we see the early accumulation of such adverse experiences already beginning to have a major impact on children's functioning—especially among those children in out-of-home care. The challenges of helping these children to achieve well-being and to reach the academic and employment goals held for children in general are significant. The pervasiveness of the delays and difficulties that children in out-of-home care experience suggest that these goals are unlikely to be achieved with services aimed only at those children leaving foster care via independent living programs. The developmental disadvantages of children in foster care begin early and, probably, last long.

Leaving Out-of-Home Placement

When children are placed in foster care, the objective for case-workers is to return them to their biological parents. Reunification is important because the law that governs parent-child relationships assumes that children's best interests are served if they live with their biological parents (Wulczyn, 2004). In the event reunification is not possible, adoption is a preferred alternative because it features a legally permanent relationship between the child and the adoptive parents. Recently, states have turned to guardianship as a third alternative to foster care in the event reunification is not possible (Testa, 2004). When children are discharged to guardians, the adults acting as guardians (they usually are, but need not be, related to the child) have a limited set of responsibilities vis-à-vis the child, but the parents retain their rights. Other exits are possible, but these exit types are not regarded as exits to permanency. For example, some children simply leave placement (i.e., run away). Other times, children leave placement because they are transferred to another child-serving agency, such as the mental health system or the juvenile justice system.

In this section, we explore whether exit patterns follow age-specific patterns. We use two measures: long-term exit probabilities, which measure the likelihood of specific exit types, and relative rates of exit, which measure the timing of exits. Relative rates of exit describe how fast exits occur relative to the date of entry. Generally, the relative rate of exit and the probability of exit are closely related. That is, exits that happen quickly (e.g., short duration) are also more probable. However, sometimes exits that happen slowly are more likely to happen. One case in point involves African American children who are adopted. In general, adoptions involving white children take less time than adoptions involving African American children of the same age. However, when specific entry cohorts are followed over the long term, African American children are more likely to be adopted (Wulczyn, 2003). To avoid confusion, we provide separate estimates for the probability of exit and the relative rate of exit.

Age and Long-Term Exit Probabilities

Over the years, researchers have documented a persistent relationship between age and how a child leaves placement (Barth, 1997;

Benedict & White, 1991; Courtney & Wong, 1996; Wulczyn, Hislop, & Goerge, 2000a). Generally, younger children are more likely to be adopted than older children, and older children are more likely to be reunified. However, when children are grouped by age, any within-group heterogeneity is concealed. The importance of understanding exit probabilities for single-year age groups is revealed in Figure 4.9. The graph shows how the children who were admitted to foster care for the first time between 1990 and 1995 left their first placement spell, if they did in fact leave foster care before December 31, 2001.

To simplify the presentation, children reunified, discharged to a relative, or placed with a guardian (regardless of whether the guardianship was subsidized) were grouped together in a category labeled "family exits." Children who were adopted, whether the adoption was subsidized or not, formed a second category. All other exit types (e.g., runaways, emancipation, and children transferred to other systems) were used to form a third category. The final category shows the children who were still in care.

The data show that age and exit type are clearly related. Notwithstanding the children who were still in care (about 4 percent of the children admitted as babies), children admitted to care prior to their first birthday were almost as likely to be reunified (42 percent) as they were to be adopted (44 percent). All other exit types accounted for fewer than 10 percent of the exits.[6] The shift in outcome between children who enter younger than 1 and those who enter as 1-year-olds is striking. Children admitted as 1-year-olds were much more

Figure 4.9
Age at First Admission by Exit Type:
Children Admitted to Foster Care from 1990 to 1995

likely to be reunified (60 percent) and much less likely to be adopted (27 percent). Even if all of the 1-year-olds still in care go on to be adopted, the likelihood of adoption would reach 1 in 3, still well below the proportion of 1-year-olds who were reunified. Among all children between the ages of 1 and 14 at the time of admission, about 60 percent were reunified. However, the likelihood of adoption declines steadily with admission age. Children who were 5 years old when they were admitted had a 1 in 5 chance of being adopted. If all the 5-year-olds still in care are eventually adopted, adoption would be half as likely as reunification for children in this age group.

As the likelihood of adoption declines with age, the likelihood of leaving foster care via a nonpermanent exit increases. Through age 6, other exits account for 9 to 10 percent of all exits (not including children still in care). Among 10-year-olds, more than 1 in 5 placements ended for other reasons. For 15-year-olds, the adolescents most likely to enter care, reunification was the most common exit type (56 percent). However, fewer than 1 percent of the 15-year-olds left placement because they were adopted. Other exits, including running away and aging out, accounted for the remaining exits.[7] The 16-year-olds either went home or left placement for some other reason; among 17-year-olds, nearly 60 percent left for other reasons; fewer than half of the 16-year-olds were discharged to their families.

The Timing of Exits

As we noted earlier, the likelihood of exit is usually, but not always related to how quickly the exit happens. To better judge the speed of exits, we calculated the relative rate of exit, using a competing risk, proportional hazards model (Courtney & Wong, 1996). Children were divided into single-year age categories; the rate of exit for each single-year age group was then compared with the rate of exit reported for infants. The competing risk model allows single exit types (e.g., reunification or adoption) to be studied separately while adjusting for the fact the children can leave for reasons other than the specified exit.

Reunification. Data that compare the speed of infant reunification with that for children of all other ages are found in Figure 4.10. Each panel of the figure shows the results for a different racial/ethnic group. Although the results show some inconsistencies, comparing the timing of exits for children of all ages with that for infants shows that all

Figure 4.10
Relative Rate of Exit to Reunification by Race/Ethnicity: First Admissions to Foster Care 1990-1995
(as of 12/31/2001)

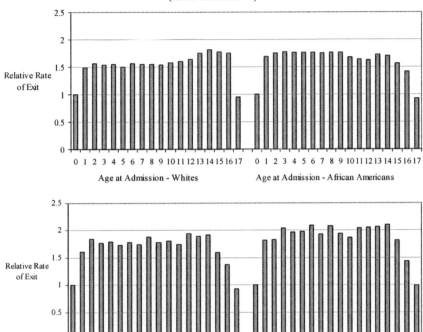

children admitted to foster care for the first time between the ages of 1 and 16 are reunified at rates that are faster than infants, regardless of the child's race or ethnicity.[8] Generally, 15- and 16-year-olds move more slowly to reunification, but the pattern is least pronounced for white children. Otherwise, a consistent pattern is difficult to discern.

Adoption. Adoption patterns are much more consistent, as shown in Figure 4.11. Regardless of race or ethnicity, children who entered placement after their first birthday move much more slowly to adoption. Moreover, the speed of adoption drops persistently with age until age 16, suggesting that the relatively few adoptions that do occur tend to happen at a pace that is somewhat faster for older youth.

Most importantly, the data in Figure 4.11 show how age-defined patterns in the data transcend matters of race/ ethnicity. African American children move more slowly through the foster care system than white children do. Although the differences are not as stark, the ex-

Figure 4.11
Relative Rate of Exit to Adoption by Race/Ethnicity:
First Admissions to Foster Care 1990-1995
(as of 12/31/2001)

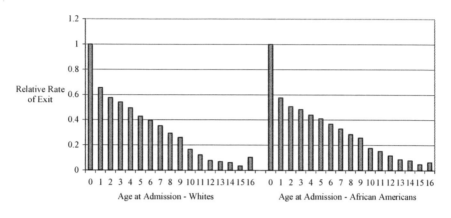

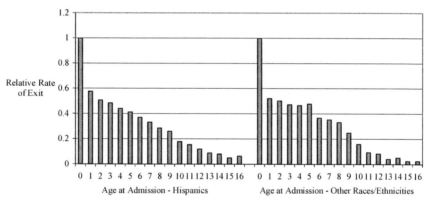

perience of Hispanic children also differs from that of white children. However, within groups of children defined by their race and ethnicity, the durable age effect is indicative of how forcefully developmental issues influence what happens to children.

Conclusion

The data presented in this chapter reinforce the notion that the likelihood of coming into contact with the child welfare system follows a distinct, age-differentiated pattern. Just as we saw with the maltreatment data, infants are by far the group of children at greatest risk of entering foster care, followed close behind by adolescents.

As we expected, the age patterns that illuminate underlying risk patterns are remarkably stable. With respect to race and ethnicity, African American infants have the highest placement rates. Differences between white and Hispanic children are smaller, although the number of Hispanic children in the FCDA may be undercounted because of coding problems. Importantly, the data suggest that although African American children of all ages are more likely to enter placement than either white or Hispanic children of the same ages, the most notable differences involve infants. That said, infants of all races and ethnicities are considerably more likely to enter foster care than are 1-year-olds, the group of children with the next-highest placement rate.

The pattern is little changed when the county-specific placement rates are calculated. When urban counties, secondary urban counties, and non-urban counties are examined separately, the pronounced risk of placement facing infants emerges yet again. So, too, does the elevated risk of placement among adolescents. The same is true when counties are divided into high- and low-poverty counties. Rates of placement are generally higher in urban counties and poorer counties, although in each instance, the risk of placement among infants is particularly elevated in the higher-risk context (i.e., urban counties, high-poverty counties). When poverty and race/ethnicity are examined together, the placement rate for African American children living in high-poverty counties reaches almost 30 per 1,000, the highest rate of placement for any population we examined.

Equally striking are the data that describe the developmental status of the children at the time they enter foster care. Historically, advocates for child welfare reform have argued for reducing the time in foster care so as to minimize the detrimental effects a period of parent-child separation has on the child. If placement has detrimental effects on children, those effects are added to the already substantial developmental problems facing children who enter the foster care system. Moreover, the problems are pervasive and in that all domains—physical, cognitive/educational, and social-emotional—indicate that children in the foster care system face serious challenges to their well-being. Young foster children are physically smaller. On age-appropriate measures of behavioral and cognitive functioning, foster children score substantially below the norms; parents report clinical and borderline CBCL scores that are nine times the rate reported in the normed population. Delinquency scores for children in NSCAW's out-of-home sample were far in excess of what one would expect to find in a general population of 6- to 15-year-olds.

Stepping back from the data, it should come as no surprise that children in the child welfare system present pervasive developmental issues. Of the children in NSCAW who went into foster care after placement, nearly 60 percent were neglected, either because the caregiver did not provide for the child or because the caregiver did not provide proper supervision. A long history of scholarship has linked poverty to pernicious developmental effects (Aber, Bennett, Conley, & Li, 1997; Duncan & Brooks-Gunn, 2000; McLoyd, 1998; and Rutter & Madge, 1976) . Although neglect is not limited to poor families and most poor families take good care of their children, there is nevertheless a link between economic hardship, parenting behavior, and child well-being (Mistry, Vandewater, Huston, & McLoyd, 2002). The parent-mediated interventions discussed in chapter 6 are designed to help mitigate these effects by promoting parenting behaviors that can influence child behaviors, even in difficult environments.

There does appear to be some type of selection effects in that more troubled children are found in more restrictive, least family-like settings. For example, caregiver reports of clinical/borderline total problem behaviors as measured by the CBCL suggest that children in group care have much higher rates of reported problems than do children in either kinship homes or foster family homes. Among other things, these findings validate the need to trace the interdependent nature of trajectories when assessing the outcomes of children involved in the foster care system. If, as is often the case, foster children exhibit higher-than-average rates of problem behavior, then the impact of child welfare services has to be adjusted for the fact that children arrive with a plethora of developmental needs. Simple measures of well-being that fail to account for the child's condition at the time services start will be of very limited value from a monitoring and service design perspective.

When all of the epidemiologic data are taken together, a coherent picture begins to emerge. Although we do not mean to imply that developmental factors are the sole explanation for why placement rates vary over the lifespan of childhood, it does appear that the likelihood a child will come in contact with the child welfare system is tied to passage through developmental stages (Pickett, Streight,

Simpson, & Brison, 2003).[9] Infants, the most vulnerable children in the biological sense, face the greatest risk of placement because of their developmental stage. Infants are totally dependent on adults and there is widespread conviction that developmental risks during this developmental period have very long-term consequences. Risks peak again in adolescence as the family processes change and adolescents become harder to manage. The NSCAW provides clear support for the idea that manifest behavior problems present parents with real parenting challenges, even if those same parenting behaviors contributed to the problems in the first instance. The long developmental period between birth and adolescence appears quieter in the sense that the overall likelihood of involvement with the child welfare system declines until about age 11. Physical abuse is one exception to the general rule.

The incidence rates computed with the NCANDS and FCDA, together with the developmental profiles constructed with the NSCAW data, form an essential base of evidence for understanding how child welfare services should be assembled to better meet the needs of at-risk children and their families. Given what the evidence tells us, we turn to the question of what works for high-risk children in the two chapters that follow.

Notes

1. When children from different states are compared, babies from states with longer-than-average placement duration will have longer duration than babies who are from other states. But, duration for babies, relative to children of other ages in a given state, will be longer. The differences are attributable to system and ecological factors; the similarities are due to placement patterns that are influenced by factors tied to human development.

2. See Wulczyn & Hislop (2002) for a description of the counties that fall into each category.

3. In Figures 4.7 and 4.8, the data show the proportion of children entering care by age at entry rather than the placement rate. The data are presented in this way because single-age population counts at the county level are not available from the 1990 census.

4. As with the severity of maltreatment, this analysis was conducted only for children with one of the four main abuse types as their most serious type of maltreatment. More description of this score is provided in U. S. DHHS (2005).

5. Two versions of the Achenbach were used in NSCAW; one covers children ages 2-3 and one is used to assess children ages 4-16 (Dowd et al., 2001).

6. For young children, none of the "other" exits involved runaways.

7. Additional analysis not covered here shows that among children who were admitted to foster care as 15-year-olds, runaway and "other" exits (e.g., transfers to other child-serving systems) accounted for one-third of the exits. Surprisingly, only 10 percent of the children who entered foster care as 15-year-olds left care because they reached the age of majority.

8.   Relative rates of exit above one imply faster movement; relative rates of exit below one imply slower exits.
9.   The importance of these other factors cannot be understated. For example, in the counties we identified as high-poverty counties, the rate of infant placement ranged between 1 per 1,000 and 40 per 1,000 with most of the counties reporting an infant placement rate between 5 and 15 placements per 1,000. Although infants may be the children most likely to enter foster care, even in these diverse counties, it is clear that contextual factors play an important role. Understanding these influences is one of the many challenges facing researchers. For example, how do system resources, human capital (worker skill levels), and community standards interact with basic developmental considerations to produce the observed rate of placement?

Part 3

Child Welfare Services in a
Developmental Context

Introduction to Part 3

The focus in this section of the book shifts away from the epidemiological perspective to examine child welfare services and promising approaches to services. Sensitivity to developmental and social ecology is a factor that distinguishes good programs from others. Service designs and their evaluations have to conceptualize interventions as changes in the life course trajectory of parents in relation to the life course of their children and vice versa (Brooks-Gunn, Phelps, & Elder, 1991). As children grow older, and patterns of maltreatment and of caregiving change, explanations of maltreatment that emphasize parental behavior need to shift to those that balance child and caretaker contributions to the need for service.

At this point, given the title of this volume, readers may be expecting a review of clinical programs in the manner of the Cochrane or Campbell reviews that are becoming the staple of evidence-based practice in health care and social welfare. Research reviews in the Cochrane and Campbell traditions are designed to synthesize evidence pertaining to interventions and public policy.[1] They follow a rigorous format designed to summarize the results of studies that test interventions. In doing a review, the reviewer must acknowledge any conflicts of interest, explicitly state the criteria for selecting studies, formulate review questions, define data extractions strategies, assess the quality of the studies, and synthesize results using recognized statistical procedures (Khan, Riet, Glanville, Sowden, & Kleijnen, 2001).

Our purpose here is broader and more thematic in that we want to connect policy and program design to a body of work that suggests quite strongly that effective interventions "regardless of the target group or the desired outcomes, can be derived from the normative theories of child development" (Shonkoff & Phillips, 2000). Our belief is that child welfare interventions have to become much more self-conscious in their theoretical and evidentiary underpinnings if they are to become more effective. The next two chapters offer a starting point for that work. To start, we focus in chapter 5 on promising services intended for young children. We start here for the simple reason that the data in Part 2 indicate that infancy and early childhood are high-risk developmental periods characterized by high utilization of child welfare services. In most, if not all jurisdictions, a successful child welfare agency will have to address the needs of families with very young children. Older children with mental health needs belong to a second high-risk developmental group marked by service trajectories that differ significantly from those of younger children. Among school-aged children, maltreatment rates are lower than those reported for infants. So, too, are rates of placement away from home. Nevertheless, the data show that school-aged children face significant psychosocial problems. From a service delivery perspective, it is important to note that adolescents are much more likely to leave foster care for reasons other than adoption or reunification. At the very least, these data reinforce the fact that adolescents' ability to walk away from placement, or to get transferred into a more restrictive facility, are important reasons why the care of adolescents has to be approached differently. These issues are taken up in chapter 6.

The discussion throughout this section is also intended to reinforce the need to match services with the developmental realities that policymakers and practitioners are likely to encounter. Typically, policy discussions in the United States promote certain approaches: family preservation, neighborhood-based services, kinship care, wrap-around services, concurrent planning, and so forth. These are useful categories of services, but they lack a clear connection to the probability that some services fit better with some populations than others. Indeed, the federal framework for child welfare services (embodied in ASFA and the main child welfare services funding streams) is almost completely silent on ways to account for age or development. As we discuss in the conclusion (chapter 7), the idea that different service types should be integrated will suffer if policymakers embrace the concept without realizing that the continuum of services must be composed of evidence-based elements best suited to the target population. For the young children entering child welfare services, the link between child welfare services and early education may be as vital to meeting their needs as the link to mental health services is for older children.

Common sense points in this direction, but the institutional and organizational challenges are anything but trivial.

Note

1.   Readers interested in obtaining an example of such a review will find one at http://www.campbellcollaboration.org/doc-pdf/teenpar.pdf (Barlow, May 21, 2001).

5

Altering the Early Life Course of Children in Child Welfare: Evidence-Based Interventions for Infants, Toddlers, and Preschoolers

As the numbers of children exposed to maltreatment have increased, interventions aimed at this unique group of children and their families have proliferated. Although there is widespread use of these intervention programs, empirical evidence regarding their effectiveness is sorely lacking. Moreover, researchers and practitioners are often working in parallel streams, without informing one another's work. The few programs with empirically documented effectiveness have not been evaluated specifically with child welfare samples and have not often found their way into mainstream child welfare practice (Barth et al., in press). Thus, the child welfare field expends many of its meager service dollars on programs— such as family preservation programs (Littell & Schuerman, 2002)— whose impact on children and families is uncertain.

This chapter will review the available evidence on interventions designed to alter the child welfare trajectory of very young children. Included in this section is an examination of interventions specifically targeted to the child welfare population, as well as more globally targeted interventions that may have an impact on this population. We will also review the literature on interventions designed to alter the developmental trajectory of children involved with child welfare services (i.e., prevent poor developmental outcomes). Before turning to the extant evidence about these specific interventions, the knowledge that the field of prevention science provides about the design of effective preventive intervention programs offers a view of the way that the child welfare system might best generate interventions of the future.

The Contribution of Prevention Science

Although the child welfare system is about far more than prevention, the prevention science framework has utility. Prevention science is a burgeoning field that is built upon a solid conceptual and empirical foundation. An important theoretical distinction that has been proffered in this field pertains to how prevention programs can be categorized. Although there is some controversy about this classification framework (Weissberg & Greenberg, 1998), the Institute of Medicine categorized preventive interventions as: (1) *universal* programs that target persons without risk factors; (2) *selective* programs that target persons with risk factors that make them more vulnerable to a disorder, such as maltreatment; and (3) *indicated* programs that target high-risk persons with identified biological or behavioral markers related to the manifestation of a disorder, but who have not been diagnosed with a specific disorder (Mrazek & Haggerty, 1994). In this vein, preventive programs for maltreated children and their caregivers (whether biological or substitute caregivers) would be classified as either selective or indicated preventive interventions. In a meta-analysis of maltreatment prevention programs, more than 90 percent of the programs were either selective or indicated (MacLeod & Nelson, 2000).[1]

Although the majority of the prevention programs that appear in the empirical literature target older children and adolescents (Weissberg & Kumpfer, 2003), there has been considerable interest in the development of effective intervention programs for families with young children. Some scholars assert that these interventions are the most cost effective in that they beget long-term benefits in children's developmental course (Heckman, 2000). For example, early intervention has been found to decrease delinquent and other externalizing behaviors in adolescence (Webster-Stratton & Taylor, 2001; Yoshikawa, 1994). Preventing these conduct problems also helps to protect children from maltreatment because, as shown previously, children who have difficult behavior are overrepresented among children who become involved with child welfare services. Although our data do not clearly indicate whether the maltreatment is the cause of the problem behavior or the result of it, some bidirectional causality is almost certain (Kadushin & Martin, 1981). Parent-mediated interventions that reduce problem behavior are likely to reduce maltreatment risks from both directions. It is further posited that higher-risk families require intervention much earlier in the life course, such as during the prenatal or early childhood period (Olds, Hill, Robinson, Song, & Little, 2000; Webster-Stratton & Taylor, 2001). Thus, recent empirical attention has been drawn to prevention programs that target very young children and their families.

As discussed in greater length below, the empirical literature has underscored several global features of effective prevention programs that are relevant to a discussion of prevention programs for young maltreated children and their families (Nation et al., 2003). Effective preventive interventions have strong theoretical and empirical foundations that inform their design, and are subject to ongoing evaluation. Unfortunately, Repucci and colleagues (1999) suggest that the majority of prevention programs that have been developed do not have a strong theoretical base. Prevention programs with proven effectiveness are comprehensive in nature and address multiple individual and ecological risk and protective processes. Importantly, participants are exposed to sufficient dosage of the program and experience a well-trained staff. Effective interventions are documented to be relationship-based and utilize an active (non-didactic) approach to altering the skills of participants. Finally, they are long-term, age-specific, and culturally appropriate. Despite the fact that these characteristics have been identified in the global prevention literature, the paucity of evidence-based prevention programs specific to the child welfare field limits our capacity to make such generalizations about effective programs to prevent child maltreatment and foster care placement.

Empirically Based Interventions for Young Children

Although the field of prevention science has concentrated heavily on programs serving school-aged children, there has nevertheless been an expansion of prevention programs serving high-risk young children and their families in the last few decades. Fueled largely by the belief and evidence that early intervention produces more long-term benefits and by the early brain development literature, programs for young children have been initiated by the health, education, and social service sectors. These programs are typically characterized by many of the features of effective prevention programs that are described above. Because many of them have not been initiated by the child welfare field specifically, and are addressing general developmental risk and protective factors, they are not necessarily designed to prevent maltreatment or placement into foster care. However, given that targeted families have risk factors similar to the families involved with child welfare services, these interventions may ultimately help to reduce child maltreatment and placement. Following are descriptions of programs that have been found to have at least a modest impact on altering the child welfare and developmental trajectories of young children—children not unlike those who become involved with child welfare services.

Preventing maltreatment of young children. The developmental and service trajectories of maltreated children who enter child welfare services are dynamic. The most common experience that maltreated children may have at any point in their child welfare services involvement is some indirect service receipt from in-home case monitoring or parent training due to maltreatment (Barth et al., in press). A second experience, in terms of likelihood, is placement into foster care. Programs that prevent maltreatment directly relate to these two case outcomes. Such interventions can prevent families from becoming involved with child welfare services as protective services cases. They can also, in concept, prevent the foster care placement of children by providing in-home support services that reduce the potential for maltreatment. The evidence from demonstration projects suggests that we are much farther along in preventing the need for in-home services than we are in preventing placement, once serious maltreatment has occurred.

The number of programs with an explicit goal of preventing or reducing child maltreatment has markedly increased since the passage of comprehensive federal child welfare legislation in the the late twentieth century (e.g., Adoption Assistance and Child Welfare Act of 1980; Adoption and Safe Families Act of 1997). Most prevention programs for families of maltreated children are focused on physical abuse. Although neglect is the most common type of maltreatment, few programs address child neglect specifically, and few are aimed at young children (Barth et al., in press). Many of these programs have not been rigorously evaluated, so it is impossible to offer a general statement regarding the effectiveness of these programs. Some interventions with effects on the prevention of maltreatment—for example, the Nurse Family Partnership Program (Olds et al., 1997)—have been conducted as part of expensive clinical trials and have not been tested for effectiveness when delivered on the community level (Peterson, Tremblay, Ewigman, & Saldana,

2003). Thus, there are almost no known effective interventions embedded into community-based family support programs or selective intervention programs.

Rigorous evaluations of child maltreatment reduction programs are also uncommon, and many methodological problems remain unresolved. One challenge that has compromised the evaluation of these programs is the level of undetected maltreatment. Because there is more surveillance in the treatment groups, and therefore increased reports of maltreatment, the use of child maltreatment reports as an outcome used to evaluate prevention programs is problematic (Brayden et al., 1993; Olds, Henderson, Kitzman, & Cole, 1995; Roberts, Kramer, & Suissa, 1996).

Despite these caveats, interventions exist that have been documented to be successful in preventing or reducing maltreatment, or in diminishing the risk factors associated with maltreatment (MacLeod & Nelson, 2000). For example, a 12-week hospital-based parent education program for urban adolescent, unmarried mothers was evaluated 3 to 5 years after the birth of the children (Britner & Reppucci, 1997). This study found that intervention mothers were less likely to have substantiated reports of child abuse and neglect than control mothers. Peterson and colleagues (2003) implemented a 4-month peer group and home-based program for mothers of children 18 months to 3 years. The program helped to develop mothers' cognitive-behavioral repertoire for managing their transition to parenthood. Intervention mothers demonstrated reductions in the use of harsh discipline, increased knowledge of the developmental needs of their children, less child-directed anger, greater understanding of their parental roles, higher levels of nurturance, and a higher sense of parenting efficacy. Child maltreatment was not directly measured in this study, but all these factors have been documented to be related to child maltreatment. The reduction in these risk factors suggests that such an intervention could have an impact on maltreatment reduction.

Another approach to reducing risk is to supplement the increasingly available postpartum home visiting programs that are provided through local public and private health and human service agencies. Bugental and colleagues (2002) evaluated the addition of a 1-year cognitive retraining program to the standard ongoing home visits provided to mothers identified as at-risk during pregnancy or early in the postnatal period. Mothers were randomly assigned to one of three groups: (1) education regarding cognitive strategies to improve their parenting behavior during home visits based on the Healthy Start model; (2) conventional Healthy Start-oriented home visits; and (3) no home visits. At the 1-year follow-up, lower levels of harsh parenting and reduced prevalence of physical abuse were found in the enhanced home visiting group in comparison with the standard home visiting group and the no home visiting control group.

The largest program in this country with an expressed goal of preventing maltreatment is the Healthy Families America (HFA) program. HFA is a national home visiting program that has hundreds of local affiliate programs across the United States. Its precursor was the Healthy Start model, which was initiated and currently operates statewide in Hawaii. HFA principles inform the design of all local programs, and include prenatal or immediate postnatal initiation of services, family assessment, voluntary nature of services, varying intensity of service depending upon family need, long-term duration of services, and comprehensive services. Specific principles relate to staffing of the program, including intensive training and supervision, cultural competence, and personal and employment-related competencies.

Several experimental and quasi-experimental evaluations of local HFA programs have been conducted (Daro & Harding, 1999; Duggan et al., 1999), some of which have documented a reduction in child maltreatment reports. However, many of the studies have methodological and attrition issues that limit their findings. In more recent randomized clinical trials of HFA, no differences were found regarding levels of maltreatment in the intervention and control groups at post-test (Duggan et al., 2004; Landsverk & Carrilio, 2000). Although HFA maltreatment effects are not conclusive, other positive benefits are evident, such as improved parent-child interactions and reduced partner violence (Duggan et al., 1999).

There are many other prevention programs that have not yielded benefits for participating families. For example, Fraser and colleagues (2000) conducted a randomized controlled trial of a child abuse and neglect home visiting intervention beginning early in the postnatal period. At follow-up (12-18 months post-birth), no differences were found in intervention and control families regarding parental stress, parenting competence, and quality of the home environment. Similarly, Barth (1991) evaluated the impact of the Child Parent Enrichment Project, which provided 6 months of paraprofessional home visitation to mothers at risk of child abuse during or soon after pregnancy. Although this program overall had no impact on child abuse reports or on maternal self-report of functioning, there was some evidence of program effectiveness with families who had less serious problems. Brayden and colleagues (1993) did not find that comprehensive health services for parents and infants, beginning in the prenatal period through age 2, reduced maltreatment in their intervention group. Their finding of increased neglect in the intervention group was attributed to detection bias (i.e., increased maltreatment surveillance in the intervention group).

Although many prevention programs do not have a specific goal of preventing maltreatment, some programs designed to promote the health and well-being of infants and their families have been found to prevent maltreatment. For example, home visiting programs designed to enhance maternal/child health outcomes have been found to affect maltreatment. Perhaps the most well known and well documented of such programs is the Nurse Family Partnership Program, originally implemented in a semi-rural community in upstate New York and now implemented in many states across the United States. In this intervention, nurses provided home visits to high-risk primiparous mothers during the prenatal and infancy periods. In the group at greatest risk (i.e., adolescents who were unmarried and had low incomes), there was a trend suggesting that intervention mothers were less likely to abuse or neglect their children in the first 2 years of life (Olds, Henderson, Chamberlain, & Tatelbaum, 1986). However, no treatment-control differences were found regarding child abuse and neglect between 25 and 40 months of age, immediately after the end of intervention (Olds, Henderson, & Kitzman, 1994). At a later follow-up of the whole sample (Olds et al., 1997), it was documented that nurse-visited mothers had fewer substantiated child maltreatment reports 4-15 years following the birth of the child, particularly if they were unmarried and of low socioeconomic status. Another finding of note in the Nurse Family Partnership program is that benefits to families are more pronounced when they are served by professional staff (i.e., nurses) rather than paraprofessional staff (Olds et al., 2002).

Comprehensive child development programs have also been found to reduce maltreatment. A large longitudinal investigation of Title I Child-Parent Centers in Chicago documented a lower rate of child maltreatment, via court petitions and child protective service records, for intervention children than for children who received kindergarten intervention (Reynolds & Robertson, 2003). This finding held throughout childhood and adolescence and was more pronounced if the children had received 4-6 years of intervention. Indeed, influences of this program have been detected as late as early adulthood— as the positive impact on educational attainment cascaded across a range of positive outcomes (Smokowski, Mann, Reynolds, & Fraser, 2004). Similarly, high-risk families participating in an interdisciplinary early intervention program that included child development and mental health services were less likely to require child protection services and to have substantiated incidents of child abuse and neglect than were a comparison group receiving standard care (Huxley & Warner, 1993). These intervention parents also exhibited better attitudes about punishment and more emotional and verbal involvement with their infants.

Promoting the Well-Being of Families with Young Children

Many parental characteristics and processes have been associated with child maltreatment, including inappropriate expectations of children, mental health difficulties, lower levels of empathy, higher levels of stress, and negative parent-child interactions (Milner, 1998). Many preventive interventions attempt to alter these processes, with the ultimate goal of preventing child maltreatment. Such interventions include home visiting services, mental health and psychotherapeutic approaches, and parent education programs.

Prevention programs with home visiting as the primary service delivery mechanism are quite varied in their targets, duration, and staffing. Many have been found to be effective in meeting the needs of families at risk for maltreatment. In one study (Black et al., 1994), trained nurses provided biweekly home visits for a 2-year period to low SES, drug-abusing mothers. Mothers in the intervention group were less likely to report ongoing drug use, were more likely to complete pediatric appointments, and exhibited greater emotional and verbal responsiveness to their infants. Gelfand and colleagues (1996) also used nurses to provide home visits to depressed mothers during their infants' first year of life. Mothers in the treatment group exhibited fewer depressive symptoms and daily hassles than did those in the control group. Additionally, control group mothers reported fewer social supports over time, and if they were depressed, became more punitive toward their children over time.

In an intervention using paraprofessional home visitors, Marcenko and Spence (1994) and Marcenko, Spence, and Samost (1996) did not find that the goal of reducing child out-of-home placement was met for their population of mothers experiencing psychiatric illness, substance abuse, or domestic violence. (This was probably not a realistic expectation for a test of a preventive intervention, given the low rate of placement for children—even those living with parents with significant problems.) However, intervention mothers reported less psychological distress and more social support over time than control mothers. Jacobson and Frye (1991) evaluated a program using volunteers as "parenting coaches" from the prenatal period through the first year of life. After the program, intervention mothers rated their children as more securely attached than did the control mothers. These interventions showed that some parenting characteristics can change through interventions, although their ability to have a major influence on parent and child trajectories are not evident.

Many other efforts have been made to influence the parenting of high-risk families, with modest results. Black and colleagues (1995) trained community workers to provide home visiting services to families of infants diagnosed with non-organic failure to thrive, a condition emanating from parental emotional neglect. Lay home visitors supervised by a community health nurse, focused on building a therapeutic alliance with the family, meeting the mother's needs, and promoting positive parent-child interaction. Although there were no effects on parent-child interaction when the intervention and control groups were compared, intervention children exhibited fewer declines in receptive language over time, and their parents provided more child-oriented environments at the end of the program.

Mental health and psychotherapeutic approaches for young high-risk children and their families have, in the main, focused on promoting positive parent-child interaction and attachment. Examining the effects of a combination home- and clinic-based preventive infant mental health program, Heineke and colleagues (1999) found that mothers receiving the intervention were less likely to be restrictive and punitive, and more likely to promote their infants' autonomy. Additionally, their infants were less likely to be insecurely attached and exhibited greater expectations that their needs would be effectively met, attributes that reduce stress in parent-child interactions.

In a program for mothers at risk for attachment disorders, infant-parent psychotherapy was provided in the home for 1 year (Leiberman, Weston, & Pawl, 1991). Although intervention dyads were not more likely to be securely attached than controls, they engaged in more frequent partnered interaction. Additionally, mothers in the intervention group expressed greater empathy toward their children and communicated more frequently with them. Infants expressed less anger, demonstrated less avoidance, and were less resistant to maternal requests. These changes should have made parenting less stressful for these young and troubled mothers—probably increasing the odds of successful parenting and positive child development.

Parent education programs are arguably the most common intervention strategy for the prevention of child maltreatment. Many of these interventions have not been subject to rigorous evaluation (Barth et al., in press). Overall, the available literature suggests that parent education groups as a *universal* intervention (i.e., for families not identified as at risk for maltreatment) have met with success (Carter & Harvey, 1996). However, such programs have limited effectiveness for high-risk families (Chalk & King, 1998). Additionally, parent education programs that rely on didactic, informational, and discussion formats tend to be less effective (Daro, 1988; Durlak, 1997). Those making the case that they are successful (e.g., Cowen, 2001; Huebner, 2002) often have methodological difficulties, such as the absence of a control group.

Some studies do suggest that parent education programs that employ a more targeted, therapeutic approach for higher-risk families are more effective. For example, parent groups used in concert with more individualized therapeutic interventions have been found to reduce child maltreatment (Daro & Cohn Donnelley, 2002). A few parent training programs focused on reducing behavior problems in young children have been rigorously evaluated and applied to young children receiving child welfare services. For example, Parent Child Interaction Training (PCIT; Chaffin et al., 2003), developed for oppositional-defiant children between the ages of 2 ½ and 7 years, has been implemented with young physically abused children and their parents. PCIT includes live coaching of parental behavior, focusing on two primary goals: (1) to enhance parent-child relationships; and (2) to improve parents' behaviorally oriented discipline. It incorporates child-directed interaction strategies (e.g., play during special time) and parent-directed interaction strategies (e.g., command giving). This intervention was found to improve parental functioning and parent-child relationships in families of young children who had been physically abused.

Another intervention aimed at reducing behavior problems in young children is "The Incredible Years" (Webster-Stratton, 1998; Webster-Stratton & Hammond, 1997). This model consists of twelve weekly group sessions led by professional therapists to train parents to manage young children's behavior problems in the home. "The Incredible Years" has been tested on children ranging from 2 to 8 years of age with risk for conduct problems. One evaluation study was conducted with a Head Start population in which almost one-quarter of the sample had a recent history of child protection service involvement. Findings suggested that negative parenting behaviors (e.g., harsh style) were reduced and positive parenting behaviors (e.g., positive affect, praise) were increased in the intervention sample.

Addressing the Needs of Young Maltreated Children

Although there are by far many more intervention programs targeted to improve the functioning of the families of young children at risk for maltreatment, some interventions have as an explicit goal the enhancement of the well-being of maltreated children. Interestingly, the bulk of these interventions have been designed to support the development of young maltreated children in the foster care system. An exception is a school-based intervention program for maltreated preschool children (Fantuzzo, Manz, Atkins, & Meyers, under review; Fantuzzo et al., 1996). This intervention entailed pairing socially competent peers with withdrawn maltreated children in the classroom, under the supervision of a parent assistant. It led to an increase in interactive peer play and a decrease in solitary play for maltreated children. Another child-centered intervention provided therapeutic day treatment services to preschool maltreated children, and also included comprehensive counseling and education services for their parents (Culp, Little, Letts, & Lawrence, 1991). Findings at post-test indicated developmental gains and enhanced self-concepts among intervention children when compared with non-intervention children.

Interventions for Foster Children

Given the broad developmental insults experienced by foster children, interventions that assist them are sorely needed. Several empirical studies regarding young foster children have focused on comprehensive assessment of the children's developmental needs (Leslie, Gordon, Ganger, & Gist, 2002; Urquiza, Wirtz, Peterson, & Singer, 1994). Horwitz and colleagues (2000) moved beyond documenting the rate of developmental delay and behavior problems in their sample of foster children to study the impact of their multidisciplinary assessment clinic. This clinic provided health, mental health, and developmental evaluations and follow-up for all children from 11 to 74 months of age entering foster care in a specific county in Connecticut. Compared with the children in a nearby county who received the usual services in that community, children in the intervention county were more likely to have their developmental and mental health problems identified, to be referred for services, and to receive follow-up care at 6 and 12 months after placement.

Another multidisciplinary assessment clinic serving children in foster care ranging from birth to 48 months of age was initiated in a parish in Louisiana (Zeanah et al., 2001). This clinic was designed to improve child welfare outcomes for young foster children and provided a broad array of services, including a comprehensive assessment of the child and the child-caregiver relationship, parent-infant psychotherapy, individual psychotherapy for the birth parents, a foster parent support/education group, crisis intervention, and case management. Interestingly, fewer children receiving the intervention were reunified with their biological parents and more were freed for adoption than similar children who were receiving child welfare services prior to the initiation of the intervention. The authors postulated that the intervention may have assisted caregivers in making more expeditious permanency decisions for their children.

Other empirically based interventions attempted to address foster child outcomes through the provision of services to the foster parents. For example, Dozier and colleagues (2002) have implemented a theoretically and empirically based intervention for foster parents, which is delivered in their homes over ten sessions. The intervention targets three caregiving needs of 12- to 24-month-old infants in the foster care system: the provision of nurturing care, the recognition of behavioral signals, and the facilitation of behavioral regulation. Preliminary findings suggest that this intervention model has a beneficial effect on young children's behavioral regulation.

Focusing on preschool children (ages 4-6), Fisher and colleagues (2000) initiated an intervention designed to improve the behavioral functioning of young foster children and their caregivers. Both caregivers and children participate in short-term psycho-educational groups, informed by a cognitive-behavioral theoretical perspective. Preliminary results of this study suggest that this intervention reduces problematic behaviors in children and has an impact on their behavioral regulation, as assessed by physiological measures. In addition, foster parents exhibited more positive parenting strategies.

Characteristics of Effective Interventions for Young Children and Families

The current review of the literature highlights the considerable variability in the effectiveness of interventions for children and families at risk for or identified with maltreatment. The prevailing evidence suggests that overall, there are very few programs that have been found to prevent/reduce maltreatment and/or foster care placement of children in high-risk families. Specific preventive intervention programs for young children have met with a modicum of success in reducing family risk factors that are associated with maltreatment. This section summarizes the specific characteristics of effective programs, with a consideration of the features discussed by Nation and colleagues (2003), as well as features of effective programs designed to address maltreatment.

The Target of the Intervention. "What works for whom?" is a question that has been pondered by evaluation researchers in the psychotherapy field for decades (Roth & Fonagy, 1996). This question, which is equally important for prevention researchers, suggests that the effectiveness of the program is inextricably tied to who the target of the intervention is. Further, the family preservation literature suggests that prevention programs should target the specific difficulties in the family that give rise to maltreatment (Littell & Schuerman, 2002). Programs serving children and families at high risk can be targeted to the children, to the parent, to the parent-child dyad, and to the family. The literature suggests that few preventive interventions for families at risk for maltreatment who have young children directly target the child, although older children are often targeted in such prevention programs. Despite the lack of child-specific services, most programs identify child development as a potential outcome of their intervention. The available literature suggests that child developmental outcomes are generally not attained by these prevention programs, which calls into question whether such goals are theoretically plausible (Olds, Hill, Robinson, Song, & Little, 2000). However, programs with child development as an outcome often have an impact on family functioning. It is conceivable that facilitating parents' focus on child well-being has a beneficial impact on their parenting knowledge and skills.

In contrast to the paucity of child-directed services, the overwhelming majority of prevention programs target parents. Programs often specify a particular type of parent, such as a first-time parent, an adolescent parent, a parent with a substance use history, or a parent who is depressed. Many programs operate from the assumption that these factors place parents at high risk for maltreatment, so often evidence of maltreatment is not a criterion for program participation. Such programs incorporate service delivery strategies that are pertinent to the particular parental risk factor. For example, effective programs for substance-using parents incorporate alcohol or drug treatment in the design of the intervention (Uziel-Miller, Lyons, Kissiel, & Love, 1998).

There has been scant attention in the literature regarding the effectiveness of programs targeted toward biological parents vs. foster parents. Clearly, these are two different types of caregiving situations that require different types of intervention. However, if child well-being is the focus, the services should theoretically follow the child and be targeted toward meeting the needs of the child. In the one study that explicitly provided services to biological and foster parents (Zeanah, 2000), permanency was achieved more quickly for participant children, at least in regard to adoptive placement. It could be argued that child-focused services could be tailored to meet the distinct needs of different types of caregivers, while maintaining the goal of meeting the needs of target children.

The extant evidence suggests that prevention programs have very modest if any beneficial impacts on parenting knowledge, attitudes, and behaviors. More didactic programs seem to improve parenting knowledge and attitudes, and the more active, experiential programs are more likely to affect parenting behavior. Dosage and duration seem to be a factor in changing behavior, yet there are few interventions funded to provide intensive and prolonged interventions. What the effective programs also have in common is a theoretically derived set of intervention strategies that are aimed at changing a specific set of parenting behaviors. Thus, addressing emotional self-regulation and anger management strategies would be an important component of preventive interventions for abusive parents. Although the data are less clear for neglecting parents, it seems that strategies to address parental mental health and substance abuse, sense of competence, motivation, and custodial care skills are important tenets of such programs. Lutzker and colleagues' (1984; 2001) work over two decades with neglecting families shows that these elements of parental capacity can be systematically developed. Additional evidence points to the positive effects of such programs for parents with specific difficulties. For example, Lyons-Ruth and colleagues (1990) found that their home-based early intervention was more beneficial for depressed mothers. Similarly, Olds and colleagues (1997) documented a greater impact of the nurse home visitation intervention on mothers with low psychological resources vs. those with higher resources (i.e., mental health, intelligence, and mastery).

Instead of targeting the parent or infant individually, some programs focus on the parent-infant dyad. Often these programs are informed by an infant mental health perspective, which emphasizes the parent-infant relationship as an important "port of entry" (Stern, 1995) for intervention. Such programs rely on a more active approach in which parents and infants are engaged in mutual activities, such as play, and the goal of the service provider is to promote a more positive relationship between the pair. Although the data on such programs are fairly recent, they do point to enhanced relationships between parents and infants. A few studies have documented a reduction in behaviors associated with maltreatment as well (Heinicke et al., 1999).

Interventions targeted at the family have received far less empirical attention although there is a large evidentiary base pointing to family factors as contributors to maltreatment. For example, marital conflict, lack of social support, mental health issues of other family members, and large households are among the family characteristics that render parents more prone to maltreat their children. Family support programs tend to target the family unit and attempt to address all these factors in a global manner. These family support programs have been found to improve overall parental functioning such as parenting cognition and child development knowledge, but they do not generally reveal any impact on child maltreatment per se (Kagan, 1998). Evaluations of family preservation programs provide further evidence on the limited effectiveness of global family support programs and brief interventions (Lindsey, Martin, & Doh, 2002; Littell & Schuerman, 2002). However, the data on programs that specifically target particular family issues, such as parenting children with externalizing problems, show more promise (see chapter 6). Comprehensive programs have also been implemented that target the child, parent, and other family members and factors. The increased intensity in service makes such programs more effective than single-level programs (Wekerle & Wolfe, 1993).

The salience of time. The timing of interventions has been documented to affect outcome in myriad ways. First, many evaluations of preventive interventions have underscored dosage effects on outcome, in relation to program intensity and duration. Regarding intensity, the preponderance of the evidence suggests that programs should attempt to intervene with maltreating families on a weekly basis to realize any positive impact (Jones Harden & Early Head Start Research and Evaluation Consortium, 2003). The reality is that a goal of weekly contacts with high-risk families often results in a 50 percent completion rate (i.e., biweekly contacts). Duration is equally important, with a long-term intervention yielding the most benefits. In a meta-analysis of maltreatment prevention programs, MacLeod and Nelson (2000) reported that lower effect sizes were found in programs of less than 6 months duration and programs in which participants received twelve or fewer visits.

Another important time-related factor is the temporal point in the family life cycle at which the intervention is initiated. The evidence strongly suggests that interventions begun prenatally or in early infancy are more likely to benefit high-risk families and their young children (Karoly et al., 1998; MacLeod & Nelson, 2000). Thus, high-risk parents can be reached during pregnancy, which many have found to be a window of opportunity for intervention. This is particularly true for first-time parents, who need support in the transition to parenthood. In situations in which prenatal interventions are not possible, scholars posit that intervention initiation in early infancy is essential so that potentially negative parent-child interactions can be improved before they become long-term relationship patterns.

From a developmental perspective, a consideration of time pertains to the implementation of interventions that are age- and developmentally sensitive. In many child welfare practice arenas, interventions that are not consistent with the developmental needs of the child have not met with success. In other arenas, programs focused on a specific child age group provide an array of services specifically germane to the families of these children (Olds, Hill, Robinson, Song, & Little, 2000). This is particularly relevant for services to families with young children. Because infancy and early childhood are rapidly changing and very complex developmental periods, it is essential that programs address the unique needs of young children but also respond to the particular challenges faced by families caring for this population. In this vein, programs have the opportunity to positively influence the well-being of young children receiving child welfare services.

Implications for Policy and Practice

The evidence reviewed in this chapter argues for the funding and implementation of prevention programs for families of young children who are at risk of or identified with maltreatment. Such an approach has the potential to reduce child protection referrals and substantiations, maintain maltreated children safely in their families of origin, and prevent child placement. From the available evidence, it also seems that such programs could foster the development and well-being of the vulnerable children and families who participate in these interventions.

There are important lessons regarding the design and delivery of prevention programs that emanate from the extant evidence. Evaluations of preventive programs for young high-risk children suggest some basic features that will optimize the effectiveness of any intervention. The program should be long-term (i.e., 6 months to 2 years) and should offer a high number of contacts to participants (i.e., weekly to biweekly) to enhance its impact on participants. Initiating programs during the prenatal or immediate post-partum period seems to be most effective. Regarding staffing, programs that hire professional staff to deliver the intervention seem to be more advantageous to participants than programs using paraprofessionals as the primary service deliverers.

It is crucial that practitioners have a "theory of change" that stipulates why and how specific services will be delivered. After a complete assessment of the program participants, program staff could reflect on the needs of the families, the services that have been found to be effective for these types of families, and the strategies the program would employ to provide such services. For example, prevention programs for substance-using mothers should consider the impact of their addiction on their parenting. Therefore, a parenting education model would not be sufficient as there would be no attempt to address the underlying factors associated with parenting dysfunction. Provision or referral/follow-up of drug treatment would be an essential component of an intervention with an appropriate "theory of change."

Equally important, there is a convergence of evidence supporting a developmental focus to preventive interventions. Regardless of the target age, practitioners must tailor their services to meet the developmental needs of the child and family. For example, parent-infant activities focusing on attachment would be appropriate for young infants. Preschoolers would benefit from child development programs in which there is a center-based component. Obviously, a consideration of the developmental functioning of the child is more useful than merely focusing on child age. A developmental focus is important for participating parents as well. Parents who are experiencing the transition to parenthood require different services (e.g., pregnancy preparation and support) than do parents who have multiple children. Knowledge of whether parents have developmental disabilities is also important in program planning.

Finally, the intervention should be comprehensive and offer a broad array of services that can be tailored to meet an individual family's needs. Thus, services should be offered that have direct benefit to the child, parent, parent-child dyad, and family. Each family should receive a different set of services that are contingent upon a comprehensive assessment of family needs. It is essential that services often perceived as ancillary (e.g., drug treatment, mental health treatment) become an integral part of the prevention program as such targeted services have more impact than global services. In addition, these services can be provided in the context of the unique experiences of parents involved with child welfare services. For example, drug treatment for mothers of young children may not focus so heavily on punitive consequences (e.g., no visits with children) and on the temporary severance of ties to social networks (e.g., living away from children).

Given the evidence pointing to the limited effectiveness of didactic parent training, conventional parent training should not be the primary service offered as it is in many prevention programs. If parent training is offered, it should be active and experiential, and should incorporate parent-child interactional approaches. It should also be theoretically grounded and designed to address specific parental needs. Additionally, it should be developmentally sensitive with all material geared to the developmental period of the children who are being served (e.g., focus on age-appropriate disciplinary techniques). Because of the low participation and retention rates reported in some group-based programs, consideration should be given to offering individual home-based parent educational experiences, particularly for parents with very low levels of parenting competence.

Conclusions

Prevention programs that are well developed and empirically validated have the potential to alter the trajectories of young children involved with child welfare services. In terms of child welfare trajectories, child protection supervision and foster care placement can potentially be avoided for this population of children. With regard to developmental trajectories, prevention programs can foster positive short- and long-term outcomes for children in all developmental domains. The evidence presented in this chapter underscores a need for careful program design that capitalizes on the rich evidentiary base on more global prevention programs for young children and their families. To be effective, these programs must be theoretically sound, developmentally sensitive, targeted, and comprehensive.

The empirical evidence regarding such programs should not just inform the program design phase. Ongoing evaluation of service delivery strategies should occur, so that program improvement is facilitated over time. Arguably, the most important evidence regarding a program's effectiveness emanates from its ongoing continuous improvement efforts. Thus, the quality of such programs can be constantly enhanced, moving them toward their ultimate goal of improving the well-being of young children and their families.

Note

1.   The relative absence of universal programs has not always been the case. For example, California, in the 1970s, developed a massive statewide pre-school and school-based program for informing all children about the risk of maltreatment. These programs were later found to be conceptually and empirically feeble and were discredited and discontinued (Barth & Derezotes, 1990; Gilbert, Berrick, & LeProhn, 1989). A substantial amount of state resources that could have been devoted to other promising child abuse interventions were used, but the funding of program evaluations limited the duration of these ineffective efforts.

6

Evidence-Based Mental Health Interventions for Children in Child Welfare

Overview

The concept of child well-being can be characterized abstractly as the level of psychosocial and/or developmental functioning observed in the child. This fits well with the dual perspectives that have been brought to bear on the data presented in this volume, namely, child development and public health. The child development perspective, as shown in prior chapters, is grounded in research studies that have demonstrated the levels of functioning that are normative for children at different ages. When children are observed to be significantly below where they are expected to be on the basis of these standards, the public health perspective suggests that services should be provided to bring their functioning within the normative range for their age group. However, providing services for the amelioration of problems in psychosocial or developmental functioning has been historically seen as at the discretion of the child welfare agency. Therefore, most service delivery for mental health and developmental problems is done through linkages to mental health and other agencies outside of child welfare. This means that the perspectives of mental health agencies and agencies linked to developmental problems need to be considered, as well as the perspective of child welfare agencies, in the discussion of child well-being.

Within child welfare, well-being is most often portrayed as conceptually distinct from the traditional child welfare mission of safety and permanency. In fact, the developmental perspective elucidated in this volume, as well as the public mental health perspective, would argue that safety and permanency are necessary for normal child development. Children are at serious risk for falling below normative standards when their physical and emotional safety is compromised and permanency of the family environment is not maintained. These perspectives argue that child well-being is the basic concept that is actually being served by the other two elements.

Chapters 3 and 4 include findings from the National Survey of Child and Adolescent Well-Being (NSCAW) that demonstrate marked departures from normative standards for children involved with the child welfare system. The NSCAW findings lead to the conclusion that from a developmental perspective, the majority of children involved with child welfare services are functioning below national norms in at least one area of functioning and that the most extreme scores are on mental health measures. Additional findings from the NSCAW relevant to the current chapter demonstrate the high risk for delinquency, with youth 6 to 15 years old in the problematic range of the CBCL delinquency sub-scale at a rate three times as great as the general population of youth in this age range, and youth in out-of-home care five times as likely to be categorized as delinquent as the general population.

This chapter will discuss the implications of these findings from a treatment perspective with an overall focus on children and adolescents involved with child welfare services during their school years from age 6. The chapter will use findings from several evidence-based bodies of literature related to the provision of treatment services for the purpose of ameliorating psychosocial and developmental problems. This chapter differs from chapter 5 in two major ways. First, this chapter focuses predominantly on services that would be categorized as "indicated," while chapter 5 included an emphasis on "universal" and "selective" programs. Second, this chapter focuses on children and adolescents in their school years, while chapter 5 discussed service programs primarily designed for children prior to school age. The chapter will include a review of evidence related to the need for ameliorative services and what is known from research studies about the provision of such services. These two evidence-based domains will serve as background to the core of the chapter—namely, the development and availability of evidence-based interventions coming primarily from the fields of mental health and developmental science that show promise for addressing the developmental and psychosocial functioning problems observed in children served by the child welfare system. The presentation of evidence-based interventions will also consider how these interventions are likely to affect not only the well-being of children, but also their safety and permanency. Finally, the section will lay out the critical dilemma of moving the evidence-based interventions from the laboratory settings where they were developed and tested for efficacy to the community-based treatment settings where children from child welfare are most likely to receive these services.

Child Welfare, Mental Health Problems, and Use of Mental Health Services

Within its overall organizational mission, the child welfare system investigates maltreatment, places children in foster care, and finds permanent families for children (their biological families, guardians, or adoptive families) as part of its mission to protect children at risk for further maltreatment. This means that child welfare services for *open cases* (i.e., open for services) are usually delivered in one of three settings: (1) in the home of origin in an attempt to preserve families, (2) in out-of-home foster care or other settings to which children are court-ordered in an effort to assure safety, or (3) in an adoptive home (or the home of a guardian). Clinical or indicated services to address problems in areas of development and psychosocial functioning need to be related to these contexts, especially if the services target parent behaviors in order to impact child behavior problems. The discussion in this chapter is structured around service delivery patterns and promising evidence-based approaches with the in-home and out-of-home contexts.

The mental health needs of children in the child welfare system are significant. Recent reviews of the literature on psychosocial functioning of children in the child welfare system (Landsverk & Garland, 1999; Landsverk, Garland, & Leslie, 2002; Pilowsky, 1995) have shown that children receiving child welfare services, especially children who have been placed, exhibit problems requiring mental health assessment and/or intervention at a considerably higher rate than what would be expected from either normative data or from community studies. Aggregated findings from these studies suggest that 50 to 75 percent of children entering foster care exhibit behavioral and social competency problems warranting mental health services. Farmer and colleagues (2001) note that this high rate may also be anticipated for children receiving in-home child welfare services. As shown in chapters 3 and 4, the findings summarized in these reviews are now confirmed for a national probability sample of children and adolescents involved in the child welfare system.

The reviews also point to the importance of externalizing problems, as observed in child welfare populations. For example, Pilowsky's review of studies published from 1974 through 1994 (1995) noted that externalizing disorders in particular may be more prevalent than internalizing in the foster care population. These findings about externalizing problems have been confirmed in a recent San Diego study conducted from 1997 through 1999 (Garland et al., 2001), which reported that 42 percent of the 426 foster youth between the ages of 6 and 18 met the criteria for one or more DSM IV diagnoses. By diagnosis, the largest proportion of children fell into the following categories: disruptive disorders (22.2 percent for oppositional defiant disorder, 16.1 percent for conduct disorder), 20.8 percent for ADHD, and much smaller proportions meeting criteria for mood disorders (5.2 percent) and anxiety disorders (8.6 percent). Again, these findings are mirrored in the NSCAW findings that youth involved in the child welfare system are five to eight times as likely to be in the borderline or clinical range on the delinquency sub-scale of the CBCL. Several studies have linked unstable living arrangements and decisions about reunification to externalizing behavior problems. A recent analysis (James, Landsverk, & Slymen, 2004) identified externalizing problems as the main predictor that distinguished children with unstable residential patterns in out-of-home care from those with stable residential patterns, a finding consistent with previous studies that have reported a link between disruptive behaviors and placement instability (Cooper, Peterson, & Meier, 1987; Teare et al., 1999). Landsverk and colleagues (1996) found that children with significant behavior problems, especially externalizing problems, were significantly less likely to be reunified with their birth parents than those without such problems. Finally, an investigation by Newton and colleagues (2000) found that behavior problems were not only a predictor, but also an outcome of multiple placement changes. These studies suggest that externalizing problems of children in foster care may affect basic decisions regarding their continuing in or exit from foster care. Taken together, the evidence about the high rates of externalizing and disruptive behavior problems and their likely role in placement trajectories support the suggestion that child well-being, safety, and permanence are interdependent.

Children with externalizing problems or disruptive behavior dis- orders are also at high risk for having continued problems that es- calate in severity as they develop (Reid & Eddy, 1997). Studies comparing levels of antisocial behavior for children receiving child welfare services with those of children in intensive mental health treatment programs have found that the two groups are statistically indistinguishable in terms of common forms of child disruptive behavior (Trupin, Tarico, Low, Jemelka, & McClellan, 1993). The risk for lifetime problems with antisocial behavior is es- pecially high for children with early onset of such problems (Patterson, DeBaryshe, & Ramsey, 1989). Therefore, it is not sur- prising that youth in child welfare are at higher risk for entering the juvenile justice system than their non-foster counterparts (Armstrong, 1998; Conger & Ross 2001), with Jonson-Reid and Barth (2000) reporting that whereas only 1 percent of children leaving foster care will go to the California Youth Authority, children with a prior his- tory of placement represent nearly 20 percent of admissions. There is also evidence to suggest that youth in child welfare are treated more harshly by the juvenile justice system than their non-foster counterparts (Conger & Ross, 2001). These findings suggest that clinical or indicated services that target externalizing problems of children in child welfare may have a selective function in prevent- ing later involvement of these children in criminal justice systems during their adolescent years.

Finally, studies in California (Halfon, Berkowitz, & Klee, 1992; Leslie et al., 2000), Washington state (Takayama, Bergman, & Connell, 1994), Pennsylvania (Harman, Childs, & Kelleher, 2000), and North Carolina (Minnis, Pelosi, Knapp, & Dunn, 2001) have demonstrated a very high rate of use of mental health services for children in foster care across all age groups, with the highest rate of 70 percent shown in children over the age of 7. The rates of use of mental health services observed in the North Carolina study were considerably higher than rates observed in the other states, but did indicate that children in both in-home and out-of-home settings were significantly more likely to receive mental health services than chil- dren in low-income families (Farmer et al., 2001). Early findings from the NSCAW study suggest that youth with mental health needs (defined by a clinical range score on the Child Behavior Checklist) were much more likely to receive mental health services than lower- scoring youth, but that only one-fourth of such youth received any specialty mental health care during the 12 months surrounding early involvement with the child welfare service system (Burns et al., 2004).

Taken together, findings from these studies provide the basis for a particular focus on bringing evidence-based interventions into settings that serve children involved with the child welfare system. The high prevalence of externalizing problems and disruptive disorders, the negative long-term trajectories of youth with these problems, and the impact of these problems on placement instability within child welfare settings and on movement out of child welfare settings, all suggest their public health significance and the importance of finding more effective ways to address them. A major focus is to find ways to more effectively transport evidence-based interventions for children with externalizing and disruptive behavior problems into the child welfare system with the aim of preventing escalations of those problems over time. The findings of widespread use of mental health services by children in foster care suggest that (1) there is a base upon which more effective interventions can be built, and (2) transporting mental health interventions will require an understanding of both the child welfare service system and the specialty mental health care system.

Parent-Mediated Interventions in Child Welfare[1]

Parent-mediated interventions refers to a class of interventions that focus on the skills that adult caregivers of children bring to their role as either biological or substitute parents. This class of interventions is focused on the conduct or externalizing behavior problems that children may develop in the course of their developmental trajectories. The interventions indirectly (therefore the term "mediated") target the externalizing behaviors of the children by focusing on changing the types of parenting behaviors that have been instrumental in the development of externalizing behavior problems, such as harsh or inconsistent responses to oppositional behaviors. The term *parent mediated* is used instead of the more common terms *parent training* or *parent education* in order to clearly indicate that the changes in specific parenting behaviors are intended to bring about a change in specific types of child conduct or externalizing behavior problems.

Parent-mediated interventions are widely used in child welfare. Parent education for biological parents, foster parents, and adoptive parents is an essential component of the service continuum. Estimates derived from the NSCAW data suggest that the parents of as many as 400,000 children a year (U.S. DHHS, 2005) will participate in voluntary or mandated parent training. In addition, among the nearly two-thirds of cases of families whose child welfare service cases were closed following investigation, approximately 28 percent (or about 448,000) will have parent classes provided, referred to, or arranged by the child welfare agency. Parent training programs are clearly a lynchpin of the government's responsibility to provide "reasonable efforts" to preserve, maintain, or reunify families who become involved with the child welfare system.

These efforts most often include parent training, drug treatment (in about half the cases), and child treatment. In some cases, these rehabilitative efforts involve in-home parent training, although quite often they are primarily child-focused, taught without a developmental focus, and presented to parents in agency settings without children in their presence (Barth et al., in press). Foster parents are increasingly expected to be partners in the rehabilitation of biological parents and to help them find culturally acceptable means for providing safe and supportive parenting. About half of these children will return home within 18 months, with the balance of the children remaining in longer-term foster care or group care, or being adopted. In a recent series of studies, Price and colleagues examined the social adjustment of maltreated children who had been returned to their biological parents following the receipt of mandated services, including parent training. Compared with low-income non-maltreated children, these children, especially those who were physically abused, were perceived by their parents and teachers to exhibit higher levels of externalizing behavior problems and problems with peers (Price, in review) and to be more likely to attribute hostility to others, especially their parents, teachers, and peers (Price & Glad, 2003).

Even when children are adopted, the need for assistance with parenting is evident. A nearly two-decade-old cross-sectional study of families that had adopted children from foster care found Behavior Problem Index (a short version of the CBCL) scores in the clinical range for a substantial percentage of the children (Barth & Berry, 1988). More recent surveys of the general population of adoptive families whose children had been in foster care found the same pattern (Smith & Howard, 1999). Yet, efforts to apply such approaches as the Homebuilders brief, intensive family preservation model to help preserve these adoptive families have not been successful (Barth & Miller, 2000; Smith & Howard, 1999) because this intervention model did not fit the needs of adoptive parents and children.

Effective child welfare services must rely on effective parent training and support—as this is the primary intervention that child welfare agencies provide in trying to preserve or reunify families. Without effective interventions, there is no chance of operating an equitable child welfare system that adequately balances child and parent (Currie, 1997). Historically, there have been many efforts to develop and deliver effective parenting interventions. Most notably, several decades of services included "homemaker" services, which worked directly with parents in their own homes to teach home economics skills and provide assistance with parenting (Hutchinson & Sudia, 2002; Kadushin, 1961). Intensive family preservation programs (IFPS), especially the Homebuilders model programs with their crisis-oriented, home-based and social learning-based interventions, had relatively widespread use in the 1980s and 1990s. Their intended use is to teach enough parenting skills and coping strategies, within a month of intensive, ecologically based services, to steer families out of their crisis and into a prolonged period of successful parenting. Yet the amount and model of parent training that occurs in IFPS programs have been poorly documented. This approach has not shown robust effects in preventing the placement of children or reducing reabuse in the most rigorous statewide and national evaluations (Schuerman, Rzepnicki, & Littell, 1994; Westat, Hall, & Bell, 2002). Thus, although they continue to be in use across the United States, they have experienced declining support and use. At the same time, federal funds for such programs are increasing, offering an opportunity for developing more effective approaches.

Especially lacking is evidence on effective parent-mediated interventions for biological parents who are working toward reunification with their children. Typically, the needs of these families are addressed through general parent education courses and specialty mental health services for the parents and their children. However, unless parenting practices are remediated, children reunified with their parents are at continued risk for maladaptive outcomes. Child welfare services agencies have tried to apply evidence-based parent-mediated interventions to address a wide range of goals. In the 1970s, Robert Wahler and his colleagues endeavored to apply techniques of applied behavior analysis to work with abusive families (Wahler, 1980); they found that maltreating parents could learn positive new parenting skills taught with a social skills-based approach and would apply these techniques until they became overwhelmed with other aspects of an aversive environment.

In summary, although parent-mediated interventions are routinely used in child welfare, there is little to suggest that these strategies are evidence based, especially for biological parents who are working toward reunification with their children. Despite the fact that the needs of these families are often addressed through general parent education courses, the research evidence suggests that unless the dynamics of these families are improved, children reunified with their parents are at continued risk for maladaptive outcomes (Taussig, Clyman, & Landsverk, 2001). Overall, however, it appears that the culture of child welfare practice is open to parent-mediated approaches.

Evidence-Based, Parent-Mediated Approaches for Externalizing Problems

Substantial previous work in the field of mental health treatment has shown that parent-mediated interventions are a promising approach for treating child externalizing problems (Graziano & Diament, 1992); basing these findings (Brestan & Eyberg, 1998; Tremblay, Masse, Perron, Leblanc et al., 1992) on longitudinal designs has demonstrated the importance of parenting practices to the later development of problems in childhood and adolescence. For example, in their re-analysis of data from several such studies, Loeber and Dishion (1983) found that composite measures of parental family management practices were the most powerful predictors of subsequent delinquency when compared with other variables such as ratings of earlier child behavior, criminality of the parents, separation from parents, and socioeconomic status. Laub and Sampson (1988) reported that family management variables (supervision and discipline) mediated 80 percent of the variance in structural variables such as household overcrowding, father's drunkenness and criminality, and economic dependence. Additionally, a number of studies have implicated poor discipline and especially inconsistent, overly harsh punishment in the development of negative outcomes, including childhood depression (Gelfand & Teti, 1990) and oppositional behavior (Dumas, Gibson, & Albin, 1989).

These findings have obvious implications for intervention studies. With parenting practices identified as contributing to later poor adjustment, they become logical targets for theory-driven intervention studies. These studies pave the way for examination of how supports for parenting in larger social systems, such as child welfare, can decrease the occurrence or likelihood of child mental disorders, as recommended by the National Advisory Mental Health Council Workgroup's report on "Priorities for Prevention Research at NIMH" (National Advisory Mental Health Council Workgroup on Mental Disorders Prevention Research, 1998).

Over time, without effective intervention, ineffective and counterproductive family processes continue and become amplified. The child's experience of early parental negativity, failure in school, rejection by peers, and exclusion from clubs and sports activities sets the stage for association with delinquent peers, school dropout, drug use, and delinquency in adolescence. Interventions aimed at teaching and supporting parents have shown promise in altering childhood negative trajectories, as has been discussed in chapter 5 (Olds et al., 1998; Reid & Eddy, 1997). A substantial body of research shows that the difficult and anti-social behavior of older children can also be minimized.

Over the past three decades, a series of studies have been conducted on the efficacy of parent-mediated treatments, beginning in the 1960s with single-case designs (Patterson & Brodsky, 1966; Patterson & Ray, 1968) and later using wait-list control (Wiltz & Patterson, 1974), placebo control (Walter & Gilmore, 1973), and randomized treatment comparison (Dishion, French, & Patterson, 1995; Prinz & Miller, 1994; Webster-Stratton & Hammond, 1997). As these studies progressed, it became increasingly clear that working with parents was a powerful means of changing child problems and nonfunctional behavior patterns. Compared with approaches that provided treatment to the individual child alone, teaching parents methods for systematically intervening with their child had more powerful and longer-lasting effects (Graziano & Diament, 1992; Serketich & Dumas, 1996). These interventions, although targeting youngsters who varied in age and severity of problems, had common elements; they emphasized having the parents track their child's prosocial and problem behaviors; provide daily encouragement; consistent, rational limits; and nonviolent discipline. Outcome data indicated that by using these tactics, rates of child problem behaviors dropped to normal levels in 75 percent of the cases. Follow-up studies (Patterson, 1985; Tremblay, Masse, Perron, Leblanc et al., 1992) showed that these effects tended to persist long-term, and that they generalized to the siblings of the referred child. Thus, parent-mediated interventions represent a highly promising approach to dealing with the externalizing behavior problems of children in high-risk families. Yet, although we expect that many of the children in these studies have had experience with child welfare services, little has been done—until recently—to test them with child welfare populations or within child welfare settings.

Evidence-Based Biological-Parent Approaches for Child Welfare Settings

The biological parent interventions with good promise to address externalizing behavior problems for children in child welfare are also the interventions with significant promise to improve the abuse and neglect behaviors of biological parents. This suggests that consideration of these approaches may improve the delivery of overall child welfare services targeting safety and permanence as well as child well-being. However, as Barth and his colleagues point out in their recent review (Barth et al., in press), there is not a single intervention that has generated a published peer-review article based on a study in which they accepted referrals from a child welfare agency, randomly assigned them to a treatment condition, and evaluated the outcome. Whereas several randomized clinical trials (RCTs) of parent training interventions have included maltreated children in their samples (e.g., Reid & Kavanagh, 1985; Webster-Stratton, 1998), the intent of these studies was not to understand the effectiveness of the intervention with child welfare clientele, per se. For example, Webster-Stratton (1998) employed an RCT to evaluate an abbreviated version of The Incredible Years with low-income children in Head Start centers. Families with recent involvement with child protective services for child abuse and neglect comprised nearly a quarter of the sample. The short- and long-term intervention effects were promising. One randomized clinical trial (RCT) (Chaffin et al., 2004) was tested with just physically abused children referred from the child welfare system to Parent Child Interaction Training (PCIT) or a standard treatment control group.

Although there are many ways to rank the effectiveness of intervention programs on behalf of children, a few interventions have been repeatedly highly ranked. Four interventions have been repeatedly nominated as meeting the highest standards of evidence in a variety of reviews. These are clearly the leading evidence-based parent training: The Incredible Years (TIY; Webster-Stratton, 1997); Multisystemic Therapy (MST; Henggeler et al., 2003)[2]; Oregon Social Learning Center's Parent Management Training (PMT; Forgatch & Martinez, 1999; Patterson, Chamberlain, & Reid, 1982); and Parent Child Interaction Training (PCIT; Eyberg & Robinson, 1982). The many evidence-based reviews that cite these programs indicate substantial consensus about their high ranking. These reviews include: *U.S. Office of Juvenile Justice and Delinquency Prevention Bulletin* (Mihalic, Irwin, Elliott, Fagan, & Hansen, 2001: TIY, MST, PMT, and PCIT); *School Psychology Quarterly* (Kratochwill & Stoiber, 2002); *Journal of Child Clinical Psychology* (Brestan & Eyberg, 1998: PMT, TIY, MST, and PCIT); *Journal of Consulting and Clinical Psychology* (Farmer, Compton, Burns, & Robertson, 2002: TIY and MST; Kazdin & Weisz, 1998: PMT, MST); the Center for Evidence-Based Practice's *Young Children with Challenging Behavior*, funded by the U.S. Office of Special Education Programs, (Dunlap, Strain, & Kern, 2003: TIY); and *Clinical Psychology Review* (Nixon, 2002: PCIT, PMT).

The time- and family-tested parent training programs described above are poised for adaptation for greater use with the child welfare system. Each has already had clinical trials that included maltreated children. Although only PCIT has met the most stringent criteria for effectiveness—involving RCTs with a target population of maltreated children—the evidence from studies on each of these interventions points to their likely success with child welfare system families. This evidence, developed over as long as three decades of study, positions these interventions as the most promising starting points for the rapid development of effective interventions with maltreating families.

There are a number of programs that the Barth review classified as "Possibly Efficacious and Commonly Used in Child Welfare." These are programs that are comprised of interventions working with the target population of child welfare cases and that were tested with quasi-experimental designs or a series of single-subject designs. These designs have the capacity to show substantial likelihood of benefit, but are not sufficiently definitive. Only four interventions fall into this category—Parenting Wisely (Gordon, 2003), Nurturing Parent

(Bavolek, 2002), STEP (Adams, 2001), and Project 12-Ways (Lutzker & Rice, 1984). Each of these parent training programs has been used in substantial amounts of research with child welfare populations; however, the research designs would only meet the level of evidence for a grade of "B or C" using the criteria of the Cochrane Collaboration (Clarke & Oxman, 2003). This would include those using single-subject designs, matched comparison control groups, pre- and post-test designs, consumer satisfaction surveys, and evaluations for master's theses. Yet, the evaluations at this level allow many challenges to the findings. These programs are welcome and promising parent training programs because they have met the test of implementation (perhaps better than they have met the test of evidence). STEP appears to be commonly used in child welfare agencies, but the more than forty evaluations of STEP are primarily those done as master's or doctoral theses and have not been rigorous or focused on child welfare populations.

The *Parenting Wisely* (Kacir & Gordon, 1997) Web site indicates that it has been selected as a *"SAMHSA/CSAP & OJJDP Model Program!"* (bold typeface and exclamation point in original) and is in use in nearly every state. Yet, a review of the research articles presented shows no rigorous evaluations involving a randomized or quasi-experimental clinical trial. The research reports provided by the developers on the use of *Parenting Wisely* include applications with high-risk populations (e.g., teenage parents, parents with children with conduct disorders, and poor families in Appalachia) but none with child welfare populations appear.

Project 12-Ways has not had widespread use but has undergone a long period of testing. This approach has been in operation for nearly two decades, in partnership with the child welfare system in Illinois and, more recently, in California and Oklahoma. Although the evidence base consists largely of a series of single-subject designs showing that social and cognitive principles (Bandura, 1976) can work with multi-problem families who are being served at home, several quasi-experimental studies also support the efficacy of Project 12-Ways (e.g., Lutzker, Tymchuk, & Bigelow, 2001). "The effect of the program…is supported by a pattern of findings, including both liberal and, more importantly, conservatively biased quasi-experimental comparison studies. To date, the SC/12 model has been implemented by small-scale university-affiliated projects using high levels of protocol adherence and service monitoring. The model has not been disseminated on a large scale to actual agency settings" (Chaffin, personal communication, June 18, 2003).

The Barth review includes a third classification of programs, *conventional child welfare parent* training programs, including those ad hoc programs that operate in many agencies and have virtually no evaluation support. These would be described in the Cochrane Collaborative literature as interventions with expert opinion without critical appraisal (Clarke & Oxman, 2003). These parent-training interventions revealed limited, if any, efforts to demonstrate program effectiveness with child welfare cases. Yet, these programs appear to be meeting other standards that are also important to the dissemination of evidence-based interventions. They are interventions that have the following attributes: they have enough face validity to have gained agency adoption; they have features that have allowed them to be broadly used, including the development of manuals and Web sites; and they have been tailored to the time, resources, and trainer skill levels that child welfare agencies now have available for parent training.

The previously described classification of evidence-based interventions is supported by work in progress from a major forthcoming meta-analysis of interventions for emotional or behavioral problems underway by John Weisz and his colleagues. Parent Management Training, the Incredible Years, and PCIT have each been examined in at least one published, peer-reviewed, randomized, between-group design study, and they have each shown efficacy with youth conduct problems (Weisz, 2003). Parenting Wisely, Nurturing Parent, Project 12-Ways, STEP, Active Parenting, Parenting 123, Love and Logic, and Common Sense Parenting were all excluded from the Weisz review because their efficacy (or lack thereof) has not been examined and reported in at least one published, peer-reviewed, randomized, between-group design study.

Evidence-Based Substitute Parent Approaches for Child Welfare Settings

Almost all foster care systems have a category that is intermediate between regular foster care and congregate care, such as group homes. These are often called treatment foster care settings and are designed to provide a more intensive approach to children in foster care who exhibit elevated levels of behavioral and emotional problems. There is only one model of treatment foster care (TFC) that has been rigorously evaluated and should be considered evidence-based at the present time. This is the Multidimensional Treatment Foster Care model that has been developed by Chamberlain and her colleagues at the Oregon Social Learning Center.

Early data on more general TFC approaches showed that TFC could provide a viable community-based residential option for youth with quite severe behavioral problems (Bogart, 1988; Bryant & Snodgrass, 1992; Chamberlain, 1990; Chamberlain & Reid, 1991; Hawkins, Almeida, Fabry, & Reitz, 1992; Meadowcroft & Trout, 1990; Moore & Chamberlain, 1994; Morrissette, 1992). Findings from research about TFC suggests that it increases placement permanency and social skills, reduces problem behavior, improves psychological adjustment, and reduces restrictiveness of post-discharge placements (Chamberlain & Moore, 1998; Chamberlain & Weinrott, 1990; Clarke, Hawkins, Murphy, & Sheeber, 1993; Fanshel, Finch, & Grundy, 1990; Hudson, Nutter, & Galaway, 1994; Reddy & Pfeiffer, 1997). Yet, these findings have not, for the most part, been generated from randomized clinical trials. Further, the variability in treatment foster care provision is quite vast (Farmer, Compton, Burns, & Robertson, 2002; James & Meezan, 2002) and provides no assurances that the results of one TFC study would generalize to other treatment foster care providers.

As noted above, the best research on TFC comes from Chamberlain and colleagues on programs run by the Oregon Social Learning Center (Chamberlain, 1994, 2002; Fisher & Chamberlain, 2000). Their model is explicitly short-term (6-9 months). A series of randomized trials has examined the effects of TFC for youth with severe conduct problems and delinquency (Chamberlain, Ray, & Moore, 1996; Chamberlain & Reid, 1998; Eddy & Chamberlain, 2000). These studies have found that very high-risk youth in TFC showed larger and more rapid improvements in behavior, fewer arrests, and higher rates of community tenure than youth in more restrictive placements. They have also shown that boys and girls in TFC have better outcomes than youth receiving group care.

Research by Chamberlain and colleagues has been instrumental in specifying moderating and mediating factors that affect outcomes. For example, they have found different trajectories of behavioral improvement for boys and girls, with boys showing more consistent positive change across time and girls (particularly adolescent girls) being at increased risk for placement disruption (Chamberlain &

Reid, 1994; Smith, Stormshak, Chamberlain, & Whaley, 2001). The strong base in a theoretical model of development and change has helped focus attention on key processes that drive outcomes. Four key mediating factors have been identified: supervision, consistent discipline, positive relationship with an adult, and low levels of interaction with deviant peers (Chamberlain, 2002; Eddy & Chamberlain, 2000).

Three important extensions of the Oregon Social Learning Center (OSLC) TFC model should be noted even though no published work is yet available on the effectiveness of the extensions. First, Patricia Chamberlain and Joseph Price are testing a Parent Management Training Intervention for regular foster and kinship parents that is based on the intervention principles of the OSLC TFC model. This is being tested in the San Diego County foster care system in a two-phase, randomized clinical trial that is also examining the effectiveness of the model when it is removed from the developer's control and implemented by a group other than the OSLC group. Preliminary results with more than 600 kinship and non-kinship foster families suggest that caregivers regularly attend training and problem-solving sessions, the number of problem behaviors reported per day is declining, placement stability is improved, and transitions to permanency (reunification and adoption, together) are more likely than for foster families in the "services as usual" control group.

Second, the OSLC TFC model is undergoing further development and testing by Betsy Farmer at Duke University and Patricia Chamberlain and Philip Fisher at the OSLC. This extension considers the broader context within which a youth exists (Farmer & Farmer, 2000) and is using an ecological model to provide a helpful framework for viewing developmental needs, opportunities, and risks (Munger, 1991, 1997). This perspective recognizes the nested contexts within which youth live and the need to bring these contexts into alignment to reach sustainable improvements in outcomes (e.g., Bronfenbrenner, 1979; Hobbs, 1982). The social learning perspective is quite consistent with this focus, and bringing the two together appears to produce a useful perspective for understanding needs and development of youth with multiple problems (such as youth in TFC). Chamberlain's evidence-based model of short-term TFC has explicitly incorporated this approach, and signified it with a re-naming as Multidimensional Treatment Foster Care (Fisher & Chamberlain, 2000). Both theoretical approaches also underlie the most prominent home-based intervention, Multisystemic Therapy (MST), for such youth. In fact, TFC is an integral part of the service continuum for MST candidates who are too difficult to maintain in their own homes (Fisher, Gunnar, Chamberlain, & Reid, 2000).

This emphasis on learning and ecology provides an excellent framework for assessing, recognizing, and addressing needs and strengths as they emerge during development. In the short-term evidence-based model of TFC, developmental issues are addressed to the extent that they are relevant during short-term treatment (e.g., teaching age-appropriate social skills, addressing sexual behavior in adolescence). In a long-term model, however, youth with serious mental health and developmental problems may spend extended periods of their key developmental years in TFC. In Farmer's studies of such an approach in North Carolina, two prominent areas have been identified where treatment and development overlap. These include issues related to adolescents' preparation for the future and resolving issues related to prior abuse (particularly sexual abuse). If unaddressed, both of these issues are associated with very poor prognoses for youth (Blackorby & Wagner, 1996; Conte & Berliner, 1988; Davis & Vander Stoep, 1997; Finkelhor, Hotaling, Lewis, & Smith, 1989; Kendall-Tackett, Williams, & Finkelhor, 1993; Noble, Honberg, Hall, & Flynn, 1997; Rohsenow, Corbett, & Devine, 1988; Wagner, 1995; Wagner, D'Amico, Marder, Newman, & Blackorby, 1992; Wagner et al., 1991). There is a risk and temptation in extending the short-term model of TFC to continue focusing only on the behavioral practices and present-oriented focus that appears to successfully modify problem behavior. In the long term, however, there is an opportunity and need to address a broader spectrum of children's mental health issues. The emergence of several evidence-based interventions to address the sequelae of trauma and prior sexual abuse (Cohen, Mannarino, Zhitova, & Capone, 2003; Kolko & Swenson, 2002) makes this more likely.

Dissemination and Implementation of Evidence-Based Mental Health Treatments

The previous section points to a number of evidence-based interventions that appear to be very promising for children and adolescents involved in child welfare systems. The promise for using these interventions to improve care in child welfare settings, however, must be balanced with a caveat about the challenges of transporting evidence-based mental health treatments from the university-based laboratory settings in which they have been developed and tested to the complex service settings that make up "usual care." This is especially true when most of the interventions were neither directly designed for children in child welfare settings nor tested in these populations.

Considerable thinking and some limited research in both the adult and child mental health fields are addressing the complexities and challenges of bringing evidence-based interventions into usual care settings. Although there is general agreement on the importance of implementing evidence-based practices in routine mental health service settings (Drake et al., 2001; National Institute of Mental Health, 1999; Schoenwald & Hoagwood, 2001; Torrey et al., 2001), there is also considerable evidence that routine mental health practices do not, by and large, provide evidence-based services to either adult or child populations (Dixon et al., 1999; Hurlburt, Zima, Lau, Culver, & Knapp, 2002; Lehman & Steinwachs, 1998). Two examples suggest the difficulties involved. In the adult mental health field, strong efforts have been made to develop and deploy standardized guidelines for evidence-based practice, especially for persons with severe mental illness (American Psychiatric Association, 1997; Drake et al., 2001; Lehman & Steinwachs, 1998; Miller et al., 1999), although these have not yet had much influence.

In the child mental health field, there has been a strong effort over the past six years to develop guidelines for both psychosocial and psychopharmacological treatments, occurring predominantly in the professional groups for clinical psychology, pediatrics, and child psychiatry (American Academy of Child and Adolescent Psychiatry, 1992; American Academy of Pediatrics, 2000; Brestan & Eyberg, 1998). Although there have been some attempts to systematically disseminate these guidelines and interventions, in general, the child mental health field has lagged behind the adult mental health field. Two prominent exceptions are the work by Olds and colleagues for the Nurse Home Visitation Model for early preventive interventions (Olds et al., 1999), and the efforts by Henggeler and colleagues to disseminate Multisystemic Therapy (MST), which explicitly used a technology transfer model coming out of diffusion of innovation literature (Schoenwald & Hoagwood, 2001). Both of these approaches were implemented in many states and communities, following relatively rigorous evaluations.

There are a number of different models for dissemination and implementation that have appeared in both adult and child mental health. A common thread among these efforts appears to be a move away from the directive, unidirectional model of diffusion to more collaborative models where community consumers, providers, and service system managers are partnered with researchers involved with the development of efficacious treatments (Henggeler, 2002; Rogers, 1995). A promising approach is based on a collaborative partnership model with a conceptual framework that treats the process as a cross-cultural exchange. So, increasing the well-being of children will require that child welfare agencies demonstrate substantial flexibility in the way that they engage mental health and other child-serving agencies and that these agencies be open to dramatically revising their service delivery methods. A classic example of the challenge at hand is the reform of parent-focused child welfare services. Because of the historic lack of funding for in-home services, and the lack of evidence that one approach to working with parents is superior to any other, the field has assumed the approach of "let a thousand [briefly opening] flowers bloom." Many child welfare agencies have given up all control of what parent training programs are provided to parents, instead referring all their parents to YMCAs or family service agencies that make that determination. Sometimes child welfare agencies pay nothing for those services and sometimes they pay little more than $100 per family (Barth et al., in press). In addition, much of the work in these groups is oriented toward helping parents understand the court proceedings and child welfare practices that are now so integrally shaping the future of their family life. In short, this is a very challenging context for mounting a program of evidence-based parent-mediated interventions.

Model evidence-based parent-training programs like Parent Management Training and The Incredible Years have capitalized on thirty years of basic research to generate interventions that are excellent at helping parents to increase their positive behavior and that of their children. They have considerable experience with children and parents with exceptionally poor relationship skills and histories of violence and irresponsibility. But, they typically have little experience with the case management-related activities of child welfare, working with parents who do not have custody of their children, or delivering services at such a low cost. Although there is much interest in sharpening the capacity to work with child welfare families, there is much to be done to develop the means for integrating this work with that of child welfare agencies. Fortunately, exploratory efforts like Project Keep in San Diego and the Parent Child Interaction Therapy approach used in Oklahoma are showing that these mutual accommodations can be made to enhance the well-being of maltreated children and parents. The deepening of these partnerships, and of the quality of our offerings to children and parents, will only occur if we are resolute in our commitment to evidence-based practice models. This common commitment to evidence will be the meeting point for the integration of old child welfare challenges and new mental health methods.

A starting point for integrating evidence-based interventions into child welfare services is to attend to the fit between the developmental characteristics of children and the interventions that we provide (Berrick, Needell, Barth, & Jonson-Reid, 1998). Whereas a sizable proportion of all children entering child welfare are younger than 3 years old, well-tested parent-meditated interventions do not exist for this population. Although demonstration projects funded under Part C of the Individuals with Disabilities Education Act of 1997 promote better links between early intervention services to children in the child welfare system and new federal legislation requires that young children involved with the child welfare system get referred to Part C services, the work is still very young and is going to require a lengthly commitment to develop fully. This work, and parallel work for each of the age groups, must begin with the awareness that parenting strategies and children's developmental characteristics must match, and that parent-mediated interventions must, in turn, also correspond. In exploratory work looking at parent training programs, we found agencies that provided the same program to parents, regardless of the ages of their families because, basically, it was convenient and the parents seemed to like it. If this chapter communicates nothing more, we hope that it argues persuasively for challenging the assumptions that the interventions already in place for children have a solid grounding in developmental and intervention science.

Notes

1.   This section on parent-mediated interventions is much indebted to the work of the Child and Adolescent Interdisciplinary Research Network (CAIRN) "Improving Care for Children in Child Welfare" that was developed under funding by the National Institute of Mental Health (R24 MH67377). The goal of the CAIRN is to develop a heuristic model, including practical strategies, for the dissemination, imple-

mentation, and maintenance of *evidence-based, parent-mediated interventions* (E-BPMI) in child welfare settings for treatment of disruptive disorders and externalizing behavior problems in children and adolescents. The CAIRN work group on evidence-based interventions (Richard P. Barth, Patricia Chamberlain, Betsy Farmer, Michael Hurlburt, Sigrid James, John Landsverk, Kristin McCabe, Joseph Price, John Reid, Jennifer Rolls) has produced two papers that provide much of the information on parent-based interventions in this chapter: (1) Richard P. Barth et al. (in press), "Parent Training in Child Welfare Services: Planning for a More Evidence-Based Approach to Serving Biological Parents," *Research on Social Work Practice*, and (2) Betsy Farmer et al. (in preparation), "Training for Substitute Parents: Current Status and Evidence Base of Training for Foster and Treatment Foster Parents."

2.   It should be noted that Julia H. Littell, in a recent presentation (Julia H. Littell. "Lessons from a systematic review of effects of multisystemic therapy," Children and Youth Services Review. 27:4 [April, 2005], 445-463), has raised substantial questions about this review and nomination process, especially in regard to Multisystemic Therapy. Her presentation questioned the strength of the evidence base for this well-known intervention based on her new, systematic review that followed guidelines used by the Campbell Collaboration and the Cochrane Collaboration.

7

Beyond Common Sense:
Future Directions for Child Welfare Policy

The Adoption and Safe Families Act of 1997 (ASFA) is generally regarded as an important piece of social legislation, second only perhaps to the Adoption Assistance and Child Welfare Act of 1980 in terms of its influence on the delivery of child welfare services.[1] The reasons why ASFA is important are straightforward. Between 1980 and 1997, the foster care caseload in the United States nearly doubled, climbing from 300,000 to 537,000. The perception was that more children were entering foster care and staying longer than ever before because child welfare policy was no longer a relevant guide to work in the field. Something clearly needed to be done. The provisions that clarified reasonable efforts, extended adoption incentives for states, and advanced measurable outcomes tied to fiscal penalties were important because they brought a renewed focus to core ideas at a time when it could be said that the child welfare system was itself adrift.

ASFA also set in motion a more fundamental shift in policy and practice, a shift that is still very much underway. Although largely a function of how the law was interpreted rather than explicit statutory language, ASFA triggered an ongoing discussion that has placed child well-being at the forefront of policy discussions. Common sense tells us that well-being ought to be on the list of child welfare outcomes. The reason safety and permanency are so important is related to a basic sense that children cannot thrive in unsafe environments and without stable relationships with caregivers. When a child welfare agency steps in to help families, the consequences for the child ought to be evaluated with well-being in mind.

Despite what common sense tells us, an earnest commitment to well-being would alter fundamentally the nature and scope of the child welfare system in the United States. The long-held focus on safety and permanency reflects the nation's desire to limit intrusions into family life to those situations in which there is a compelling state interest. With the commitment to safety, the government has outlined a range of responsibilities that is easily contained within a doctrine that limits government involvement in family life to situations in which the risk of harm is significant. The commitment to permanency flows from the belief that governmental interventions should be time limited, and that the parents are the most flexible and responsive entities able to act on behalf of their children.

The concept of well-being does not fit within the rationale of a limited government for the simple reason that well-being has to be evaluated from a variety of perspectives, including but not limited to whether the parents are fulfilling their responsibilities. Even good parents cannot overcome the tough circumstances they face trying to raise a challenging child in what are sometimes very difficult neighborhoods. It is hard to guarantee a minimum level of well-being, and indeed public policy does not hold parents to such a standard. Instead, policy looks to give assistance to parents who are trying to address those problems.

Of course, the risk is that the state will treat parents as though they are the single reason why children are not doing as well as they should be. This could lead to allegations against perfectly adequate parents who have, for many other possible reasons, children who are falling below community standards. This is the very sort of expanded involvement in family life that gives rise to the idea that intrusions into family life ought to be limited in the first place.

That said, the child welfare system cannot ignore the well-being of the children it serves, and a place for well-being has to be found. Our view about the proper role of well-being in child welfare services derives from the basic framework of this book. We have tried to outline the implications of moving the child welfare field beyond the common-sense appeal of well-being and onto firmer footing. From our perspective, doing so means proceeding cautiously and with an emphasis on evidence—evidence that speaks to who uses child welfare services and when during their childhood—so that policy and the resources that flow from policy can be allocated in proportion to demand *and* evidence that points to what works for which children, given their age and circumstances.

An evidence base requires two things. Theory helps the field organize what it knows and what it does not know. With respect to well-being, this is especially important. Although the quality of child welfare services research has improved dramatically in the last two decades, the bridge to knowledge from other research disciplines is only getting started. We have tried to advance that process. The bio-ecological/life course perspective reflects current knowledge in relation to child development. Two features of the theories stand out. The bio-ecological perspective accommodates the view that child well-being is at its core a developmental concept best understood in reference to the interactions between the child, parents, and the context in which the family is situated. Moving past the parent-child interaction is, of course, what generates the policy tension. Second, the life course perspective offers an orientation to empirical work and the notion that well-being and development are about how children are functioning, across time, relative to their biological endowments and the assets embedded in their situation. In particular, the notion of interdependent trajectories alerts us to the fact that assessing whether a child is moving adequately along a well-being trajectory, as the focus on outcomes implies, means that someone will have to make note of where the child was developmentally when services started, and that the impact of services has to be evaluated relative to that starting point and how long the service trajectory overlapped with the developmental trajectory. At this time, there are no resources or mechanisms in place to consistently collect such information on the more than 3 million children who come to the face-to-face attention of child welfare services each year.

Of course, an evidence base also requires evidence. Our argument is that an evidence base for child welfare policy has to evolve in two interrelated directions. Most often, discussions of the need for evidence focus on the issue of what works. Practitioners have, for the most part, always been interested in providing services that offer the best chance of helping the client. What has changed, albeit slowly, are the standards used to judge whether a given service helps relative to the alternatives (including no treatment). Whereas choosing an intervention used to be somewhat idiosyncratic within a broader context of schools of thought, today interventions that rely on intervention theory (e.g., social learning theory) and that have been tested using rigorously designed evaluations earn credibility faster because the interventions build on a foundation. Unfortunately, very few interventions that address maltreatment and placement have met the standard scientific criteria of effectiveness.

All else being equal, the fact that resources for child welfare services are scarce means that policy ought to support interventions that work. However, an evidence base that relies solely on studies of clinical efficacy is unacceptably narrow. Policymakers want service providers to use the services that work best, but a policymaker also has to make judgments regarding how much service to make available, for whom, and under what circumstances. For this evidence, policymakers have to draw on an epidemiological perspective to identify the most pressing needs and then use knowledge about what works.

Fortunately, investments in information systems and research have added considerably to the quantity and quality of data available to policymakers, practitioners, and academic researchers. In particular, the combination of NSCAW, NCANDS, and the Multistate Foster Care Data Archive provides an unprecedented opportunity to establish a basic epidemiology of reported maltreatment and foster care placement together with baseline information about the well-being of children using child welfare services as close as possible to the time the service careers start. The theoretical importance of these synchronized data is substantial. The administrative data (NCANDS and FCDA) provide the perspective needed to understand whether the incidence of reported maltreatment and placement fits within a life phase view of child development that anticipates elevated risks during different developmental periods (Brooks-Gunn, Phelps, & Elder, 1991; Elder, 1998).[2] The NSCAW data reinforce and extend the administrative data because the NSCAW data describe child well-being at the point in time when the service trajectory first intersects with the developmental trajectory. Taken together, these data help us to understand the extent to which our basic assumptions about the child welfare system square with its current operation.

What the Data Tell Us

We expected to find discernible patterns in the maltreatment and foster care data pointing to a strong link to child development. We also expected to find that children involved in the child welfare system are behind their age group peers developmentally. Last, we expected to find research that reinforced the idea that effective child welfare services are designed to take developmental issues into account. Our expectations were framed by research that ties risk patterns in childhood to passage through developmental stages, research that says maltreatment adversely affects child development, and research that suggests that interventions work best when the theory of change invokes developmental themes.

Broadly speaking, the data support the view that a developmental perspective is critical to understanding who uses the child welfare system and how well-being fits within the broader policy context. For as far back as the data go, the child welfare system in the United States has served three developmentally distinct populations: children starting out, children starting school, and children starting adolescence. Although these patterns could change in time, and we recognize local variation along with the importance of within-population differences, this relatively simple reality has profound implications for how we ought to think about child welfare, child well-being, and child welfare policy.

Starting Out

When reports and investigations are included, more children start child welfare services during their first year of life than at any other time. Indeed, the most striking patterns observed in the NCANDS and foster care data concern the rates of maltreatment and placement among children under the age of 1. Although levels of maltreatment and placement were generally higher in poor counties and urban counties, in each subset of counties, the rates were substantially higher for children under the age of 1 than for children of all other ages. From a developmental perspective, the fact that neglect is the single most frequent type of abuse involving infants reinforces the idea that the capacity to provide care and an infant's need for attention are often mismatched during this critical developmental period.

The placement data also point to the fact that infants placed in foster care leave placement differently. Compared with children who started placement as 1-year-olds, infants are about 60 percent more likely to be adopted. Of course, higher rates of adoption mean that infants are also much less likely to return home following their first placement in foster care. In the starkest possible terms, the data point to the fact that almost half of all infants—the largest group of children entering foster care—will leave with a new set of adults acting as their legal parents.

For a significant subset of the children using child welfare services, the onset of services occurs early in the child's developmental trajectory. From a service design perspective, the importance of interweaving child welfare services and development so early is hard to mistake. More than half of all children ages 3 to 24 months whose families were investigated for maltreatment were classified as being at high risk for developmental delay or neurological impairment. Early language skills also show signs of substantial impairment. Finally, the fraction of young children (2- to 3-year-olds) who are already showing signs of problem behavior is twice the norm. Although children who receive child welfare services, as a group, sometimes showed greater impairment than the cases that were closed at intake, the levels of developmental risk were exceptionally high among the closed cases.

Children placed in foster care have a higher incidence of problem behaviors, even at this young age, than children placed in kinship care or children who go on to receive in-home services. Later, the data will tell us whether these children are the ones with high levels of problem behavior who are still in care after a period of several years. Similarly, among children who are re-reported for maltreatment, the longitudinal perspective built into NSCAW will offer some insight into how initial service decisions (services/no services) and developmental standing influence what happens next.

Starting School

Generally speaking, children entering school have lower rates of substantiated maltreatment and placement away from home. Their rates are, however, somewhat elevated compared with toddlers and children old enough to be in the upper grades of elementary school. This is particularly true in the case of physical abuse. The likelihood of a substantiated report of physical abuse is highest among children between the ages of 5 and 9, with a peak near age 6. Reports of physical abuse are also elevated for babies and adolescents. With respect to neglect, the rate of substantiated neglect rises slightly as children enter school, especially among African American and Hispanic children living in counties with low poverty rates. It is important to remember, however, that neglect is still the most common reason children in this age group come to the attention of child welfare services.

The increase in substantiated maltreatment as children move into their school years illustrates why the ecological/life course perspective is so important. First, the data beg the question: Does the likelihood of maltreatment/physical abuse increase at that age, or does the likelihood of detection, given school attendance, account for increased reporting? Unfortunately, the data do not speak directly to this point. The NSCAW data suggest that about 12 percent of the children in the 3- to 5-year-old group experienced maltreatment earlier in life. Of 6- to 10-year-olds, the comparable figure is 20 percent. However, the NSCAW data also indicate that children in these groups are somewhat less likely to be referred for services or placed in foster care, given an allegation of physical abuse. Yet, when they are placed into foster care, these 6- to 10-year-olds have higher rates of problem behavior than any other age group, indicating that these children have long exposure to maltreatment, few services, and high risk. One might expect slightly higher rates of service referral if the onset of maltreatment occurred earlier and was, therefore, more chronic. As for the meaning of these data in an ecological context, the data illustrate the embeddedness of individuals in a larger social context that shapes lives. Elder (1998) refers to timing as an illustration of the principle that the "developmental impact of a succession of life transitions or events is contingent on when they occur" (pg. 3). Design of child welfare services requires an understanding of developmental trajectories and what they portend.

When school-aged children do enter foster care (about 10 percent of the 6- to 10-year-olds in NSCAW), the exit patterns differ markedly from those of both younger and older children. Children between the ages of 6 and 10 are much more likely to leave foster care and live with their families (parents and other relatives). The likelihood of adoption is much lower than it is for younger children, and the likelihood of running away or leaving for some other reason is much less among members of this age group than among adolescents. The data also show that children in this age group spend less time in foster care before going home. However, when adoptions do occur, the timing of the adoption takes longer than it does with much younger children, especially infants. Finally, it is important to point out that the children in this age group were the most likely to still be in care. Thus, the data say that children fitting into this age group return home quickly, but if reunification does not happen, other exits are slower and there is a good chance the child will still be in care even after a considerable period of time (6 years) has elapsed. Although relatively small compared with all the other groups of children placed in foster care, it is this group of children for whom the service trajectory and the developmental trajectory are most closely intertwined. Again, NSCAW data will in time point to whether developmental issues apparent at the time of placement have anything to do with why some children in this age group have a difficult time leaving foster care. New federal policies that reward states for increasing the likelihood adoption of children aged 9 or older will also contribute information to our understanding of their long spells of in care.

The poor well-being of children between the ages of 4 and 10 also reveals significant challenges. Although tests of cognitive skills described in chapters 3 and 4 show that most maltreated and services-involved children ages 4 and older fall within one standard deviation of the norm, a higher proportion of the child welfare population has scores that are more than two standard deviations below the mean. Reading and math abilities follow the same pattern. Generally speaking, a fair number of school-aged children fall well within the normed ranges, yet a substantially higher proportion of children in the child welfare system show significant educational delays.

Measures of adaptive skills, social functioning, emotional well-being, and problem behaviors all indicate that school-aged children are behind their age-group peers at the time they enter child welfare services. Reports of low daily living skills were about twice as high in the NSCAW sample as one would expect in a normed sample. Slightly more than a third of the 4- to 10-year-olds scored in the clinical range on the CBCL. CBCL scores in the clinical and borderline ranges were reported for half the 6- to 10-year-olds who received some sort of child welfare services (other than placement) after the investigation. Clinical and borderline scores were reported for almost 60 percent of the 6- to 10-year-olds placed out of home; the figure was nearly two-thirds among all children placed in out-of-home care.

In short, children in this age group already face significant developmental challenges. Child welfare services may help resolve safety concerns, but only one-third of the children in this group receive any ongoing child welfare services (at least at this juncture). Interestingly enough, children who get in-home services have clinical and borderline CBCL scores that are higher than those reported for children who do not receive services. That said, the 6- to 10-year-olds who did not go on to receive child welfare services were three times as likely to score in the clinical range as the normed population. Safety may not be a grievous issue, but problem behaviors are common.

Starting Adolescence

As noted, reported rates of neglect and physical abuse are slightly higher among adolescents than among children approaching adolescence. In particular, physical abuse rises sharply after about age 10. Rates of substantiated physical abuse peak near age 14, about the same age that foster care placements peak. Age-differentiated patterns associated with physical abuse show a striking similarity even across urban, secondary-urban, and non-urban counties. Physical abuse rates are higher in counties with higher poverty levels, but again the underlying consistency of association between age and the rate of substantiated physical abuse is far more striking than the local variation. Neglect rates, which are generally higher than rates of physical abuse, also rise as children move deeper into adolescence. In primary urban areas, neglect rates reach nearly 5 per thousand 14-year-olds. Although we have not delved into the area of sexual abuse in any detail, the incidence of sexual abuse reported in the NSCAW data is highest among children ages 11 and above. The NSCAW data also indicate that, for the most part, the maltreatment that led to the most recent contact with the child welfare system occurred contemporaneously with that contact. Only 14 percent of the children who were above the age of 10 (11+) reported an onset of maltreatment that was much earlier. In the vernacular of juvenile justice, most of these adolescent child maltreatment cases are "late onset" cases rather than chronic or "early onset" cases (Eley, Lichtenstein, & Moffitt, 2003). If the analogy to the juvenile justice research holds, then a positive developmental resolution for children who experienced early onset will be more difficult to achieve.

Along with children between the ages of 0 and 2, children starting adolescence were the children most likely to get some form of service following the investigation. Including both in-home and out-of-home services, about 4 in 10 children in this age group received services. Children in this age group were among the most likely to be placed outside of the home (e.g., 13 percent compared with 10 percent of 6- to 10-year-olds). Compared with other types of maltreatment, the adolescents reported for sexual maltreatment and failure to supervise were the ones most likely to get in-home services.

When placed in foster care, adolescents are the least likely to start their placement experience in a family setting. In a separate analysis of the Foster Care Data Archive, nearly half the children with late placement onset entered group care of some sort as their initial placement type. With regard to how adolescents leave foster care, historical data are equally revealing. Although children above age 10 at the *time of entry* are about as likely to go home as other, younger children are, the likelihood of adoption is below 10 percent and quickly approaches zero. Among children who entered foster care at age 14 or above, an exit by way of completed adoption was rare. The large number of *other* exits experienced by children who come into foster care as teenagers is perhaps the most troubling finding. Other exits include running away, discharge to other (usually more restrictive) child-serving systems, and emancipation, so one might expect these exits to be more common among older children and indeed they are. However, for 6-year-olds, the likelihood of other exits is about 10 percent (although it could go higher depending on the outcomes recorded for the children who were still in care). For 10-year-olds, the likelihood is 20 percent, double the figure reported for 6-year-olds. Among children who entered placement as 13-year-olds, "other" exits account for 40 percent. Finally, 16-year-olds are as likely to leave for other reasons as they are to go home.

The developmental status of adolescents coming into the child welfare system is not so different from the status reported for younger children. Adolescents in the child welfare system face significant adaptive and behavioral challenges. Caregivers reported than more than half of the adolescents had clinical or borderline CBCL scores. Nearly 80 percent of the adolescents placed in group care had borderline/clinical CBCL scores. Adolescents also had high rates of delinquency as captured by the CBCL and suicidality as captured by a variety of indicators of plans and means to do self-harm.[3]

Race, Maltreatment, and Placement

Given what the data say, we would be remiss if we neglected to comment on the higher rates of child maltreatment and foster care placement reported for African American children, especially those living in the high-poverty counties we examined. Racial disproportionality, usually defined as the overrepresentation of children of color on the child welfare caseload relative to the general population, has been an ongoing concern in child welfare debates for a long period of time (Billingsley & Giovannoni, 1972; Courtney & Skyles, 2003; Roberts, 2002). Recent research has tried to untangle whether overrepresentation is a function of intake (e.g., more African Americans reported for maltreatment or placed in foster care) or duration (e.g., African American children stay longer in foster care) with some success (Barth, Miller, Green, & Baumgartner, 2000).

Our chapters on the epidemiology of maltreatment and placement add to this debate in a fundamental way insofar as they place disproportionality in a developmental context. Specifically, if we define disproportionality as a function of heightened rates of maltreatment for African American children (or other children of color) relative to children of other races, then the data presented earlier lend support to the contention that African American children are more likely to be subject of a substantiated maltreatment report. They are also more likely to be placed in foster care. However, the data also suggest that disproportionality is not even across the age span of childhood. In particular, for African American children residing in poor counties, the rate of maltreatment among children under the age of 1 was more than 5 times the rate for white children of the same age who were also living in high-poverty counties. Among all other older children, disproportionality was evident, but the differential was significantly smaller.

The placement data revealed a similar pattern: placement rates among African American children are higher than those reported for white and Hispanic children, but the differential that characterizes the rates for infants is substantially higher than it is for children of other ages.

When these data are coupled with the fact that infants come in contact with the child welfare system primarily for reasons of neglect (failure to supervise and failure to provide) and that infants and toddlers are more likely to be placed following a investigation (see Table 3.4), then one sees in the data a need to consider disproportionality in more nuanced terms. Specifically, the data presented in chapters 3 and 4 suggest quite strongly that disproportionality in the child welfare system is a function of how the system responds to African American families with babies. For example, in the counties we examined, the rate of maltreatment among African American children above the age of 1 in high-poverty counties is nearly the same as the rate reported in low-poverty counties.[4] Indeed, the only substantial difference within the African American population concerns the higher rates of maltreatment among infants.

Why are African American babies so much more likely than other children, including other African American children, to enter the child welfare system? Unfortunately, the answer to this important question is beyond the scope of this volume. We can, however, offer the following as a guide to future research. First, the data reinforce the importance of using a bio-ecological/life course perspective in combination with basic epidemiology. When set in a developmental context, the data on maltreatment and placement rates raise the possibility that over representation does not adequately represent what happens across all sectors of the child welfare system. For example, one might expect higher-than-observed maltreatment rates among African American teenagers in poor counties, given the general sense that poverty and maltreatment are positively correlated (McLoyd, 1990). Thus, the data invite an alternative hypothesis that points to the underrepresentation of African American teenagers in the child welfare system because of their overrepresentation in the juvenile justice system. Given the more coercive nature of juvenile detention, the underrepresentation of African American teenagers in the child welfare system may be as troubling as the overrepresentation of African American babies in the child welfare system.

The point is this. The debate over whether children of color are overrepresented in the child welfare system has tended to treat the child welfare system in monolithic terms—responding to all African American children and other children of color in a more or less uniform, but biased, way. The epidemiological data presented earlier suggest a wider set of hypotheses that includes both over serving and under serving. More important, the data suggest the need to explore the case processing mechanisms and systemic factors that give rise to a differential response using a lens that considers race, child development, and the interaction between race and age in the way workers understand and respond to perceived threats to children.

These are clearly important and difficult research questions. In the meantime, policymakers will have to respond to the fact that disproportionality in the child welfare system in the United States is to a very large extent a function of how well the needs of African

American families with very young children are addressed. In doing so, however, policymakers and practitioners may well leverage the fact that families with very young children of all races and ethnicities are overrepresented in the child welfare system. Everybody involved with the child welfare system has to do a better job of facing a common challenge–supporting children as they make the transition from birth to adulthood and beyond. If developmental theorists are right, then the realities of child development give a contour to the organization of services that ought to fit, with some modification, in all communities. The structure of the service delivery system, in light of developmental theory, concludes our analysis of child welfare, child well-being, and the evidence for policy reform.

Public Policy and Service Designs

Developmental theory suggests that interventions ought to be designed with an understanding of developmental processes in clear view. Shonkoff and Phillips (2000) articulate this most forcefully. "All strategies of intervention, regardless of the target group or the desired outcomes, can be derived from the normative theories of child development. That is to say, the general principles of development apply to all children independent of their biological variability or the range of environments in which they live."

From a public policy standpoint, the earlier chapters point in several directions. To begin our discussion of the policy implications, we focus first on language. As we noted in chapter 1, the policy discussions that followed passage of the Adoption and Safe Families Act of 1997 inflated the extent to which the law emphasized well-being as an outcome for the child welfare system. It was only after the development of ASFA entered into the regulatory phase that well-being moved closer to the fore. The ease with which this happened is attributable in part to the fact that well-being in the context of the child welfare system has face validity, or what we call common-sense appeal. The mere fact that so many children are reported for maltreatment during the most critical developmental periods signifies why the system has to take a holistic view of children, their families, and the communities where they live.

The data presented through chapters 3 and 4 do nothing to dispel the notion that the children in the child welfare system face real challenges, whether those challenges are described in terms of safety, permanency, or well-being. Yet, contemporary theories of child development call into question the division of child welfare outcomes into three parts: safety, permanency, and well-being. When well-being is couched in developmental terms, the idea that safety and permanency are separable from well-being loses its allure. A long history of research in child development suggests that children develop best when living in safe and stable families. In other words, safety and permanency are a part of, not separate from, a larger concept generally referred to as well-being.

The shift in language is subtle, but nevertheless important. Policymakers, especially those who are elected, want to know that their child welfare system cares about the well-being of children. Separating well-being from safety and permanency in the way the current language does creates the impression that securing safe, permanent homes for children leaves a large domain of concerns untended, when in fact well-being is largely contingent on whether the home is safe and stable. Second, the term well-being is really shorthand for health, education, and mental health, facets of well-being that are for the most part programmatically beyond the scope of the child welfare system. By using a vague term such as well-being when something much more specific is intended, advocates for expanded services for children weaken their position. The child welfare system cannot be accountable for safety, permanency, *and* education, health, and mental health because the resources needed to influence the well-being outcomes are outside the boundaries of the system. Instead, if the mandate for the child welfare system were expressed as *achieving* safety and permanency outcomes and *ensuring* the child welfare system engages the education, health and mental health systems, two things would be clearer. First, by working to create safe and stable families for children, the child welfare system *is* accomplishing a great deal when it comes to the well-being of children. Second, separating well-being into its constituent parts makes clear that which is obvious to most child welfare administrators: When well-being is couched in terms of health, mental health, and education, the general public and policymakers alike quickly realize that the child welfare system has a limited range of options without using the health care system, schools, and the mental health system as *collaborators*. If children in the child welfare system are not moving along their age-appropriate trajectory, these other systems will have to shoulder their share of the responsibility in conjunction with, not in spite of, the child welfare system.

The shift in language leads to a second policy direction supported by the evidence. Again, contemporary child development theories treat the various strands of development as a web of interacting events that mutually influence each other through time. The interplay of safety and permanency in relation to well-being represents an excellent example of developmental reciprocity. On the one hand, if a child is in a safe and stable environment, the long-term developmental impact of noxious influences may be muted. On the other hand, children who are otherwise normal in a developmental sense could spiral in another direction if the home environment turns unstable over even a short period of time, depending of course on when in the unfolding trajectory the instability occurs.

To account for the highly interactive nature of child development, child welfare policy has to move cautiously but deliberately towards strategies that promote integrated approaches to service delivery. A relatively simple notion in theory, integrated service delivery is not new or peculiar to child welfare (Waldfogel, 1997). Contemporary reform initiatives in mental health services for children and adults, school services, health care and juvenile justice are all rooted in the idea that a full-service continuum is best suited to meeting the interconnected needs of children (and adults). Moreover, as the idea of integrated services has matured, the approach has adapted such ideas as serving children in the least restrictive community-based setting possible; supporting families in their efforts to raise their children; and individualizing service plans using strengths-based, culturally relevant approaches (Stroul & Freidman, 1986). Each of these ideas has already found its way onto the child welfare reform agenda in some way or another. In the case of serving children in the least restrictive, most family-like setting, the idea has been around for more than a quarter-century.

The notion that services should be linked in integrated bundles that are developmentally oriented is an appealing idea, but it has to be approached carefully. There are at least two reasons why. First, child welfare agencies have a tendency to rush good ideas into service long before they are ready to go to scale. Family preservation services are a good case in point. Family preservation services share their origins with the multi-systemic therapies (MST) described in chapter 6. However, family preservation services lost their cachet nearly a decade ago after the results from the first full-scale randomized trials demonstrated that the programs failed to produce the promised results (Littell & Schuerman, 2002).[5]

Second, some efforts to increase service integration have failed to provide client benefits. Bickman (2002); Bickman, Lambert, Andrade, & Penaloza (2000); and Bickman, Noser, & Summerfelt (1999) have studied mental health systems of care (systems of care are a variant of integrated service strategies) and found that although service access improved, the outcomes for children were not better when compared with children who received services outside the system. Similarly, the evaluation of the Comprehensive Child Development Program (CCDP), a case management, home visiting model offering a range of educational, health, and social services, failed to produce positive effects consistent with the underlying theory of change (Goodson, Layzer, St. Pierre, Bernstein, & Lopez, 2000).

Advocates of integrated services were disappointed by the results from these two studies, but the findings suggest why the programs described in chapters 5 and 6 have been modestly more successful. In the case of Bickman's Fort Bragg study, systems integration was not coupled with evidence-based treatments. Facilitating greater access to relatively weak services, as usual, did not impact client outcomes. The problems uncovered in the CCDP study were similar. The program sought changes in child functioning but directed the treatment at parents rather than through direct intervention with children, a choice the evaluators ultimately questioned.

Thus the evidence favors a deeper interpretation of what integrated services mean for the child welfare system. First, we start with the three critical periods when child welfare services are most likely to be used. Then, from each of these developmental stanchions, we must examine the necessary mix of developmentally relevant services. Then, we must examine how, in fact, these services need to be organized around the most common developmental trajectories. Children starting out (i.e., infants) and those starting adolescence are in some respects the most unique populations, by virtue of their developmental characteristics, the number entering foster care, and their trajectories through child welfare services. The most common infant outcomes that child welfare workers should expect to achieve are adoption/guardianship and reunification—in about equal measure—and the services most able to fulfill the health, education, and mental health needs are those provided by early intervention services.[6] There are specialized units that are designed to provide high levels of expertise at assessment and intervention with newborns (Clyman & Harden, 2002). The Miami/Dade County Juvenile Court and the Family Court in New York City both have efforts focused on issues relating to the specialized needs of infants and toddlers in the courts (Dicker & Gordon, 2004; Lederman & Osofsky, 2004). We are also aware of unique, and promising, efforts to assist mothers to reunify with their drug-exposed newborns (Usher & Wildfire, 2003). Although each of these programs embodies different approaches to organizational improvement, their initial success suggests a need for broader, more rigorous testing of the underlying models.

Children starting adolescence have starkly different outcomes. The chance of adoption is negligible; the likelihood of running away or being transferred to a juvenile justice or mental health facility is relatively high; and the need for independent living services is common.[7] When they do go home, adolescents have high reentry rates. The most significant and knowledgeable providers of adolescent health, education, and mental health services have almost no overlap with those of infants. Knowledge of group and residential treatment resources—and their alternatives—is critically important because a significant proportion of adolescents will spend at least some time in group care, and the evidence indicates that the residential treatment can be as harmful as helpful (Barth, in press; Dishion, McCord, & Poulin, 1999). If treatment foster care is available for youth, child welfare workers need to be able to identify more evidence-based approaches, because treatment foster care programs vary markedly (Farmer, Compton, Bums, & Robertson, 2002; Fisher & Chamberlain, 2000). Productive interactions with mental health services, juvenile justice, special and regular education, and reproductive health services are key to achieving well-being. Special programs are available for foster and group home youth in each of these areas, but they are unlikely to be known to those with generalized caseloads.[8] Further, agency personnel are unlikely to justify the time away from a generalized caseload in order to master new approaches to intervention.

Even as we argue for services integrated around specific developmental periods, we recognize that children live in families with children who belong to other age groups. Although this complicates the use of specialized units organized around a life phase interpretation of developmental needs, the opportunity for innovation is nevertheless significant. We also recognize that services for children starting school have received scant attention. That said, strategies that reorganize services to accommodate explicit developmental theory might promote greater success in both of these areas. The scientific work has to be done, but the growing body of epidemiological evidence and our expanding knowledge of life course trajectories suggests that interweaving these themes in service design is essential.

Flexible funding is a third feature of integrated service systems that has to be adapted to the child welfare system before the full potential of integrated services can be realized. Flexibility is important because the funds for services can be aligned with client needs more easily than categorical funds that are tied to specific service types. Most important, as a child's needs change, the services can be more easily transformed if the funding is flexible.

The primary sources of federal funds earmarked specifically for child welfare services emanate from Titles IV-B and IV-E of the Social Security Act, as noted in chapter 1. Of those two sources, Title IV-B funds are the most flexible in that states can allocate those funds for a broad range of services. The Title IV-E funds are the least flexible in that those funds, and the matching state and local dollars, can only be spent on board and maintenance and related expenses. Board and maintenance refer to the costs associated with placing a child in foster care. The Title IV-E program also covers administration and training expenses, but the range of services that can be financed with Title IV-E funds is extremely limited.[9] Finally, the IV-E funds can only be used to provide room and board to a child, not to a parent.[10]

The key to understanding why the Title IV-E program is inflexible can be found in the way IV-E funds flow to the states. In the simplest possible terms, a state claim for a day of foster care provided is at the heart of the process. Each time a state provides a day of foster care for a federally eligible child, the federal government reimburses the state for its share of the board, maintenance, and other associated costs. Without the claim for a day of foster care provided on behalf of an eligible child, no IV-E revenue for foster care placements flows to the state (Wulczyn, 2000).

In practical terms, the limited use of Title IV-E funds means that when states elect to serve children at home rather than in foster care or the state decides to change the mix of services provided while a child is in foster care, the state risks losing federal funding if those services result in a net reduction in the use of foster care. For example, if states work with communities to better serve families with very young children and reduce the utilization of foster care (e.g., placement rates go down, length of time in care goes down, or less restrictive levels of care are used), then aggregate funding for child welfare services on behalf of those young children in those communities will decline in direct proportion to the drop in the use of foster care. If, on the other hand, those funds could be captured and redirected, then the base of available services in the community would expand and diversify.[11]

By itself, however, the Title IV-E program cannot be expected to serve as the source of flexible funds for services that address the wide variety of safety, permanency, and well-being needs found in the population of children who come into contact with the child welfare system.[12] The main problem has to do with the fact that Title IV-E funds now are dedicated to the purpose of providing suitable living arrangements for children who are not able to live with their families. If the child is again able to live with the family, then they leave care and those federal funds are lost (often before the needs of the family are truly met). Flexible funding proposals are evolving to offer the possibility that this large sum of funds for placement could be used to prevent re-placement back into care.

Proposals for flexible funding that involve real discretion over the use of federal Title IV-E board and maintenance payments have to contend, however, with the fact that if the money is going to support alternatives to foster care, then the state has to find ways to safely reduce the need for foster care. Only then can the state use the flexible revenue for something other than foster care. Otherwise, it is the state's first obligation to protect the child. If credible alternatives to foster care do not exist, for whatever reason, then board and maintenance payments must be the first priority for those dollars.

We raise this issue because the NSCAW data reveal clearly that a large proportion of the population of children in contact with the child welfare system have clear developmental needs even though they do not receive either in-home or foster care services. The tension this creates over the flexible use of federal, state, and local funds for foster care is clear. If flexible funds are used to address the broad social, emotional, health, and educational needs of children touching the child welfare system, the funding will not go very far or deep. The likelihood that such an approach would reduce foster care placements is very low.[13] Flexibility and accountability must be linked to evidence-based interventions that can be expected to generate specific outcomes in a way that is direct and unambiguous with respect to the original purpose of those funds. For this reason, and others, the outcome measures used by the federal government to evaluate state child welfare programs have to recognize the age-differentiated outcomes the data so clearly reveal.

The need for both flexibility and accountability highlights a theme that has surfaced throughout this book. Well-being outcomes stretch the boundaries of the child welfare system because the system is set up to intervene whenever parents fail to provide a safe home for their children. Questions about a child's well-being might shade the interpretation of what constitutes safety, but in the end safety is the issue that most clearly defines the system's boundary relative to other human service systems. The push on the part of states to rationalize state protective services investigations, using carefully delineated safety assessments, is the most tangible manifestation of those boundaries.

The boundaries generally mean that resources—in the form of human capital and funding—are also divided in a way that reflects the core purposes of the program. Child welfare services, whether they are funded out of Title IV-B or Title IV-E, are earmarked fundamentally to address safety and permanency. To the extent safety and permanency facilitate well-being, which is the presumption, then those funds can be said to have an *indirect* effect on well-being. However, the primary resources that offer the best chance of affecting child well-being are quite simply outside the child welfare system. The child welfare system *is* concerned about health, education, and mental health, but the human capital and infrastructure to alter developmental trajectories rests with doctors, teachers, and therapists who are attached to those systems. In other words, it is hard to find a place for well-being on the list of outcomes, if putting it on the list means that the child welfare system is accountable for altering developmental trajectories with the kind of resources the system has on hand, or else face the consequences of failure.

But that should not be construed to mean providers of child welfare services should remain passive with respect to how children are doing. On the contrary, the child welfare system has the job of securing safe and stable families for children. Safe and stable families are fundamental to well-being and the language we use should reflect this sense of priorities. The child welfare system has to serve as an impassioned advocate for children who are in difficult circumstances and whose long-term well-being is in jeopardy if ameliorative services are not available. The parents of those children need a powerful voice to help them hold service providers accountable so that the needs of their children are being met in the health care, day care, educational, and other allied settings with the primary responsibility of making sure children have the best chance of finding their way. If the child is in foster care, the need for that sort of cross-system advocacy on behalf of children is paramount, lest the child be denied services simply because the state is acting as the parent, even temporarily. The infrastructure of services to help maltreated children develop along a trajectory comparable to that of their nonmaltreated peers is, in many respects, already in place—at least for infants. The Maternal and Child Health Services Block Grant—Title V of the Social Security Act (United States Code, §701-710, subchapter V, chapter 7, Title 42)—already has broad responsibility for at-risk mothers and infants. For example, home visiting programs are funded under the mandate to develop and expand health education services, and related social services in the home of pregnant women and families with young children. In 2002, the Administration for Children and Families released $10 million to fund Early Head Start Programs with a specific focus on children in the child welfare system (Program Announcement No. ACF/ACYF/HS 2002-04). This initial step set the stage for expanded new efforts to integrate children in the child welfare system with those services that offer the best hope of improving child well-being. New requirements from CAPTA require greater integration of child welfare services with early intervention services and greater involvement of medical centers (that identify children born with positive drug toxicology tests) with reporting to child welfare services.

Much less is in place, however, for getting necessary evidence-based services to the older groups of children and their parents. This is not likely to change under existing funding constraints because there is not enough flexibility, under IV-E, to amass support for new approaches to services. Even if child welfare services focuses on its primary commitment to safety and permanency, in the end, Title IV of the Social Security Act (as currently configured) is not a useful base on which to build a new generation of evidence-based interventions. The IV-E waivers were intended to spawn innovation in child welfare services, but they have largely been a disappointment in this regard. The most heralded efforts have not been focused on improving the offering of evidence-based services but in providing new options for leaving the child welfare system, most notably via guardianship. Federal funding, whether a portion of IV-E or otherwise, is needed to stimulate and reward states that engage in serious research and development of new approaches to service. The evolution of child welfare services requires that we bring the same evidence-oriented sensibility to examining the alternatives to the current child welfare services funding scheme as we do to critiques of child welfare services.

Notes

1.   Not everyone agrees with this position. Stein et al. (2003), for example, argue that ASFA was unnecessary because the goals of ASFA were reachable given existing laws.

2.   It is important to point out that the idea of critical life phases is not restricted to children. Returning to a key point from chapter 2, developmental trajectories are interdependent. Maternal and paternal circumstances, not just characteristics, can have an impact on child outcomes (Brooks-Gunn, Phelps, & Elder, 1991; Forehand & Nouisianen, 1993).

3.   More than one-quarter of the children 11 and older in NSCAW expressed suicidal intent at entrance into the child welfare system, and this is more than halved (to about 10 percent) for children in out-of-home and in-home care (Wall, Green, Barth, & Group, April 15, 2004); about one in five children was involved in delinquent activity at intake, regardless of setting, and this remained the same across the 18 months, regardless of setting.

4.   The data for this comparison can be found in Figures 3.8 and 3.9. For example, in high-poverty counties, the rate of maltreatment among African American children between the ages of 9 and 11 was 8.8, 7.6, and 7.1 per 1,000, respectively. The comparable rates for African American children in low-poverty counties were 8.3, 7.7, and 8 per 1,000, respectively. These differences stand in sharp contrast to the data for African American babies. In high-poverty counties, the infant placement rate was 49 per 1,000; in low-poverty counties, the infant placement rate was 27 per 1,000. In statistical terms, one could say that the relationship between poverty and placement depends on the age of the child. Notwithstanding the fact that the analysis considers only poverty and age as explanatory variables, the data suggest that except for babies, poverty has a small impact on rates of maltreatment among African Americans (when high- and low-poverty counties are compared).

5.   Although no single reason accounts for why family preservation programs failed to deliver the promised results, part of the reason may be the failure to target services. Littell and Schuerman (2002) and Ryan and Schuerman (2004) examined whether targeted family preservation services were more effective, but their findings are not persuasive. However, Denby and Curtis (2003) did not find much evidence that caseworkers matched services to specific subpopulations of children.

6.   The Child Abuse Prevention and Treatment Act now requires that all children ages 0-3 be referred to early intervention services. These services are the downward

extension of special education services and are intended to generate an individualized family service plan to help address the child and family conditions that might reduce the need for special education services.

7. We want to be very careful when talking about age-specific outcomes. For example, advocates of adoption might argue that the adoption rate among adolescents is unacceptably low. We agree. At the same time, even in states where adolescents are more likely to be adopted, the likelihood of adoption is still much lower than it is for children of other ages (Wulczyn, Hislop, & Goerge, 2000b). In sum, the outcome trajectories are baselines against which improvements can be measured. The age effects suggest ways in which expectations should reflect an awareness of developmental issues.

8. For example, Kolko and Swenson (2002) and Cohen and colleagues (2003) have developed and tested important new treatment programs for children and youth experiencing post-maltreatment trauma; educational programs that are most promising for helping youth include foster youth services (Ayasse, 1995). Specialized approaches to reducing reproductive risk that have been developed and evaluated for foster youth have provided some guidance to those endeavoring to improve the delivery of mental health services to foster youth (Becker & Barth, 2000; Simms, Freundlich, Battistelli, & Kaufman, 1999).

9. Funding to meet the needs of children in the child welfare system comes from a variety of sources. Titles IV-B and IV-E are the sources of dedicated funding (Bess, Andrews, Jantz, Russell, & Geen, 2002)

10. A single exception is that IV-E can be used for care for a dependent adolescent who gives birth to a child (and becomes a parent).

11. The need for fiscal reform in child welfare has been addressed off and on for the past twenty-five years, if not longer. The Adoption Assistance and Child Welfare Act of 1980 contained a transferability provision that would have allowed states to transfer unused funds from the Title IV-E program into the Title IV-B program. More recently, the federal government has used waivers to grant states greater authority (Section 1130 of the Social Security Act, as amended by Public Law 105-89). Waivers allow states to set aside federal rules regarding the uses toward which federal Title IV-E funds are allocated provided the state operates the program in a cost-neutral way. The waivers are, however, limited to five years and do not represent a long-term solution of the problem of flexibility. The PEW Commission on Children in Foster Care (http://pewfostercare.org/) has been charged with the task of proposing policy changes that would address the problem of flexibility.

12. Here again, the arguments are too complicated to describe at length. The essential issue has to do with the entitlement nature of the Title IV-E program. It is relatively easy to propose flexible funding solutions if the amount of revenue that can be claimed is unlimited. However, the federal government will not create open-ended social service entitlements. On the contrary, flexible funding streams usually come with some limit on the government's fiscal exposure. Block grants are one way to limit funding levels while offering greater flexibility. The discussion presented here is based on the idea that if states do not reduce foster care expenditures, then the cost of providing foster care will shift to the state and local governments. For a discussion of risk sharing in the Title IV-E program, see Wulczyn (2000).

13. We are reminded of Bickman's aforementioned findings that having additional flexibility in funding—as was achieved in Fort Bragg via the Medicaid waiver—offers no insurance that outcomes will improve.

References

Aber, J. L., Bennett, N. G., Conley, D. C., & Li, J. (1997). The effects of poverty on child health and development. *Annual Review of Public Health, 18,* 463-483.

Achenbach, T. (1992). *Manual for child behavior checklist 2-3 and 1992 profile.* Burlington, VT: University of Vermont, Department of Psychiatry.

Achenbach, T. M. (1991a). *Manual for the child behavior checklist 2-3 and 1991 profile.* Burlington, VT: University of Vermont, Department of Psychiatry.

Achenbach, T. M. (1991b). *Manual for the child behavior checklist 4-18 and 1991 profile.* Burlington, VT: University of Vermont, Department of Psychiatry.

Achenbach, T. M. (1991c). *Manual for the teacher's report form and 1991 profile.* Burlington, VT: University of Vermont, Department of Psychiatry.

Achenbach, T. M. (1991d). *Manual for the youth self-report and 1991 profile.* Burlington, VT: University of Vermont, Department of Psychiatry.

Ackerman, B. P., Brown, E. D., D'Eramo, K. S., & Izard, C. E. (2002). Maternal relationship instability and the school behavior of children from disadvantaged families. *Development Psychology, 38,* 694-704.

Adams, J. F. (2001). Impact of parent training on family functioning. *Child & Family Behavior Therapy, 23*(1), 29-42.

Administration for Children and Families. (1998). Program Instruction (ACYF-CB-PI-98-02). Washington, DC: U. S. Department of Health and Human Services.

Adoption and Safe Families Act of 1997, Public Law 105-89. Title IV, Section 401. 111 Stat. 215.

Alexander, K. L., Entwisle, D. R., & Horsey, C. S. (1997). From first grade forward: Early foundations of high school dropout. *Sociology of Education, 70*(2), 87-107.

Allen, M. L. (1997). *Statement of Mary Lee Allen Before the Subcommittee on Human Resources of the House Committee on Ways and Means.* Retrieved November 30, 2003, from http://waysandmeans.house.gov/legacy.asp?file=legacy/humres/105cong/4-8-97/4-8alle.htm

Amenta, E., Bonastia, C., & Caren, N. (2001). U. S. social policy in comparative historical perspective: Concepts, images, arguments, and research strategies. *Annual Review of Sociology, 27,* 213-234.

American Academy of Child and Adolescent Psychiatry. (1992). Practice parameters for the assessment and treatment of conduct disorders. *Journal of the American Academy of Child & Adolescent Psychiatry, 31*(2), iv-vii.

American Academy of Pediatrics. (2000). Clinical practice guidelines: Diagnosis and evaluation of children with attention-deficit/hyperactivity disorder. *Pediatrics, 105,* 1158-1170.

American Psychiatric Association. (1997). Practice guidelines for the treatment of patients with schizophrenia. *American Journal of Psychiatry, 154*(4 Suppl), 1-63.

Armstrong, M. L. (1998). *Adolescent pathways: Exploring the intersection between child welfare and juvenile justice, PINS, and mental health.* New York: Vera Institute of Justice.

Ayasse, R. H. (1995). Addressing the needs of foster children: The Foster Youth Services Program. *Social Work in Education, 17*(4), 207-216.

Aylward, G. (1995). *Bayley infant neurodevelopmental screener manual.* San Antonio, TX: Harcourt Brace.

Azar, S., & Wolfe, D. (1998). Child physical abuse and neglect. In E. Mash & R. Barkley (Eds.), *Treatment of childhood disorders* (pp. 501-544). New York: Guilford.

Bandura, A. (1976). *Social learning theory.* London: Prentice-Hall.

Barlow, C. E. (May 21, 2001). *Individual and group-based parenting programmes for improving psychosocial outcomes for teenage parents and their children,* from http://www.campbellcollaboration.org/doc-pdf/teenpar.pdf

Barth, R. P. (1991). An experimental evaluation of in-home child abuse prevention services. *Child Abuse and Neglect, 15*(4), 363-375.

Barth, R. P. (2002). *Institutions vs. foster homes: The empirical base for a century of action.* Chapel Hill, NC: University of North Carolina, School of Social Work, Jordan Institute for Families.

Barth, R. P. and the NSCAW Research Group. *National Survey of Child and Adolescent Well-Being (NSCAW): Developmental characteristics of maltreated children at intake.* 16th Annual Research Conference: A System of Care for Children's Mental Health: Expanding the Research Base, Tampa, Fl, March 4, 2003.

Barth, R. P. (in press). Residential care: From here to eternity. *International Journal of Social Welfare.*

Barth, R., Miller, J. M., Green, R. L., & Baumgartner, J. N. (2000). *Children of color in the child welfare system: Toward explaining their disproportionate involvement in comparison to their numbers on the general population.* Chapel Hill and Research Triangle Park, NC: University of North Carolina School of Social Work, Jordan Institute for Families and Research Triangle Institute.

Barth, R. P. (1997). Effects of age and race on the odds of adoption versus remaining in long-term out-of-home care. *Child Welfare, 76*(2), 285-308.

Barth, R. P., & Berry, M. (1988). Adoption and disruption: Rates, risks, and resources. xiv, 247. New York: Aldine.

Barth, R. P., & Derezotes, D. S. (1990). *Preventing adolescent abuse: Effective intervention strategies and techniques.* Lexington, MA: Lexington Books.

Barth, R. P., Landsverk, J., Chamberlain, P., Reid, J., Rolls, J., Hurlburt, M., Farmer, B., et al. (in press). Parent training in child welfare services: Planning for a more evidence-based approach to serving biological parents. *Research on Social Work Practice.*

Barth, R. P., & Miller, J. M. (2000). Building effective post-adoption services: What is the empirical foundation? *Family Relations: Interdisciplinary Journal of Applied Family Studies, 49*(4), 447-455.

Barth, R. P., Wildfire, J., & Green, R. L. (in press). Placement into foster care and the interplay of urbanicity, child behavior problems, and poverty. *American Journal of Orthopsychiatry.*

Bavolek, S. J. (2002). *Research and validation report of...The nurturing parenting programs,* from http://www.nurturingparenting.com/npp/Research%20&%20Validation%20of%20NPP.pdf

Becker, M., & Barth, R. P. (2000). Power through choices: Evaluation of a pregnancy prevention program for foster youth. *Child Welfare, 79,* 269-284.

Belsky, J. (1993). Etiology of child maltreatment: A developmental-ecological analysis. *Psychological Bulletin, 114*(3), 413-434.

Benedict, M. I., & White, R. B. (1991). Factors associated with foster care length of stay. *Child Welfare, 70*(45-58).

Berkman, L. F., & Kawachi, I. (Eds.). (2000). *Social epidemiology.* New York: Oxford University Press, Inc.

Berlin, L. J., & Cassidy, J. (2001). Enhancing early child-parent relationships: Implications of adult attachment research. *Infants and Young Children, 14*(2), 64-76.

Bernstein, N. (2001). *The lost children of wilder: The epic struggle to change foster care.* New York: Pantheon Books.

Berrick, J., Needell, B., Barth, R. P., & Jonson-Reid, M. (1998). *The tender years: Toward developmentally sensitive child welfare services.* New York: Oxford.

Bess, R., Andrews, C., Jantz, A., Russell, V., & Geen, R. (2002). *The cost of protecting vulnerable children III: What factors affect states fiscal decisions?*, from http://www.urban.org/url.cfm?ID=310596

Bess, R., Leos-Urbel, J., & Geen, R. (2001). *The cost of protecting vulnerable children II: How has it changed since 1996?* (Occasional Paper No. 46). Washington, DC: The Urban Institute.

Bickman, L. (2002). Evaluation of the Ft. Bragg and Stark County systems of care for children and adolescents. *The American Journal of Evaluation, 23*(1), 67.

Bickman, L., Lambert, E. W., Andrade, A. R., & Penaloza, R. V. (2000). The Fort Bragg continuum of care for children and adolescents: Mental health outcomes over 5 years. *Journal of Consulting & Clinical Psychology, 68*(4), 710-716.

Bickman, L., Noser, K., & Summerfelt, W. T. (1999). Long-term effects of a system of care on children and adolescents. *The Journal of Behavioral Health Services Research, 26*(2), 185-202.

Billingsley, A., & Giovannoni, J. M. (1972). *Children of the storm: Black children and American child welfare.* New York: Harcourt, Brace, Jovanovich, Inc.

Black, M., Dubowitz, H., Hutcheson, J., Berenson-Howard, J., & Starr, R. (1995). A randomized trial of home intervention for children with failure to thrive. *Pediatrics, 95*, 807-814.

Black, M., Nair, P., Kight, C., Wachtel, R., Roby, P., & Schuler, M. (1994). Parenting and early development among children of drug-abusing women: Effects of home intervention. *Pediatrics, 94*, 440-448.

Black, N. (2001). Evidence based policy: Proceed with care. *British Medical Journal, 323*(7307), 275-279.

Blackorby, J., & Wagner, M. (1996). Longitudinal postschool outcomes of youth with disabilities: Findings from the national longitudinal transition study. *Exceptional Children, 62*(5), 399-413.

Blank, S. W., & Blum, B. B. (1997). A brief history of work expectations for welfare mothers. *Future of Children, 7*(1), 28-38.

Bogart, N. (1988). A comparative study of behavioural adjustment between therapeutic and regular foster care in the treatment of child abuse and neglect. Unpublished doctoral dissertation, Memphis State University.

Boyer, D. K., & Fine, D. (1992). Sexual abuse as a factor in adolescent pregnancy and child maltreatment. *Family Planning Perspectives, 24*(1), 4-11.

Brayden, R., Altemeier, W., Dietrich, M., Tucker, D., Christensen, M., McLaughlin, F., & Sherrod, K. (1993). A prospective study of secondary prevention of child maltreatment. *Pediatrics, 122*(4), 511-516.

Brestan, E. V., & Eyberg, S. M. (1998). Effective psychosocial treatments of conduct-disordered children and adolescents: 29 years, 82 studies, and 5,272 kids. *Journal of Clinical Child Psychology, 27*(2), 180-189.

Britner, P., & Reppucci, N. (1997). Prevention of child maltreatment: Evaluation of a parent education program for teen mothers. *Journal of Child and Family Studies, 6*(2), 165-175.

Bronfenbrenner, U. (1979). *The ecology of human development: Experiments by nature and design.* Cambridge, MA: Harvard University Press.

Bronfenbrenner, U., & Ceci, S. (1994). Nature-nurture reconceptualized in developmental perspective: A bioecological model. *Psychological Review, 101*(4), 568-586.

Brooks-Gunn, J., Han, W., & Waldfogel, J. (2002). Maternal employment and child cognitive outcomes in the first three years of life. *Child Development, 73*, 1052-1072.

Brooks-Gunn, J., Phelps, E., & Elder, G. H. (1991). Studying lives through time: Secondary data analyses in developmental psychology. *Developmental Psychology, 27*(6), 899-910.

Bryant, B., & Snodgrass, R. D. (1992). Foster family care application with special populations: People Places, Inc. *Community Alternatives, 4*(2), 1-25.

Bugental, D., Ellerson, P., Lin, E., Rainey, B., Kokotovic, A., & O'Hara, N. (2002). A cognitive approach to child abuse prevention. *Journal of Family Psychology, 16*(3), 243-258.

Burns, B. J., Phillips, S. D., Wagner, H. R., Barth, R. P., Kolko, D. J., Campbell, Y., and Landsverk, J.(2004). Mental health need and access to mental health services by youth involved with child welfare. *Journal of the American Academy of Child and Adolescent Psychiatry, 43*, 960-970. A National Survey.

Butler, C. (1995). Outcomes that matter. *Developmental Medicine & Child Neurology, 37*, 753-754.

Campbell, F. A., Pungello, E., Miller-Johnson, S., Burchinal, M., & Ramey, C. T. (2001). The development of cognitive and academic abilities: Growth curves from an early childhood educational experiment. *Developmental Psychology, 37*, 231-242.

Campbell, F. A., & Ramey, C. T. (1994). Effects of early intervention on intellectual and academic achievement—A follow-up study of children from low-income families. *Child Development, 65*(2), 684-698.

Carneiro, P., Cunha, F., & Heckman, J. (2003). Interpreting the Evidence of Family Influence on Child Development. Retrieved January 20, 2005, from http://lily.src.uchicago.edu/%7Eklmcarn/FILES/minnesota/paper.pdf

Carpenter, S. C., Clyman, R. B., Davidson, A. J., & Steiner, J. F. (2001). The association of foster care or kinship care with adolescent sexual behavior and first pregnancy. *Pediatrics, 108*(3), e46.

Carter, N., & Harvey, C. (1996). Gaining perspective on parenting groups. *Zero to Three, 16*(6), 1, 3-8.

Chaffin, M., Silovsky, J. F., Funderburk, B., Valle, L.A., Brestan, E.V., Balachova, T., Jackson, S., Lensgraf, J., Bonner, B.L. (2004). Parent-Child Interaction Therapy with physically abusive parents: Efficacy for reducing future abuse reports. *Journal of Consulting and Clinical Psychology, 72*(3), 500-510.

Chaffin, M., Silovsky, J. F., Funderburk, B., Valle, L. A., Breston, E. V., Balachova, T., et al. (2003). *Physical abuse treatment outcome project: Application of parent child interaction therapy (PCIT) to physically abusive parents.* Washington, DC: U.S. Department of Health and Human Services, The Administration on Children, Youth and Families, Children's Bureau, Office on Child Abuse and Neglect.

Chalk, R., & King, P. (Eds.). (1998). *Violence in families: Assessing prevention and treatment programs.* Washington, DC: National Academy Press.

Chalk, R., Moore, K. A., & Gibbons, A. (2003). *The development and use of child well-being indicators in the prevention of child abuse and neglect: Executive summary and introduction.* Washington, DC: Child Trends, Inc.

Chamberlain, P. (1990). Comparative evaluation of specialized foster care for seriously delinquent youths: A first step. *Community Alternatives: International Journal of Family Care, 13*(2), 21-36.

Chamberlain, P. (1994). *Family connections: A treatment foster care model for adolescents with delinquency.* Eugene, OR: Castalia Publishing Company.

Chamberlain, P. (2002). Treatment foster care. In B. J. Burns & K. Hoagwood (Eds.), *Community Treatment for Youth: Evidence-Based Interventions for Severe Emotional and Behavioral Disorders* (pp. 117-138). New York: Oxford University Press.

Chamberlain, P., & Moore, K. (1998). A clinical model for parenting juvenile offenders: A comparison of group care versus family care. *Clinical Child Psychology & Psychiatry, 3*(3), 375-386.

Chamberlain, P., Ray, J., & Moore, K. J. (1996). Characteristics of residential care for adolescent offenders: A comparison of assumptions and practices in two models. *Journal of Child and Family Studies, 5,* 259-271.

Chamberlain, P., & Reid, J. (1991). Using a specialized foster care community treatment model for children and adolescents leaving the state mental hospital. *Journal of Community Psychology, 19,* 266-276.

Chamberlain, P., & Reid, J. B. (1994). Differences in risk factors and adjustment for male and female delinquents in treatment foster care. *Journal of Child & Family Studies, 3*(1), 23-39.

Chamberlain, P., & Reid, J. B. (1998). Comparison of two community alternatives to incarceration for chronic juvenile offenders. *Journal of Consulting & Clinical Psychology, 66*(4), 624-633.

Chamberlain, P., & Weinrott, M. (1990). Specialized foster care: Treating seriously emotionally disturbed children. *Children Today, 19,* 24-27.

Chapman, M. V., Gibbons, C.B., Barth, R. P., McCrae, J.S., & The NSCAW Research Group. (2003). Parent views of in-home services: What predicts satisfaction with child welfare workers? *Child Welfare.* 82 (5), 571-596.

Children's Bureau. (1997). *Adoption 2002: The president's initiative on adoption and foster care.* Washington, DC: U.S. Department of Health and Human Services.

Children's Research Center. (2003). *Response priority.* Retrieved December 1, 2003

Cicchetti, D., & Lynch, M. (1993). Toward an ecological, transactional model of community violence and child maltreatment: Consequences for child development. In D. Reiss, J. E. Richters & M. Radke-Yarrow (Eds.), *Children and violence* (pp. 96-118). New York: Guilford Press.

Cicchetti, D., & Manly, J. T. (2001). Operationalizing child maltreatment: Developmental processes and outcomes. *Development and Psychopathology, 13,* 755-757.

Cicchetti, D., & Toth, S. L. (2000). Developmental processes in maltreated children. In D. Hanson (Ed.), The Nebraska Symposium on Motivation: Child Maltreatment. Lincoln: University of Nebraska Press.

Cicchetti, D., Toth, S., & Maughan, A. (2000). An ecological-transactional model of child maltreatment. In A. Sameroff (Ed.), *Handbook of developmental psychopathology* (2nd ed., pp. 689-722). New York: Kluwer.

Clarke, G. N., Hawkins, W., Murphy, M., & Sheeber, L. (1993). School-based primary prevention of depression symptomatology in adolescents: Findings from two studies. *Journal of Adolescent Research, 8,* 183-204.

Clarke, M., & Oxman, A. D. (2003). *Cochrane Reviewers' Handbook 4.2.0.*, from http://www.cochrane.dk/cochrane/handbook/handbook.htm

Clyman, R., & Harden, B. J. (2002). Infants in out-of-home placement. *Infant Mental Health Journal, 23*(5).

Cohen, J. A., & Mannarino, A. P. (1998). Factors that mediate treatment outcome of sexually abused preschool children: Six- and 12-month follow-up. *Journal of the American Academy of Child and Adolescence Psychiatry, 37,* 44-51.

Cohen, J. A., Mannarino, A. P., Zhitova, A. C., & Capone, M. E. (2003). Treating child abuse-related posttraumatic stress and comorbid substance abuse in adolescents. *Child Abuse and Neglect, 27*(12), 1345-1365.

Committee for the Study of the Future of Public Health. (1988). *The future of public health.* Washington, DC: National Academy Press.

Committee on Ways and Means. (2000). *Green book: Background material and data on programs within the jurisdiction of the Committee on Ways and Means.* Washington, DC: U.S. House of Representatives.

Conger, D., & Ross, T. (2001). *Reducing the foster care bias in juvenile detention decisions: The impact of project confirm.* New York: Vera Institute of Justice.

Conte, J. R., & Berliner, L. (1988). The impact of sexual abuse on children: Empirical findings. In L. E. Walker (Ed.), *Handbook on sexual abuse of children: Assessment and treatment issues* (pp. 72-93). New York: Springer Publishing.

Cooper, C. S., Peterson, N. L., & Meier, J. H. (1987). Variables associated with disrupted placement in a select sample of abused and neglected children. *Child Abuse and Neglect, 11,* 75-86.

Costello, E. J., Erkanli, A., Federman, E., & Angold, A. (1999). Development of psychiatric comorbidity with substance abuse in adolescents: Effects of timing and sex. *Journal of Clinical Child Psychology, 28,* 298-311.

Coulton, C., Korbin, J., & Su, M. (1999). Neighborhoods and child maltreatment: A multilevel study. *Child Abuse & Neglect, 23*(11), 1019-1040.

Coulton, C., Korbin, J., Su, M., & Chow, J. (1995). Community level factors and child maltreatment rates. *Child Development, 66,* 1262-1276.

Courtney, M., & Skyles, A. (2003). Racial disproportionality in the child welfare system. *Children and Youth Services Review, 25*(5/6), 355-358.

Courtney, M. E., & Wong, Y. L. (1996). Comparing the timing of exits from substitute care. *Children and Youth Services Review, 18,* 307-334.

Cowen, P. (2001). Effectiveness of a parent education intervention for at-risk families. *Journal of the Society of Pediatric Nurses, 6*(2), 73-82.

Crittenden, P., & DiLalla, D. (1988). Compulsive compliance: The development of an inhibitory coping strategy in infancy. *Journal of Abnormal Child Psychology, 16,* 585-599.

Crozier, J., & Barth, R. P. (in press). Cognitive and academic functioning in maltreated children. *Children and Schools.*

Culp, R., Little, V., Letts, D., & Lawrence, H. (1991). Maltreated children's self-concept: Effects of a comprehensive treatment program. *American Journal of Orthopsychiatry, 61*(1), 114-121.

Culp, R., Watkins, R., Lawrence, H., Letts, D., Kelly, D., & Rice, M. (1991). Maltreated children's language and speech development: Abused, neglected, and abused and neglected. *First Language, 11,* 377-389.

Currie, J. M. (1997). Choosing among alternative programs for poor children. *Future of Children, 7*(2), 113-131.

Curtis, P. A., & McCullough, C. (1993). The impact of alcohol and other drugs on the child welfare system. *Child Welfare, 72,* 533-542.

Daro, D. (1988). *Confronting child abuse for effective program design.* New York: Free Press.

Daro, D., & Cohn Donnelley, A. (2002). Child abuse prevention: Accomplishments and challenges. In J. Myers, L. Berliner, J. Briere, C. Hendrix, C. Jenny & T. Reid (Eds.), *APSAC handbook on child maltreatment.* Thousand Oaks, CA: Sage.

Daro, D., & Harding, K. (1999). Healthy Families America: Using research in going to scale. *Future of Children, 9*(1), 152-176.

Davis, M., & Vander Stoep, A. (1997). The transition to adulthood for youth who have serious emotional disturbance: Development transition and young adult outcomes. *Journal of Mental Health Administration, 24*(4), 400-427.

Dawson, T. (2003). A stage is a stage is a stage: A direct comparison of two scoring systems. *Journal of Genetic Psychology, 164*(3), 335-364.

Deater-Deckard, K., Dodge, K. A., Bates, J. E., & Pettit, G. S. (1998). Multiple risk factors in the development of externalizing behavior problems: Group and individual differences. *Development and Psychopathology, 10*, 469-493.

DeBellis, M., Keshaven, M., Clark, D., Giedd, J., Broing, A., Frustaci, K., & Ryan, N. (1999). Bennett research award: Developmental traumatology: Part II. Brain development. *Biological Psychiatry, 45*(10), 1271-1284.

Delaney-Black, V., Covington, C., Templin, T., Ager, J., Nordstrom-Klee, B., Martier, S., Leddick, L., et al. (2000). Teacher-assessed behavior of children prenatally exposed to cocaine. *Pediatrics, 106*, 782-791.

Denby, R. W., & Curtis, C. M. (2003). Why special populations are not the target of family preservation services: A case for program reform. *Journal of Sociology and Social Welfare, 30*(2), 149-173.

Dicker, S., & Gordon, E. (2004). *Ensuring the healthy development of infants in foster care: A guide for advocates and child welfare professionals.* Washington, DC: Zero to Three.

DiPietro, J. A. (2000). Baby and the brain: Advances in child development. *Annual Review of Public Health, 21*, 455-471.

Dishion, T. J., French, D. C., & Patterson, G. R. (1995). The development and ecology of antisocial behavior. In D. Cicchetti & D. J. Cohen (Eds.), *Developmental psychopathology: Risk, disorder, and adaptation* (Vol. 2, pp. 421-471). New York: Wiley.

Dishion, T. J., McCord, J., & Poulin, F. (1999). When interventions harm: Peer groups and problem behavior. *American Psychologist, 54*(9), 755-764.

Dixon, L., Lyles, A., Scott, J., Lehman, A., Postrado, L., Goldman, H., & McGlynn, E. (1999). Services to families of adults with schizophrenia: From treatment recommendations to dissemination. *Psychiatric Services, 50*(2), 233-238.

Djeddah, C., Facchin, P., Ranzato, C., & Romer, C. (2000). Child abuse: Current problems and key public health challenges. *Social Science & Medicine, 51*, 905-915.

Dodge, K. A. (2000). Conduct disorders. In A. J. Sameroff, M. Lewis & S. Miller (Eds.), *Handbook of developmental psychopathology*. New York: Kluwer.

Dodge, K. A., Bates, J. E., & Pettit, G. S. (1990). Mechanisms in the cycle of violence. *Science, 250*(4988), 1678-1683.

Dowd, K., Kinsey, S., Wheeless, S., Suresh, R., & NSCAW Research Group. (2002). National Survey of Child and Adolescent Well-Being (NSCAW): Wave 1 Data File User's Manual. Research Triangle Park, NC: Research Triangle Institute.

Dozier, M., Albus, K., Fisher, P., & Sepulveda, S. (2002). Interventions for foster parents: Implications for developmental theory. *Development and Psychopathology, 14*(4), 843-860.

Drake, R. E., Goldman, H. H., Leff, H. S., Lehman, A. F., Dixon, L., Mueser, K. T., & Torrey, W. C. (2001). Implementing evidence-based practices in routine mental health service settings. *Psychiatric Services, 52*(2), 179-182.

Drotar, D., & Robinson, J. (2000). Developmental psychopathology of failure to thrive. In A. J. Sameroff, M. Lewis & S. M. Miller (Eds.), *Handbook of developmental psychopathology* (Vol. 2, pp. 351-364). New York: Kluwer Academic/Plenum.

Dryfoos, J. (1997). The prevalence of problem behaviors: Implications for Programs. In R. Weissberg & T. Gullotta (Eds.) *Healthy children 2010: Enhancing children's wellness*, p. 17-46. Thousand Oaks, CA: Sage.

Dube, S. R., Anda, R. F., Felitti, V. J., Chapman, D. P., Williamson, D. F., & Giles, W. H. (2001). Childhood abuse, household dysfunction, and the risk of attempted suicide throughout the life span-Findings from the adverse childhood experiences study. *Journal of the American Medical Association, 286*, 3089-3096.

Dubowitz, H. (1999). Neglect of children's health care. In H. Dubowitz (Ed.), *Neglected children: Research, practice and policy*. Thousand Oaks, CA: Sage.

Duggan, A., McFarlane, E., Fuddy, L., Burrell, L., Higman, S. M., Windham, A., & Sia, C. (2004). Randomized trial of a statewide home visiting program: Impact in preventing child abuse and neglect. *Child Abuse and Neglect 28*(6): 597-622.

Duggan, A., McFarlane, E., Windham, A., Rohde, C., Salkever, D., Fuddy, L., Rosenberg, L., et al. (1999). Evaluation of Hawaii's Healthy Start Program. *Future of Children, 9*(1), 66-90.

Dumas, J. E., Gibson, J. A., & Albin, J. B. (1989). Behavioral correlates of maternal depressive symptomatology in conduct-disorder children. *Journal of Consulting & Clinical Psychology, 57*(4), 516-521.

Duncan, G., & Brooks-Gunn, J. (2000). Family poverty, welfare reform, and child development. *Child Development, 71*, 188-196.

Duncan, G., Brooks-Gunn, J., & Klebanov, P. (1994). Economic deprivation and early childhood development. *Child Development, 65*, 296-318.

Dunlap, G., Strain, P., & Kern, L. (2003). *Evidence-based practice for young children with challenging behavior*, from http://www.challengingbehavior.org/presentations.html

Durlak, J. (1997). *Successful prevention programs for children and adolescents*. New York: Plenum Press.

Earls, F., & Carlson, M. (2001). The social ecology of child health and well-being. *Annual Review of Public Health, 22*, 143-166.

Eddy, J. M., & Chamberlain, P. (2000). Family management and deviant peer association as mediators of the impact of treatment condition on youth antisocial behavior. *Journal of Consulting & Clinical Psychology, 68*(5), 857-863.

Egeland, B. (1997). Mediators of the effects of child maltreatment on developmental adaptation in adolescence. In D. Cicchetti & S. Toth (Eds.), *Rochester symposium on developmental psychopathology: Volume VIII. The effects of trauma on the developmental process* (pp. 403-434). Rochester, NY: University of Rochester Press.

Egeland, B., Yates, T., Appleyard, K., & van Dulmen, M. (2002). The long-term consequences of maltreatment in the early years: A developmental pathway model to antisocial behavior. *Children's Services: Social Policy, Research, and Practice, 5*, 249-260.

Elder, G. H. (1975). Age differentiation and the life course. *Annual Review of Sociology, 1*, 165-190.

Elder, G. H. (1994). Time, human agency, and social change: Perspectives on the life course. *Social Psychological Quarterly, 57*(1), 4-15.

Elder, G. H. (1998). The life course as developmental theory. *Child Development, 69*(4), 1-12.

Eley, T. C., Lichtenstein, P., & Moffitt, T. E. (2003). A longitudinal behavioral genetic analysis of the etiology of aggressive and nonaggressive antisocial behavior. *Development and Psychopathology, 15*(2), 383-402.

Erickson, M., Egeland, B., & Pianta, R. (1989). The effects of maltreatment on the development of young children. In D. Cicchetti & V. Carlson (Eds.), *Child maltreatment: Theory and research on the causes and consequences of child abuse and neglect* (pp. 647-684). New York: Cambridge University Press.

Eyberg, S. M., & Pincus, D. (1999). *Eyberg child behavior inventory & sutter-eyberg student behavior inventory - Revised*. Odessa, FL: Psychological Assessment Resources.

Eyberg, S. M., & Robinson, E. A. (1982). Parent-child interaction therapy: Effects on family functioning. *Journal of Clinical Child Psychology, 11*, 130-137.

Fanshel, D., (1992). Foster Care as a 2-tiered system. *Children and Youth Services Review, 14*, 49-60.

Fanshel, D., Finch, S., & Grundy, J. (1990). *Foster children in life course perspectives*. New York: Columbia University Press.

Fanshel, D., & Shinn, E. (1978). *Children in foster care: A longitudinal study*. New York: Columbia University Press.

Fantuzzo, J., Manz, P., Atkins, M., & Meyers, R. (under review). Peer-mediated treatment of socially withdrawn maltreated preschool children: Cultivating natural community resources. *Journal of Clinical Child and Adolescent Psychology*.

Fantuzzo, J., Sutton-Smith, B., Atkins, M., Meyers, R., Stevenson, H., Coolahan, K., Weiss, A., et al. (1996). Community-based resilient peer treatment of withdrawn maltreated children. *Journal of Consulting and Clinical Psychology, 64*(6), 1377-1386.

Fantuzzo, J. W., Weiss, A. D., Atkins, M., Meyers, R., & Noone, M. (1998). A contextually relevant assessment of the impact of child maltreatment on the social competencies of low-income urban children. *Journal of the American Academy of Child and Adolescence Psychiatry, 37*(11), 1201-1208.

Farmer, B. (under review). Trainings for substitute parents: Current status and evidence base of training for foster and treatment foster parents. *Social Service Research*.

Farmer, E. M., Compton, S. N., Burns, B. J., & Robertson, E. (2002). Review of the evidence base for treatment of childhood psychopathology: Externalizing disorders. *Journal of Consulting & Clinical Psychology, 70*(6), 1267-1302.

Farmer, E. M. Z., Burns, B. J., Chapman, M. V., Phillips, S. D., Angold, A., & Costello, E. J. (2001). Use of mental health services by youth in contact with social services. *Social Service Review, 75*(4), 605-624.

Farmer, E. M. Z., & Farmer, T. W. (2000). The role of schools in outcomes for youth: Implications for children's mental health services research. *Journal of Child & Family Studies, 8*, 377-396.

Felitti, V. J., Anda, R. F., Nordenberg, D., Williamson, D. F., Spitz, A. M., Edwards, V., Koss, M. P., et al. (1998). Relationship of childhood abuse and household dysfunction to many of the leading causes of death in adults. The adverse childhood experiences (ACE) study. *American Journal of Preventive Medicine, 14*, 245-258.

Finkelhor, D. (1994). The international epidemiology of child sexual abuse. *Child Abuse & Neglect, 18*(5), 409-417.

Finkelhor, D., Hotaling, G. T., Lewis, I. A., & Smith, C. (1989). Sexual abuse and its relationship to later sexual satisfaction, marital status, religion, and attitudes. *Journal of Interpersonal Violence, 4*(4), 379-399.

Fisher, A. (2001). *Finding Fish*. New York: Harper Collins.

Fisher, P., Gunnar, M., Chamberlain, P., & Reid, J. (2000). Preventive intervention for maltreated preschool children: Impact on children's behavior, neuroendocrine activity, and foster parent functioning. *Journal of the American Academy of Child and Adolescent Psychiatry, 39*(11), 1356-1364.

Fisher, P. A., & Chamberlain, P. (2000). Multidimensional treatment foster care: A program for intensive parenting, family support, and skill building. *Journal of Emotional & Behavioral Disorders, 8*(3), 155-164.

Forehand, R., & Nouisianen, S. (1993). Maternal and paternal parenting: Critical dimensions in adolescent functioning. *Journal of Family Psychology, 7*, 213-221.

Forgatch, M. S., & Martinez, J. C. R. (1999). Parent management training: A program linking basic research and practical application. *Journal of Consulting and Clinical Psychology, 67*, 711-724.

Fox, L., Long, S. H., & Langlois, A. (1988). Patterns of language comprehension deficits in abused and neglected children. *Journal of Speech and Hearing Disorders, 53*, 239-244.

Frasch, K., Brooks, D., & Barth, R. P. (2000). Openness and contact in foster care adoptions: An eight year follow-up. *Family Relations, 49*, 435-445.

Fraser, J., Armstrong, K., Morris, J., & Dadds, M. (2000). Home visiting intervention for vulnerable families with newborns: Follow-up results of a randomized controlled trial. *Child Abuse and Neglect, 24*(11), 1399-1429.

Fraser, M. W., Pecora, P. J., & Haapala, D. A. (1991). Family preservation services to prevent out-of-home placement : The family-based intensive treatment project. In M. W. Fraser, P. J. Pecora & D. A. Haapala (Eds.), *Families in crisis: The impact of intensive family preservation services* (pp. 17-47). Hawthorne, NY: Aldine de Gruyter.

Freeman, J. B., Levine, M., & Doueck, H. J. (1996). Child age and caseworker attention in child protective services investigations. *Child Abuse and Neglect, 20*, 907-920.

Friedrich, W., Dittner, C., Action, R., Berliner, L., Butler, J., Damon, L., Davies, W., et al. (2001). Child sexual behavior inventory: Normative, psychiatric, and sexual abuse comparisons. *Child Maltreatment, 6*, 37-49.

Galambos, N., Sears, H., Almeida, D., & Kolaric, G. (1995). Parents' work overload and problem behavior in young adolescents. *Journal of Research on Adolescence, 5*, 201-223.

Garland, A. E., Hough, R. L., McCabe, K. M., Yeh, M., Wood, P. A., & Aarons, G. A. (2001). Prevalence of psychiatric disorders in youth across five sectors of care. *Journal of the American Academy of Child & Adolescent Psychiatry, 40*(4), 409-418.

Garland, A. F., Landsverk, J. L., Hough, R. L., & Ellis-MacLeod, E. (1996). Type of maltreatment as a predictor of mental health service use for children in foster care. *Child Abuse and Neglect, 20*(8), 675-688.

Gelfand, D., Teti, D., Seiner, S., & Jameson, P. (1996). Helping mothers fight depression: Evaluation of a home-based intervention program for depressed mothers and their infants. *Journal of Clinical Child Psychology, 25*, 406-422.

Gelfand, D. M., & Teti, D. M. (1990). The effects of maternal depression on children. *Clinical Psychology Review, 10*, 329-353.

Gilbert, N., Berrick, J. D., Le Prohn, N., & Nyman, N. (1989). *Protecting young children from sexual abuse: Does preschool training work?* Lexington, MA: Lexington Books.

Glied, S., & Pine, D. S. (2002). Consequences and correlates of adolescent depression. *Archives of Pediatric and Adolescent Medicine, 156*(10), 1009-1014.

Golden, O. (1997). *Statement of Olivia Golden Before the Subcommittee on Human Resources of the House Committee on Ways and Means*. Retrieved November 30, 2003, from http://waysandmeans.house.gov/legacy.asp?file=legacy/humres/105cong/4-8-97/4-8gold.htm

Goodson, B. D., Layzer, J. I., St. Pierre, R. G., Bernstein, L. S., & Lopez, M. (2000). Effectiveness of a comprehensive, five year family support program for low-income children and their families: Findings from the comprehensive child development program. *Early Childhood Research Quarterly, 15*(1), 5-39.

Gordon, D. A. (2003). Intervening with troubled youth and their families: Functional family therapy and parenting wisely. In J. McGuire (Ed.), *Treatment and rehabilitation of offenders*. Sussex, England: John Wiley & Sons.

Gorman-Smith, D., Tolan, P. H., Loeber, R., & Henry, D. B. (1998). Relation of family problems to patterns of delinquent involvement among urban youth. *Journal of Abnormal Child Psychology, 26*, 319-333.

Graziano, A. M., & Diament, D. M. (1992). Parent behavioral training. An examination of the paradigm. *Behavior Modification, 16*(1), 3-38.

Gresham, F., & Elliott, S. (1990). *Social skills rating system manual*. Circle Pines, MN: American Guidance Service.

Gunnar, M. (1998). Quality of early care and buffering of neuroendocrine stress reactions: Potential effects on the developing human brain. *Preventive Medicine, 27*, 208-211.

H. Res. 134, 105th Cong., 143 Cong. Rec. H2022 (1997) (enacted).

Halfon, N., Berkowitz, G., & Klee, L. (1992). Mental health service utilization by children in foster care in California. *Pediatrics, 89*(6), 1238-1244.

Halfon, N., Mendonca, A., & Berkowitz, G. (1995). Health status of children in foster care. *Archives of Pediatric and Adolescent Medicine, 149*, 386-392.

Harman, J. S., Childs, G. E., & Kelleher, K. J. (2000). Mental health care utilization and expenditures by children in foster care. *Archives of Pediatric and Adolescent Medicine, 154*(11), 1114-1117.

Hawkins, R. P., Almeida, M. C., Fabry, B., & Reitz, A. L. (1992). A scale of measure restrictiveness of living environments for troubled children and youth. *Hospital and Community Psychiatry, 43*(1), 54-58.

Heckman, J.J. (2000). Policies to Foster Human Capital. *Research in Economics,* 54, 3-56.

Heinicke, C., Fineman, N., Ruty, G., Recchia, S., Guthrie, D., & Rodning, C. (1999). Relationship-based intervention with at-risk mothers: Outcome in the first year of life. *Infant Mental Health Journal, 20,* 349-374.

Helfer, R. E., & Kempe, H. C. (Eds.). (1968). *The battered child.* Chicago: University of Chicago Press.

Henggeler, S. W. (2002). *Moving MST into the field.* Paper presented at the A System of Care for Children's Mental Health: Expanding the Research Base, Tampa, Florida.

Henggeler, S. W., Rowland, M., Halliday-Boykins, C., Sheidow, A. J., Ward, D. M., Randall, J., et al. (2003). One-year follow-up of multisystemic therapy as an alternative to the hospitalization of youths in psychiatric crisis. *Journal of the American Academy of Child and Adolescent Psychiatry, 42,* 543-551.

Herrenkohl, E., Herrenkohl, R., & Egolf, B. (2003). The psychosocial consequences of living environment instability on maltreated children. *American Journal of Orthopsychiatry, 73*(4), 367-380.

Herrenkohl, E., Herrenkohl, R., Egolf, B., & Russo, M. (1998). The relationship between early maltreatment and teenage parenthood. *Journal of Adolescence, 21,* 291-303.

Herrenkohl, T. I., Maguin, E., Hill, K. G., Hawkins, J. D., Abbot, R. D., & Catalano, R. F. (2000). Developmental risk factors for youth violence. *Journal of Adolescent Health, 26,* 176-186.

Hildyard, K., & Wolfe, D. (2002). Child neglect: Developmental issues and outcomes. *Child Abuse and Neglect, 26,* 679-695.

Hoagwood, K., Burns, B., Kiser, L., Ringeisen, H., & Schoenwald, S. K. (2001). Evidence-based practice in child and adolescent mental health services. *Psychiatric Services, 52*(9), 1179-1189.

Hobbs, N. (1982). *The troubled and troubling child.* San Francisco: Jossey-Bass.

Hoff-Ginsberg, E. (1998). The relation of birth order and socioeconomic status to children's language experience and language development. *Applied Psycholinguistics, 19*(4), 603-629.

Horwitz, S., Balestracci, K., & Simms, M. (2001). Foster care placement improves children's functioning. *Annals of Pediatric and Adolescent Medicine, 155,* 1255-1260.

Horwitz, S., Owens, P., & Simms, M. (2000). Specialized assessments for children in foster care. *Pediatrics, 106,* 59-66.

Hudson, J., Nutter, R. W., & Galaway, B. (1994). Treatment foster care programs: A review of evaluation research and suggested directions. *Social Work Research, 18*(4), 198-210.

Huebner, C. (2002). Evaluation of a clinic-based parent education program to reduce the risk of infant and toddler maltreatment. *Public Health Nursing, 19*(5), 377-389.

Hurlburt, M. S., Zima, B. T., Lau, A., Culver, S., & Knapp, P. (2002). *Characteristics of California Outpatient Specialty Mental Health Service Providers.* Paper presented at the 15th International Conference on Mental Health Services Research: Evidence in Mental Health Services Research: What types, how much, and then what? Washington, DC.

Hutchinson, J. R., & Sudia, C. E. (2002). *Failed child welfare policy: Family preservation and the orphaning of child welfare.* New York: University Press of America.

Huxley, P., & Warner, R. (1993). Primary prevention of parenting dysfunction in high-risk cases. *American Journal of Orthopsychiatry, 63*(4), 582-588.

Hyder, A. A., Rotlant, G., & Morrow, R. H. (1998). Measuring the burden of disease: Healthy life years. *American Journal of Public Health, 88*(2), 196-202.

Institute of Applied Research. (2002). *St. Louis neighborhood network evaluation report: Analysis of child abuse and neglect statistics for the SLNN area.* St. Louis, MO: Institute of Applied Research.

Institute of Medicine. (1988). *The future of public health.* Washington, DC: National Academy Press.

Jacobson, S., & Frye, K. (1991). Effect of maternal social support on attachment: Experimental evidence. *Child Development, 62,* 572-582.

James Bell Associates. (2004). *Preliminary findings of the child and family services reviews in fiscal years 2001 and 2002.* Washington, DC: James Bell Associates.

James, S., Landsverk, J. A., & Slymen, D. J. (2004). Placement movement in out-of-home care: patterns and predictors. *Children and Youth Services Review.*

James, S., & Meezan, W. (2002). Refining the evaluation of treatment foster care. *Families in Society—The Journal of Contemporary Human Services, 83*(3), 233-244.

Jessor, R., Vandenbos, J., Vanderryn, J., Costa, F. M., & Turbin, M. S. (1995). Protective factors in adolescent problem behavior - Moderator effects and developmental change. *Developmental Psychology, 31,* 923-933.

Johnson, J., Smailes, E., Cohen, P., Brown, J., & Bernstein, D. (2000). Associations between four types of childhood neglect and personality disorder symptoms during adolescence and early adulthood: Findings of a community-based longitudinal study. *Journal of Personality Disorders, 14,* 171-187.

Jones Harden, B. (2002). Congregate care for infants and toddlers: Shedding new light on an old question. *Infant Mental Health Journal, 23*(5), 476-495.

Jones Harden, B. (2004). Safety and stability for foster children: A developmental perspective. *Future of Children, 14*(1), 31-47.

Jones Harden, B., & Early Head Start Research and Evaluation Consortium. (2003). Early Head Start home visitation: Implementation and effects. Unpublished manuscript.

Jones, L. M., & Finkelhor, D. (2003). Putting together evidence on declining trends in sexual abuse: A complex puzzle. *Child Abuse & Neglect, 27,* 133-135.

Jonson-Reid, M., & Barth, R. P. (2000). From maltreatment to juvenile incarceration: The role of child welfare services. *Child Abuse and Neglect, 24*(4), 505-520.

Jonson-Reid, M., & Barth, R. P. (2003). Probation foster care as an outcome for children exiting child welfare foster care. *Social Work, 48* (3), 348-361.

Kacir, C. D., & Gordon, D. A. (1997). Interactive videodisk parent training for parents of difficult pre-teens. *Child and Family Behavior Therapy, 21*(4), 1-22.

Kadushin, A. (1961). *Child welfare services.* New York: Prentice Hall.

Kadushin, A., & Martin, J. (1981). *Child welfare services.* New York: Macmillan.

Kagan, S. L. (1998). Using a theory of change approach in a national evaluation of family support programs. In K. Fulbright-Anderson, A. Kubisch, & J. Connell (Eds.), *New approaches to evaluating community initiatives* (pp. 113-121). Washington, DC: Aspen Institute.

Kahn, J. A., Rosenthal, S. L., Succop, P. A., Ho, G. Y. F., & Burk, R. D. (2002). Mediators of the association between age of first sexual intercourse and subsequent human papillomavirus infection. *Pediatrics, 109*(1), e5.

Kahn, K.S., Riet, G., Glanville, J., Sowden, A., & Kleijnen, J. (eds.) (2001). Undertaking systematic reviews of research on effectiveness, CRD's guidance for those carrying out or commissioning reviews. CRD Report Number 4 (2nd Edition). York, UK: York Publishing Ltd.

Karoly, L., Greenwood, P., Everingham, S., Hoube, J., Kilburn, M., Rydell, C., Sanders, M., et al. (1998). *Investing in our children: What we know and don't know about the costs and benefits of early childhood interventions.* Santa Monica, CA: RAND.

Kasen, S., Cohen, P., Skodol, A. E., Johnson, J. G., Smailes, E., & Brook, J. S. (2001). Childhood depression and adult personality disorder-Alternative pathways of continuity. *Archives of General Psychiatry, 58*(3), 231-236.

Kazdin, A. E., & Weisz, J. R. (1998). Identifying and developing empirically supported child and adolescent treatments. *Journal of Consulting & Clinical Psychology, 66*(1), 19-36.

Kelley, B. T., Thornberry, T. P., & Smith, C. (1997). *In the wake of childhood maltreatment, Juvenile Justice Bulletin (NCJ No. 165257).* Washington, DC: U.S. Department of Justice, Office of Juvenile Justice and Delinquency Prevention.

Kendall-Tackett, K. A., & Eckenrode, J. (1996). The effects of neglect on academic achievement and disciplinary problems: A developmental perspective. *Child Abuse & Neglect, 20,* 161-169.

Kendall-Tackett, K. A., Williams, L. M., & Finkelhor, D. (1993). Impact of sexual abuse on children: A review and synthesis of recent empirical studies. *Psychological Bulletin, 113*(1), 164-180.

Kerman, B., Wildfire, J., & Barth, R. (2002). Outcomes for young adults who experienced foster care. *Children and Youth Services Review, 24*(5), 319-344.

Kerr, M., Black, M. M., & Krishakumar, A. (2000). Failure-to-thrive, maltreatment and the behavior and development of 6-year-old children from low-income, urban families: A cumulative risk model. *Child Abuse & Neglect, 24,* 587-598.

Khan, K. S., Gerbenter, R., Glanville, J., Sowden, A., & Kleijnen, J. (2001). *Undertaking systematic reviews of research on effectiveness: CRD's guidance for those carrying out or commissioning reviews*: NHS Centre for Reviews and Dissemination, University of York.

Kochanska, G., Coy, K. C., & Murray, K. T. (2001). The development of self-regulation in the first four years of life. *Child Development, 72,* 1091-1111.

Koenig, A., Cicchetti, D., & Rogosch, F. (2000). Child compliance/non-compliance and maternal contributors to internalization in maltreating and non-maltreating dyads. *Child Development, 71,* 1018-1032.

Kolko, D. J., & Swenson, C. C. (2002). *Assessing and treating physically abused children and their families: A cognitive-behavioral approach.* Thousand Oaks, CA: Sage Publications.

Kratochwill, T. R., & Stoiber, K. C. (2002). Evidence-based interventions in school psychology: Conceptual foundations of the Procedural and Coding Manual of Division 16 and the Society for the Study of School Psychology Task Force. *School Psychology Quarterly, 17,* 341-389.

Kuczmarski, R. J., Ogden, C. L., Grummer-Strawn, L. M., Flegal, K. M., Guo, S. S., Wei, R., Mei, Z., et al. (2000). *CDC growth charts: United States. Advanced data from vital and health statistics; no. 314.* Hyattsville, MD: National Center for Health Statistics.

Landsverk, J. (1997). Foster care and pathways to mental health services. In P. Curtis & J. Dale (Eds.), *The foster care crisis: Translating research into practice and policy.* Lincoln: University of Nebraska Press.

Landsverk, J., & Carrilio, T. (2000). *San Diego Healthy Families America clinical trial.* San Diego: San Diego (CA) Children's Hospital and Health Center.

Landsverk, J., Davis, I., Ganger, W., & Newton, R. (1996). Impact of child psychosocial functioning on reunification from out-of-home placement. *Children and Youth Services Review, 18*(4-5), 447-462.

Landsverk, J., & Garland, A. F. (1999). Foster care and pathways to mental health services. In P. A. Curtis, G. J. Dale & e. al. (Eds.), *The foster care crisis: Translating research into policy and practice. Child, youth, and family services.* (pp. 193-210). Lincoln:

University of Nebraska Press.

Landsverk, J. A., Garland, A. F., & Leslie, L. K. (2002). Mental health services for children reported to child protective services. In J. E. B. Myers, C. T. Hendrix, L. Berliner, C. Jenny, J. Briere & T. Reid (Eds.), *APSAC Handbook on child maltreatment, 2nd edition* (pp. 487-507). Thousand Oaks, CA: Sage.

Laub, J. H., & Sampson, R. J. (1988). Unraveling families and delinquency: A reanalysis of the Gluecks' data. *Criminology, 26*(3), 355-381.

Lederman, C., & Osofsky, J. (2004). *Court Teams for Maltreated Infants and Toddlers.* Retrieved March 28, 2004, from http://www.zerotothree.org/aboutus/dialogue.html

Lehman, A. F., & Steinwachs, D. M. (1998). Translating research into practice: The Schizophrenia Patient Outcomes Research Team (PORT) treatment recommendations. *Schizophrenia Bulletin, 24*(1), 1-10.

Leiberman, A., Weston, D., & Pawl, J. (1991). Preventive intervention and outcome with anxiously attached dyads. *Child Development, 62*, 199-209.

Lerner, R., Easterbrooks, M., & Mistry, J. (Eds.). (2003). *Infancy, childhood, and adolescence* (Vol. 6). New York: Wiley.

Leslie, L., Gordon, J., Ganger, W., & Gist, K. (2002). Developmental delay in young children in child welfare by initial placement type. *Infant Mental Health Journal, 23*(5), 496-516.

Leslie, L. K., Landsverk, J., Ezzet-Lofstrom, R., Tschann, J. M., Slymen, D. J., & Garland, A. F. (2000). Children in foster care: factors influencing outpatient mental health service use. *Child Abuse and Neglect, 24*(4), 465-476.

Lester, B. M., Tronick, E. Z., LaGasse, L., Seifer, R., Bauer, C. R., Shankaran, S., Bada, H. S., et al. (2002). The maternal lifestyle study: Effects of substance exposure during pregnancy on neurodevelopmental outcome in 1-month-old infants. *Pediatrics, 110*(6), 1182-1192.

Lewin, K. (1976). *Field theory in social science: Selected theoretical papers.* Chicago: University of Chicago Press.

Lilienfeld, A. M., & Lilienfeld, D. E. (1980). *Foundations of epidemiology* (2nd ed.). New York: Oxford University Press.

Lindsey, D., Martin, S., & Doh, J. (2002). The failure of intensive casework services to reduce foster care placements: An examination of family preservation studies. *Children and Youth Services Review, 24*(9-10), 743-775.

Littell, J. H., & Schuerman, J. R. (1995). *A synthesis of research on family preservation and family reunification programs.* Washington, DC: U.S. Department of Health and Human Services.

Littell, J. H., & Schuerman, J. R. (2002). What works best for whom?: A closer look at intensive family preservation services. *Children and Youth Services Review, 24*(9-10), 673-699.

Littell, J. H. (2003, November). *Systematic and nonsystematic reviews of empirical evidence on the outcomes of multisystemic treatment.* Paper presented at the Seminar on Evidence-based Policy and Practice, Copenhagen, Denmark.

Loeber, R., & Dishion, T. (1983). Early predictors of male delinquency: A review. *Psychological Bulletin, 94*(1), 68-99.

Loeber, R., & Farrington, D. P. (Eds.). (1998). *Serious and violent juvenile offenders: Risk factors and successful interventions.* Thousand Oaks, CA: Sage.

Lowe, E., & Weigner, T. (2001). "You have to push it—who's gonna raise your kids?" Situating child care into the daily routines of low-income families. Working Paper, Next Generation Research Consortium.

Lutzker, J. R., & Rice, J. M. (1984). Project 12-ways: Measuring outcome of a large in-home service for treatment and prevention of child abuse and neglect. *Child Abuse and*

Neglect, 8, 519-524.

Lutzker, J. R., Tymchuk, A. J., & Bigelow, K. M. (2001). Applied research in child maltreatment: Practicalities and pitfalls. *Children's Services: Social Policy, Research, and Practice, 4*, 141-156.

Lyons-Ruth, K., Connell, D., Grunebaum, J., & Botein, S. (1990). Infants at social risk: Maternal depression and family support services as mediators of infant development and security of attachment. *Child Development, 61*, 85-98.

Maas, H., & Engler, R. (1959). *Children in need of parents.* New York: Columbia University Press.

Macdonald, G. (2001). *Effective interventions for child abuse and neglect: An evidence-based approach to planning and evaluating interventions.* Chicester, England: John Wiley & Sons, Ltd.

MacDonald, H. (1994). The ideology of "family preservation." *Public Interest, 94*(115), 45-60.

Mackner, L. M., Starr, R. H., & Black, M. M. (1997). The cumulative effect of neglect and failure to thrive on cognitive functioning. *Child Abuse & Neglect, 21*, 691-700.

MacLeod, J., & Nelson, G. (2000). Programs for the promotion of family wellness and the prevention of child maltreatment: A meta-analytic review. *Child Abuse and Neglect, 24*(9), 1127-1149.

Maguin, E., & Loeber, R. (1996). Academic performance and delinquency. *Crime and Justice, 20*, 145-264.

Manly, J. T., Cicchetti, D., & Barnett, D. (1994). The impact of subtype, frequency, chronicity, and severity of child maltreatment on social competence and behavior problems. *Development and Psychopathology, 6*, 121-143.

Manly, J. T., Kim, J. E., Rogosch, F. A., & Cicchetti, D. (2001). Dimensions of child maltreatment and children's adjustment: Contributions of developmental timing and subtype. *Development and Psychopathology, 13*, 759-782.

Marcenko, M., & Spence, M. (1994). Home visitation services for at-risk pregnant and postpartum women: A randomized trial. *American Journal of Orthopsychiatry, 64*, 468-476.

Marcenko, M., Spence, M., & Samost, L. (1996). Outcomes of a home visitation trial for pregnant and postpartum women at-risk for child placement. *Children and Youth Services Review, 18*, 243-259.

Masten, A. S. (1994). Resilience in individual development: Successful adaptation despite risk and adversity. In M. C. Wang & E. W. Gordon (Eds.), *Educational resilience in inner-city America: Challenges and prospects* (pp. 3-25). Hillsdale, NJ: Erlbaum.

McCluskey, C. P., Krohn, M. D., Lizotte, A. J., & Rodriguez, M. L. (2002). Substance use and school achievement among Latino, White, and African American youth. *Journal of Drug Issues, 32*(3), 921-943.

McCrone, E., Egeland, B., Kalkoske, M., & Carlson, E. (1994). Relations between early maltreatment and mental representations of relationships assessed with projective storytelling in middle childhood. *Development and Psychopathology, 6*, 99-120.

McLoyd, V. (1998). Socioeconomic disadvantage and child development. *American Psychologist, 53*, 185-204.

McLoyd, V. (personal communication, 2002).

McLoyd, V. C. (1990). The impact of hardship on black families and children: Psychological distress, parenting, and socioemotional development. *Child Development, 61*(2), 311-346.

Meadowcroft, P., & Trout, B. A. (1990). *Troubled youth in treatment homes: A handbook of therapeutic foster care.* Washington, DC: Child Welfare League of America.

Menaghan, E., & Parcel, T. (1995). Determining children's home environments: The impact of maternal characteristics and current occupational and family conditions. *Journal of Marriage and the Family, 53*, 417-431.

Mihalic, S., Irwin, K., Elliott, D., Fagan, A., & Hansen, D. (July 2001). *Juvenile justice bulletin: Blueprints for violence prevention*, from http://www.ncjrs.org/html/ojjdp/jjbul2001_7_3/contents.html

Miller, A. L., Chiles, J. A., Chiles, J. K., Crismon, M. L., Rush, A. J., & Shon, S. P. (1999). The Texas Medication Algorithm Project (TMAP) schizophrenia algorithms. *Journal of Clinical Psychiatry, 60*(10), 649-657.

Milner, J. (1998). Individual and family characteristics associated with intrafamilial child physical and sexual abuse. In P. Trickett & C. Schellenbach (Eds.), *Violence against children in the family and community*. Washington, DC: American Psychological Association.

Minnis, H., Pelosi, A. J., Knapp, M., & Dunn, J. (2001). Mental health and foster carer training. *Archives of Disease in Childhood, 84*(4), 302-306.

Mistry, R. S., Vandewater, E. A., Huston, A. C., & McLoyd, V. (2002). Economic well-being and children's social adjustment: The role of family process in an ethnically diverse low income sample. *Child Development, 73*(3), 935-951.

Mitchell, L. B., Barth, R. P., Green, R., Wall, A., Biemer, P., Berrick, J. D., Webb, M. B., et al. (2005). Child welfare reform in the United States: Findings from a local agency survey. *Child Welfare, 84* (1), 5-29.

Mnookin, R. H. (1978). *Child, family, and state: Problems and materials on children and the law*. Boston: Little, Brown.

Moe, V. (2002). Foster-placed and adopted children exposed in utero to opiates and other substances: Prediction and outcome at four and a half years. *Journal of Developmental and Behavioral Pediatrics, 23*(5), 330-339.

Moffitt, T. E., Caspi, A., Dickson, N., Silva, P. A., & Stanton, W. (1996). Childhood-onset versus adolescent-onset antisocial conduct in males: Natural history from age 3 to 18. *Development and Psychopathology, 8*, 399-424.

Moore, K. J., & Chamberlain, P. (1994). Treatment foster care: Toward development of community-based models for adolescents with severe emotional and behavioral disorders. *Journal of Emotional & Behavioral Disorders, 2*(1), 22-30.

Morrissette, P. J. (1992). Treatment foster care: Bridging troubled waters. *Journal of Family Psychotherapy, 3*(2), 53-70.

Mrazek, P., & Haggerty, R. (Eds.). (1994). *Reducing the risk for mental disorders: Frontiers for preventive intervention research*. Washington, DC: Mental Academy Press.

Munger, R. L. (1991). *Child mental health practice from the ecological perspective*. New York: University Press of America.

Munger, R. L. (1997). Ecological trajectories in child mental health. In S. Henggeler & A. Santos (Eds.), *Innovative Approaches for Difficult-to-Treat Populations*. Washington, DC: American Psychiatric Press.

Nation, M., Crusto, C., Wandersman, A., Kumpfer, K., Seybolt, D., Morrissey-Kane, E., & Davino, K. (2003). What works in prevention: Principles of effective prevention programs. *American Psychologist, 58*(6-7), 449-456.

National Advisory Mental Health Council Workgroup on Mental Disorders Prevention Research. (1998). *Priorities for prevention research at NIMH*. Washington, DC.

The national child abuse and neglect data system (NCANDS): The detailed case data component (DCDC) child data file record layout. (June 2000). from http://www.acf.dhhs.gov/programs/cb/dis/ncands98/record/recorda1.pdf

National Data Archive on Child Abuse and Neglect (NCANDS). from http://www.ndacan.cornell.edu/

National Institute of Mental Health. (1999). *Bridging science and service: A report by the*

National Advisory Mental Health Council's Clinical Treatment and Services Research Workgroup (NIH Publication No. 99-4353). Rockville, MD: National Institute of Mental Health.

Newton, R. R., Litrownik, A. J., & Landsverk, J. A. (2000). Children and youth in foster care: Disentangling the relationship between problem behaviors and number of placements. *Child Abuse and Neglect, 24*, 1363-1374.

Nixon, R. D. V. (2002). Treatment of behavior problems in preschoolers: A review of parent training programs. *Clinical Psychology Review, 22*, 525-546.

Noble, J. H., Honberg, R. S., Hall, L. L., & Flynn, L. M. (1997). *A legacy of failure: The inability of the federal-state vocational rehabilitation system to serve people with severe mental illness*. Arlington, VA: National Alliance for the Mentally Ill.

NSCAW Research Group. (2002). Methodological lessons from the National Survey of Child and Adolescent Well-being: The first three years of the USA's first national probability study of children and families investigated for abuse and neglect. *Children & Youth Services Review, 24*, 513-543.

NSCAW Research Group. (2005). *National survey of child and adolescent well-being: The characteristics of children and families entering child welfare services*. Washington, DC: U.S. Department of Health and Human Services, Administration for Children and Families.

Olds, D., Eckenrode, J., Henderson, C., Kitzman, H., Powers, J., Cole, R., Sidors, K., et al. (1997). Long-term effects of home visitation on maternal life course and child abuse and neglect. *Journal of the American Medical Association, 278*, 637-643.

Olds, D., Henderson, C., Chamberlain, R., & Tatelbaum, R. (1986). Preventing child abuse and neglect: A randomized trial of nurse home visitation. *Pediatrics, 78*, 65-78.

Olds, D., Henderson, C., & Kitzman, H. (1994). Does prenatal and infancy nurse home visitation have enduring effects on qualities of parental caregiving and child health at 25 to 50 months of life? *Pediatrics, 93*, 89-98.

Olds, D., Henderson, C., Kitzman, H., & Cole, R. (1995). Effects of prenatal and infancy nurse home visitation on surveillance of child maltreatment. *Pediatrics, 95*, 365-372.

Olds, D., Hill, P., Robinson, J., Song, N., & Little, C. (2000). Update on home visiting for pregnant women and parents of young children. *Pediatrics, 30*(4), 105-148.

Olds, D., Pettitt, L. M., Robinson, J., Henderson, C. J., Eckenrode, J., Kitzman, H., Cole, B., et al. (1998). Reducing risks for antisocial behavior with a program of prenatal and early childhood home visitation. *Journal of Community Psychology, 26*(1), 65-83.

Olds, D., Robinson, J., O'Brien, R., Luckey, D., Pettitt, L., Ng, R., Sheff, K., et al. (2002). Home visiting by paraprofessionals and by nurses: A randomized control trial. *Pediatrics, 110*(3), 486-497.

Olds, D. L., Henderson, C. R., Jr, Kitzman, H. J., Eckenrode, J. J., Cole, R. E., & Tatelbaum, R. C. (1999). Prenatal and infancy home visitation by nurses: Recent findings. *Future Child, 9*(1), 44-65, 190-191.

Patterson, G. R. (1985). Beyond technology: The next stage in the development of a parent training technology. In L. L'Abate (Ed.), *Handbook of family psychology and therapy* (Vol. 2, pp. 1344-1379). Homewood, IL: The Dorsey Press.

Patterson, G. R., & Brodsky, G. (1966). A behaviour modification program for a child with multiple problem behaviours. *Journal of Child Psychology and Psychiatry, 7*, 277-295.

Patterson, G. R., Chamberlain, P., & Reid, J. B. A. (1982). Comparative evaluation of a parent-training program. *Behavior Therapy, 13*(5), 638-650.

Patterson, G. R., DeBaryshe, B. D., & Ramsey, E. (1989). A developmental perspective on antisocial behavior. *American Psychologist, 44*(2), 329-335.

Patterson, G. R., & Ray, R. S., Shaw, D.A. (1968). Direct intervention in families of deviant children. *Oregon Research Institute Research Bulletin, 8*(9).

Paxson, C., & Waldfogel, J. (2001). *Welfare reforms, family resources, and child maltreatment.* Paper presented at the Association for Public Policy Analysis and Management 23rd Annual Research Conference, Washington DC.

Perez, C., & Widom, C. (1994). Childhood victimization and long term intellectual and academic outcomes. *Child Abuse and Neglect, 18*, 617-633.

Perry, B. D. (2000). *Traumatized children: How childhood trauma influences brain development.* Retrieved December 17, 2002, from http://www.bcm.tmc.edu/cta/trau_CAMI.htm

Perry, B. D., & Pollard, R. A. (1998). Homeostasis, stress, trauma, and adaptation: A neurodevelopmental view of childhood trauma. *Child and Adolescent Psychiatric Clinics of North America, 7*, 33-51.

Perry, B. D., Pollard, R. A., Blakley, T. L., Baker, W. L., & Vigilante, D. (1995). Childhood trauma, the neurobiology of adaptation, and "use-dependent" development of the brain: How "states" become "traits." *Infant Mental Health Journal, 16*, 271-291.

Peterson, L., Tremblay, G., Ewigman, B., & Saldana, L. (2003). Multilevel selected primary prevention of child maltreatment. *Journal of Consulting and Clinical Psychology, 71*(3), 601-612.

Petticrew, M., & Roberts, H. (2003). Evidence, hierarchies, and typologies: Horses for courses. *Journal of Epidemiology and Community Health, 57*, 527-529.

PEW Commission on Children in Foster Care. from http://pewfostercare.org/

Pickett, W., Streight, S., Simpson, K., & Brison, R. J. (2003). Injuries experienced by infant children: A population-based epidemiological analysis. *Pediatrics, 111*(4), e365-370.

Pilowsky, D. (1995). Psychopathology among children placed in family foster care. *Psychiatric Services, 46*(9), 906-910.

Pollack, S., Cicchetti, D., Hornung, K., & Reeda, A. (2000). Recognizing emotion in faces: Developmental effects of child abuse and neglect. *Developmental Psychology, 36*, 679-688.

Pollard, J. A., Hawkins, J. D., & Arthur, M. W. (1999). Risk and protection: Are both necessary to understand diverse behavioral outcomes in adolescence? *Social Work Research, 23*(2), 145-158.

Price, J. M. (in review). Social and behavioral adjustment of maltreated children in early grade school. *Developmental Psychology.*

Price, J. M., & Glad, K. (2003). Hostile attributional tendencies in maltreated children. *Journal of Abnormal Child Psychology, 31*(1), 329-343.

Prinz, R. J., & Miller, G. E. (1994). Family-based treatment for childhood antisocial behavior: experimental influences on dropout and engagement. *Journal of Consulting & Clinical Psychology, 62*(3), 645-650.

Prior, V., Lynch, M.A., & Glaser, D. (1999). Responding to child sexual abuse: An evaluation of social work by children and their carers. *Child and Family Social Work, 4*, 131-143.

Putnam, F. W. (2000). Dissociative disorders. In A. Sameroff, M. Lewis & S. Miller (Eds.), *Handbook of developmental psychopathology.* New York: Kluwer.

Qi, C. H., & Kaiser, A. P. (2003). Behavior problems of preschool children from low-income families: Review of the literature. *Topics in Early Childhood Special Education, 23*(4), 188-216.

Raver, C., & Spagnola, M. (2002). "When my mommy was angry, I was speechless:" Children's perceptions of maternal emotional expressiveness within the context of economic hardship. *Marriage and Family Review, 23*, 63-88.

Reddy, L. A., & Pfeiffer, S. I. (1997). Effectiveness of treatment foster care with children and adolescents: A review of outcome studies. *Journal of the American Academy of*

Child & Adolescent Psychiatry, 36(5), 581-588.

Reid, J. B., & Eddy, J. M. (1997). The prevention of antisocial behavior: Some considerations in the search for effective interventions. In D. M. Stoff, J. Breiling et al. (Eds.), *Handbook of antisocial behavior* (pp. 343-356). New York: John Wiley & Sons, Inc.

Reid, J. B., & Kavanagh, K. (1985). A social interactional approach to child abuse: Risk, prevention, and treatment. In M. A. Chesney & R. H. Rosenman (Eds.), *Anger and hostility in cardiovascular and behavioral disorders*. Washington, DC: Hemisphere Publishing.

Repucci, N., Woolard, J., & Fried, C. (1999). Social, community, and preventive interventions. *Annual Review of Psychology, 50*, 387-418.

Reynolds, A., & Robertson, D. (2003). School-based early intervention and later child maltreatment in the Chicago Longitudinal Study. *Child Development, 74*(1), 3-26.

Roberts, D. (2002). *Shattered bonds: The color of child welfare*. New York: Basic Books.

Roberts, I., Kramer, M., & Suissa, S. (1996). Does home visiting prevent childhood injury? A systematic review of randomised controlled trials. *British Medical Journal, 312*(7022), 29-33.

Rogers, F. (1995). *Diffusion of innovations* (4th ed). New York: Free Press.

Rogosch, F., Cicchetti, D., Shields, A., & Toth, S. (1995). Parenting dysfunction in child maltreatment. In M. Bornstein (Ed.), *Handbook of Parenting*, Vol. 4. Hillsdale, NJ: Erlbaum.

Rohsenow, D. J., Corbett, R., & Devine, D. (1988). Molested as children: A hidden contribution to substance abuse? *Journal of Substance Abuse Treatment, 5*(1), 13-18.

Roth, A., & Fonagy, P. (1996). *What works for whom? A critical review of psychotherapy research*. New York: Guilford.

Rutter, M. (1989). Age as an ambiguous variable in developmental research: Some epidemiological considerations from developmental psychopathology. *International Journal of Behavioral Development, 12*(1), 1-34.

Rutter, M. (2000). Children in substitute care: Some conceptual considerations and research implications. *Children and Youth Services Review, 22*(9-10), 685-703.

Rutter, M., Champion, L., Quinton, D., Maughan, B., & Pickles, A. (1995). Understanding individual differences in environmental-risk exposure. In P. Moen, G. H. Elder, & K. Luescher (Eds.), *Examining lives in context: Perspectives on the ecology of human development*. Washington, DC: American Psychological Association.

Rutter, M., & Madge, N. (1976). *Cycles of disadvantage: A review of research*. London: Heinemann.

Rutter, M., & Rutter, M. (1993). *Developing minds: Challenge and continuity across the life span*. New York: Basic Books.

Ryan, J., & Schuerman, J. (2004). Matching family problems with specific family preservation services: A study of service effectiveness. *Children and Youth Services Review*, unpublished manuscript.

Rychetnik, L., Frommer, M., Hawe, P., & Shiell, A. (2002). Criteria for evaluating evidence on public health interventions. *Journal of Epidemiology and Community Health, 56*, 119-127.

Sackett, D. L., Rosenberg, W.M.C., Gray, J.A.M., Haynes, R. B., & Richardson, W. S. (1996). Evidence-based medicine: What it is and what it isn't. *British Medical Journal, 312*, 71-72.

Sameroff, A. J., & Fiese, B. H. (2000). Models of development and developmental risk. In C. H. Zeanah (Ed.), *Handbook of infant mental health* (2nd ed., pp. 3-19). New York: Guilford Press.

Savelsberg, J. J. (1992). Law that does not fit society: Sentencing guidelines as a neoclassical reaction to the dilemmas of substantivized law. *American Journal of Sociology*,

97(5), March.

Schoenbach, V. J., & Rosamond, W. D. (2000). *Fundamentals of epidemiology: An evolving text*. Chapel Hill: University of North Carolina.

Schoenwald, S. K., & Hoagwood, K. (2001). Effectiveness, transportability, and dissemination of interventions: What matters when? *Psychiatric Services, 52*(9), 1190-1197.

Schuerman, J., Rzepnicki, T., & Littell, J. (1994). *Putting families first: An experiment in family preservation*. New York: Aldine de Gruyter.

Schuler, M. E., Nair, P., Black, M. M., & Kettinger, L. (2000). Mother-infant interaction: Effects of a home intervention and ongoing maternal drug use. *Journal of Clinical Child Psychology, 29*, 424-431.

Schwappach, D. L. B. (2002). Resource allocation, social values, and the QALY: A review of the debate and empirical evidence. *Health Expectations, 5*, 210-222.

Schwartz, S., Susser, E., & Susser, M. (1999). A future for epidemiology? *Annual Review of Public Health, 20*, 15-33.

Sedlak, A., & Broadhurst, D. (1996). *The third national incidence study of child abuse and neglect*. Washington, DC: U.S. Department of Health and Human Services.

Semidei, J., Feig-Radel, L., & Nolan, C. (2001). Substance abuse and child welfare: Clear linkages and promising responses. *Child Welfare, 80*, 109-128.

Serketich, W. J., & Dumas, J. E. (1996). The effectiveness of behavioral parent training to modify antisocial behavior in children: A meta-analysis. *Behavior Therapy, 27*(2), 171-186.

Shapiro, M. (1999). *Solomon's sword: Two families and the children the state took away*. New York: Times Books.

Shonkoff, J. P., & Phillips, D. A. (Eds.). (2000). *From neurons to neighborhoods: The science of early childhood development*. Washington, DC: National Academy Press.

Shore, N., Sim, K. E., & LeProhn, N. S. (2002). Foster parent and teacher assessments of youth in kinship and non-kinship foster care placements: Are behaviors perceived differently across settings? *Children & Youth Services Review, 24*, 109-134.

Simms, M. D., Freundlich, M., Battistelli, E., & Kaufman, N. (1999). Delivering health and mental health care services to children in family foster care after welfare and health care reform. *Child Welfare, 78*(1), 166-183.

Singer, J., Fuller, B., Keiley, M., & Wolfe, A. (1998). Early child care selection: Variation by geographic location, maternal characteristics, and family structure. *Developmental Psychology, 34*, 1129-1144.

Singer, L. T., Arendt, R., Minnes, S., Salvator, A., Siegel, A. C., & Lewis, B. A. (2001). Developing language skills of cocaine-exposed infants. *Pediatrics, 107*, 1057-1064.

Skocpol, T. (1992). *Protecting soldiers and mothers: The political origins of social policy in the United States*. Cambridge, MA: Belknap Press.

Skocpol, T., & Amenta, E. (1986). States and social policy. *Annual Review of Sociology, 12*, 131-157.

Smith, D. K., Stormshak, E., Chamberlain, P., & Whaley, R. B. (2001). Placement disruption in treatment foster care. *Journal of Emotional & Behavioral Disorders, 9*(3), 200-205.

Smith, S. L., & Howard, J. A. (1999). *Promoting successful adoptions: Practice with troubled families*. Thousand Oaks, CA: Sage Publications, Inc.

Smokowski, P., Mann, E., Reynolds, A., & Fraser, M. (2004). Childhood risk and protective factors and late adolescent adjustment in inner city minority youth. *Children & Youth Services Review, 26*, 63-91.

Stanton, B., Li, X. M., Cottrell, L., & Kaljee, L. (2001). Early initiation of sex, drug-relation risk behaviors, and sensation-seeking among urban, low-income African-American adolescents. *Journal of the National Medical Association, 93*, 129-

138.

Stein, M. T., Faber, S., Berger, S. P., Kliman, G., Albers, L., & Wang, P. P. (2003). International adoption: A four-year-old child with unusual behaviors adopted at six months of age. *Journal of Developmental and Behavioral Pediatrics, 24*(1), 63-69.

Steinberg, L., & Morris, A. S. (2001). Adolescent development. *Annual Review of Psychology, 52*, 83-110.

Sterling, J. S., & Moore, W. E. (1987). Weber's analysis of legal rationalization: A critique and constructive modification. *Sociological Forum, 2*(1), 67-89.

Stern, D. (1995). *The motherhood constellation.* New York: Basic Books.

Stinchcombe, A. (1986). Reason and rationality. *Sociological Theory, 4*(2), 151-166.

Stock, J., Bell, M. A., Boyer, D. K., & Connell, F. A. (1997). Adolescent pregnancy and sexual risk-taking among sexually abused girls. *Family Planning Perspectives, 29*(4), 200-203.

Stormont, M. (2001). Preschool family and child characteristics associated with stable behavior problems in children. *Journal of Early Intervention, 24*(4), 241-251.

Stormshak, E., Bierman, K. L., Bruschi, C., Dodge, K. A., & Coie, J. D. (1999). The relation between behavior problems and peer preference in different classroom contexts. *Child Development, 70*, 169-182.

Stouthamer-Loeber, M., Loeber, R., Homish, D. L., & Wei, E. (2001). Maltreatment of boys and the development of disruptive and delinquent behavior. *Development and Psychopathology, 13*, 941-955.

Strein, W., Hoagwood, K., & Cohn, A. (2003). School psychology: A public health perspective—I. Prevention, populations, and systems change. *Journal of School Psychology, 41*, 23-38.

Stroul, B. A., & Freidman, R. M. (1986). *A system of care for severely emotionally disturbed children and youth.* Washington, DC: CASSP Technical Assistance Center.

Takayama, J. I., Bergman, A. B., & Connell, F. A. (1994). Children in foster care in the state of Washington: Health care utilization and expenditures. *Journal of the American Medical Association, 271*(23), 1850-1855.

Taussig, H., Clyman, R., & Landsverk, J. (2001). Children who return home from foster care: A 6-year prospective study of behavioral health outcomes in adolescence. *Pediatrics, 108*(1).

Teare, J. F., Larzelere, R. E., Smith, G. L., Becker, C. Y., Castrianno, L. M., & Peterson, R. W. (1999). Placement stability following short-term residential care. *Journal of Child and Family Studies, 8*(1), 59-69.

Teicher, M. H., Andersen, S. L., Polcari, A., Anderson, C. M., & Navalta, C. P. (2002). Developmental neurobiology of childhood stress and trauma. *Psychiatric Clinics of North America, 25*, 397-426.

Terris, M. (1992). The society for epidemiologic research (SER) and the future of epidemiology. *American Journal of Epidemiology, 136*, 909-915.

Testa, M. (2004). When children cannot return home: Adoption and guardianship. *The Future of Children, 14*(1), 115-129.

Thornberry, T. P., Huizinga, D., & Loeber, R. (1995). The prevention of serious delinquency and violence: Implications from the program of research on the causes and correlates of delinquency. In J. C. Howell, B. Krisberg, J. D. Hawkins, and J. J. Wilson (Eds.), *A sourcebook: Serious, violent and chronic juvenile offenders* (pp. 213-237). Newbury Park: Sage.

Thornberry, T. P., Ireland, T. O., & Smith, C. (2001). The importance of timing: The varying impact of childhood and adolescent maltreatment on multiple problem outcomes. *Development and Psychopathology, 13*, 957-979.

Torrey, W. C., Drake, R. E., Dixon, L., Burns, B. J., Flynn, L., Rush, A. J., Clark, R. E., et al. (2001). Implementing evidence-based practices for persons with severe mental illnesses. *Psychiatric Services, 52*(1), 45-50.

Toth, S. L., Cicchetti, D., Macfie, J., Rogosch, F. A., & Maughan, A. (2000). Narrative representations of moral-affiliative and conflictual themes and behavioral problems in maltreated preschoolers. *Journal of Clinical Child Psychology, 29*, 307-378.

Tremblay, R. E., Masse, B., Perron, D., Leblanc, M., et al. (1992). Early disruptive behavior, poor school achievement, delinquent behavior, and delinquent personality: Longitudinal analyses. *Journal of Consulting & Clinical Psychology, 60*(1), 64-72.

Triseliotis, J. (2002). Long-term foster care or adoption: The evidence examined. *Child and Family Social Work, 7*, 23-33.

Trocme, N., Fallon, B., MacLaurin, B., Daciuk, J., Bartholomew, S., Ortiz, J., Tompson, J., et al. (2002). *Ontario incidence study of reported child abuse and neglect (OIS 1998)*. Toronto: Centre of Excellence for Child Welfare, University of Toronto.

Trupin, E. W., Tarico, V. S., Low, B. P., Jemelka, R., & McClellan, J. (1993). Children on child protective service caseloads: Prevalence and nature of serious emotional disturbance. *Child Abuse and Neglect, 17*(3), 345-355.

Tuma, N. and M. Hannan (1984). *Social Dynamics: Models and Methods*. Orlando: Academic Press.

U.S. Department of Health and Human Services. (2003a). *Child maltreatment 2001*. Washington, DC: U.S. Government Printing Office.

U.S. Department of Health and Human Services. (2003b). *National adoption and foster care statistics*. Retrieved November 27, 2003, from http://www.acf.hhs.gov/programs/cb/dis/afcars/publications/afcars.htm

U.S. Department of Health and Human Services, Administration for Children and Families. (2005). National Survey of Child and Adolescent Well-Being: Characteristics of children and families at intake into child welfare services. Washington, DC: Administration for Children and Families, U. S. Department of Health and Human Services.

U.S. Department of Health and Human Services Administration for Children, Youth and Families. (2003). *National Survey of Child and Adolescent Well-Being: One year in foster care report*. Wave 1 Data Anlysis Report. Washington, DC: U.S. Government Printing Office.

U.S. Department of Health and Human Services, Administration on Children, Youth and Families/Children's Bureau, & Office of the Assistance Secretary for Planning and Evaluation. (2003). *National study of child protective services systems and reform efforts: Review of state CPS policy*. Washington, DC: U.S. Government Printing Office.

U.S. Department of Health and Human Services, & Children's Bureau. (1997). *National study of protective, preventive, and reunification services delivered to children and their families*. Washington, DC: U.S. Government Printing Office.

U.S. Department of Health and Human Services Administration for Children Youth and Families. (2003). *Child maltreatment 2001*. Washington, DC: U.S. Government Printing Office.

U.S. Department of Health, Education and Welfare Children's Bureau. (1978). *System of social services for children and families*. Washington, DC: U.S. Government Printing Office.

U.S. Department of Health and Human Services Children's Bureau. (1994). *National study of protective, preventive, and reunification services delivered to children and their families*. Washington, DC: U.S. Government Printing Office.

U.S. General Accounting Office. (2003). *Child welfare and juvenile justice: Federal agencies could play a stronger role in helping states reduce the number of children placed solely to obtain mental health services.* (No. 03-397). Washington, DC: Government Accounting Office.

Urquiza, A., Wirtz, S., Peterson, M., & Singer, V. (1994). Screening and evaluating abused and neglected children entering protective custody. *Child Welfare, 73*(2), 155-171.

Usher, C. L., & Wildfire, J. B. (2003). Evidence-based practice in community-based child welfare systems. *Child Welfare, 82*, 597-614.

Uziel-Miller, N., Lyons, J., Kissiel, C., & Love, S. (1998). Treatment needs and initial outcomes of a residential recovery program for African-American women and their children. *American Journal of Addiction, 7*(1), 43-50.

Vance, J. E., Bowen, N. K., Fernandez, G., & Thompson, S. (2002). Risk and protective factors as predictors of outcome in adolescents with psychiatric disorder and aggression. *Journal of the American Academy of Child and Adolescent Psychiatry, 41*(1), 36-43.

Wagner, M. M. (1995). Outcomes for youths with serious emotional disturbance in secondary school and early adulthood. *Future of Children, 5*(2), 90-112.

Wagner, M. M., D'Amico, R., Marder, C., Newman, L., & Blackorby, J. (1992). *What happens next?: Trends in postschool outcomes for youth with disabilities.* Menlo Park, CA: SRI International.

Wagner, M. M., Newman, L., D'Amico, R., Jay, E. D., Butler-Nalin, P., Marder, C., & Cox, R. (1991). *Youth with disabilities: How are they doing?* Menlo Park, CA: SRI International.

Wahler, R. G. (1980). The insular mother: Her problems in parent-child treatment. *Journal of Applied Behavior Analysis, 13*(2), 207-219.

Wald, M., Carlsmith, J., Leiderman, P., Smith, C., & French, R. (1988). *Protecting abused and neglected children.* Palo Alto, CA: Stanford University Press.

Waldfogel, J. (1997). The new wave of service integration. *Social Service Review, 71*(3), 465-484.

Wall, A., Green, R., Barth, R. P., & Group, NSCAW Research Group. (April 15, 2004). *Child well-being at 18-months.* Paper presented at the Paper presented at the sixth annual meeting of the NSCAW Technical Work Group, Washington, DC.

Wall, A. E., & Barth, R. P. (2005). Aggressive and delinquent behavior of maltreated adolescents: Risk factors and gender differences. *Stress, Trauma, and Crisis: An International Journal, 8*, 1-24.

Walter, H. I., & Gilmore, S. K. (1973). Placebo vs. social learning effects in parent training procedures designed to alter the behavior of aggressive boys. *Behavior Research and Therapy, 4*, 361-377.

Webster-Stratton, C. (1984). A randomized trial of two parent training programs for families with conduct-disordered children. *Journal of Consulting and Clinical Psychology, 52*, 66-678.

Webster-Stratton, C. (1998). Preventing conduct problems in Head Start children: Strengthening parenting competencies. *Journal of Consulting and Clinical Psychology, 66*(5), 715-730.

Webster-Stratton, C., & Hammond, M. (1997). Treating children with early-onset conduct problems: A comparison of child and parent training interventions. *Journal of Consulting and Clinical Psychology, 65*(93-99).

Webster-Stratton, C., & Taylor, T. (2001). Nipping early risk factors in the bud: Preventing substance abuse, delinquency and violence in adolescence through interventions targeted at young children. *Prevention Science, 2*, 165-192.

Weissberg, R., & Greenberg, M. (1998). School and community competence-enhancement and prevention programs. In W. Damon (Series Ed.), I. Sigel & K. Renninger (Volume Eds.), *Handbook of child psychology: Child psychology in practice* (Vol. 4, pp. 877-954). New York: Wiley.

Weissberg, R., & Kumpfer, K. (2003). Special issue: Prevention that works for children and youth. *American Psychologist, 58*(6/7).

Weisz, J. (2003). Personal Communication.

Wekerle, C., & Wolfe, D. (1993). Prevention of child physical abuse and neglect: Promising new directions. *Clinical Psychology Review, 13*, 501-540.

Wennberg, J. E. (1999). Understanding geographic variations in health care delivery. *New England Journal of Medicine, 340*(1), 52-53.

Westat, Hall, C., & Bell, J. (2002). *Evaluation of family preservation and reunification programs: Final report.* Rockville, MD: Westat.

Whynes, D. K. (1996). Towards an evidence-based national health service? *The Economic Journal, 106*(439), 1702-1712.

Widom, C. (2000). Understanding the consequences of childhood victimization. In R. Reece (Ed.), *Treatment of child abuse: Common ground for mental health, medical, and legal practitioners.* Baltimore, MD: Johns Hopkins University Press.

Widom, C., & Kuhns, J. (1996). Childhood victimization and subsequent risk for promiscuity, prostitution, and teenage pregnancy: A prospective study. *American Journal of Public Health, 86*, 1607-1612.

Widom, C. S., Weiler, B. L., & Cottler, L. B. (1999). Childhood victimization and drug abuse: A comparison of prospective and retrospective findings. *Journal of Consulting and Clinical Psychology, 67*, 867-880.

Williams, J. H., Ayers, C. D., & Arthur, M. W. (1997). Risk and protective factors in the development of delinquency and conduct disorders. In M. W. Fraser (Ed.), *Risk and resilience in childhood: An ecological perspective* (pp. 140-170). Washington, DC: NASW Press.

Wiltz, N. A., & Patterson, G. R. (1974). An evaluation of parent training procedures designed to alter inappropriate aggressive behavior of boys. *Behavior Therapy, 5*, 215-221.

Wohlwill, J. F. (1970). The age variable in psychological research. *Psychological Review, 77*(1), 49-64.

Wulczyn, F. (1991). Caseload dynamics and foster-care reentry. *Social Services Review, 65*(1), 133-156.

Wulczyn, F. (2003). Closing the gap: Are changing exit patterns reducing the time African American children spend in foster care relative to Caucasian children? *Children and Youth Services Review, 25*(5/6), 431-462.

Wulczyn, F. (2004). Family reunification. *The Future of Children, 14*(1), 95-113.

Wulczyn, F., & Hislop, K. B. (2002). *Foster care dynamics in urban and non-urban counties.* Washington, DC: Assistant Secretary for Planning and Evaluation, Department of Health and Human Services.

Wulczyn, F., Hislop, K. B., & Goerge, R. (2000a). *Foster care dynamics, 1983-1998: An update from the Multistate Foster Care Data Archive.* Chicago: Chapin Hall Center for Children, University of Chicago.

Wulczyn, F., Hislop, K. B., & Harden, B. J. (2002). The placement of infants into foster care. *Infant Mental Health Journal, 23*(5), 454-475.

Wulczyn, F., Kogan, J., & Jones Harden, B. (2003). Placement stability and movement trajectories. *Social Service Review, 77*(June), 212-226.

Yoshikawa, H. (1994). Prevention as cumulative protection: Effects of early family support and education on chronic delinquency and its risks. *Psychological Bulletin, 115*, 28-54.

Yoshikawa, H. (1999). Welfare dynamics, support services, mothers' earnings, and child cognitive development: Implications for contemporary welfare reform. *Child Development, 70*, 779-801.

Zeanah, C. (Ed.). (2000). *Handbook of infant mental health.* New York: Guilford.

Zeanah, C., Boris, N., & Leiberman, A. (2000). Attachment disorders of infancy. In M. Lewis & A. Sameroff (Eds.), *Handbook of developmental psychopathology* (2nd ed.). New York: Basic.

Zeanah, C., Larrieu, J., Heller, S., Valliere, J., Hinshaw-Fuselier, S., Aoki, Y., & Drilling, M. (2001). Evaluation of a preventive intervention for maltreated infants and toddlers in foster care. *Journal of the American Academy of Child and Adolescent Psychiatry, 40*(2), 214-221.

Index

215